PRAISE FOR

THE MAP OF ENOUGH

"The Map of Enough is moving, poetic, and addictive. May's sense of wonder at her new world and adventurous spirit is admirable and contagious, but even more important is the way she inspires us to question our own deeply-held beliefs about home and happiness." —*Elle*

"In an impressive debut memoir, a self-proclaimed 'Woman of the World' chronicles her journey to find a home. May joins the ranks of Gretel Ehrlich and Annie Proulx, celebrants of sagebrush, big skies, and journeys of self-discovery... May's poetic, gleaming prose makes palpable the wildness and wind, freezing and thawing earth, delicate fragrances of grass and budding trees—and her own profound transformation." —*Kirkus*, Starred Review

"... [A] more homegrown version of *Eat, Pray, Love*... readers will find much to ponder in this journey to home and family. An obvious choice for book groups eager for rich discussions on the road less traveled." —*Booklist*

"Could a woman brought up without survival skills learn to build her own shelter, split firewood, grow food? Could a browser of the Internet keep from drowning in the electronic sea of possibilities? Could she learn to be fully present to her life without hankering to be elsewhere? May tackles all these questions and more in prose as candid and lucid as an April morning. She holds the hard-won answers lightly, open to correction from fresh experience."
—Scott Russell Sanders, *Earth Works: New & Selected Essays*

"This is a book about possibilities—about the author's, yes, but also about all of us. Read it and be implicated!"
—Bill McKibben, *Oil and Honey: The Education of an Unlikely Activist*

"*The Map of Enough* is the record of a life deeply lived, of a woman tuning herself to the earthly resonances of a severe and beautiful place. With winks and jokes and moments so heartbreakingly rendered you'll feel the mountain wind, May turns the old ideas of what it means to find home inside out. Molly Caro May has written the next great Montana memoir."
—Joe Wilkins, *The Mountain and the Fathers: Growing Up on the Big Dry*

"*The Map of Enough* is a joyful adventure. It doesn't hurt that our guide on that adventure is the exuberant, complex, thoughtful, and boisterous Molly Caro May, a placeless woman trying to find her place. It turns out that that place is a yurt in Montana, as archetypal as Thoreau's cabin. In sentences that are beautiful and lyric, May makes us think about our own lives and how we choose to pass our days on earth."   —David Gessner, *My Green Manifesto*

"In Molly Caro May's debut memoir, May and her fiancée, Chris, move to her family's land in Montana for a one-year stay... May's exceptional use of imagery effortlessly captures the atmosphere of Montana countryside, making it familiar yet mysterious... For Molly, the move is more than just breaking away from mundane life; it is an exploratory process of finding purpose and connection with her inner self. May's clean writing and excellent use of sensory detail produces a tangible effect of the land. The reader can smell the earth; feel the cold, damp snow; hear twigs snapping and birds chirping. The landscape comes alive on every page. May's thought-provoking journey will challenge the reader to question their own lives."   —*Billings Gazette*

"In her beautifully written memoir, [May] explores the challenge and allure of creating a real home in an age of ever-more-virtual interactions—and reminds us why we love the West."
            —*Sunset Magazine*

"*The Map of Enough* follows the author and her fiancée's move to 107 acres in Montana—which her family owns but rarely visits—and provides a rare glimpse into what it takes to build a traditional Mongolian yurt from scratch in an area that receives sub-zero temperatures. More than a story of building an adobe, it's about yurt life and its connections to nature and the elements, and offers keys to understanding the lure of a nomadic home that can be disassembled and moved at the blink of an eye. Anyone interested in mobile living and yurts will find this an inspirational, revealing autobiography packed with insights and encouragement."
            —*Midwest Book Review*

The Map of Enough

THE MAP OF
ENOUGH

One Woman's Search for Place

Molly Caro May

COUNTERPOINT
BERKELEY

Library of Congress Cataloging-in-Publication Data

May, Molly Caro.

The map of enough : one woman's search for place / Molly Caro May.

pages cm

ISBN 978-1-61902-474-8 (paperback)

1. May, Molly Caro. 2. Women travelers—United States—Biography. 3. Nomads—United States—Biography. 4. Home—United States. 5. Group identity—United States. I. Title.

G226.M328A3 2014

917.30092—dc23

2013031385

Interior design by VJB/Scribe

COUNTERPOINT

2560 Ninth St., Suite 318

Berkeley, CA 94710

www.counterpointpress.com

Printed in the United States of America

Distributed by Publishers Group West

10 9 8 7 6 5 4 3 2 1

For CQK
who lived this with me
and lives it with me still

↓

The peace is partly in being free of the suspicion that pursued me for most of my life, no matter where I was, that there was perhaps another place I *should* be, or would be happier or better in.

Wendell Berry

When we love the earth, we are able to love ourselves more fully.

bell hooks

Contents

What is enough?

Prologue

S ome say that your first ten years of life organize your entire perception of who you are. That's a serious statement. I sat under a cottonwood tree, wind rustling the grass by my legs, and thought it out. But not for long, because how could I not agree right away?

That young girl occupied a literal present tense in my adult life. No matter where I went, she would surface in my memory with flashbacks that came to me during the most common moments—buying cucumbers at the grocery store, petting my dog on the porch, filling my car with gas in the middle of nowhere. She spoke as if she were still alive, and always close. Maybe that girl was bolder than me. Maybe I wanted to retain her. Her stories populated my body. And she always appeared when I needed her most—somehow her presence overshadowed, for an instant, the many small disappointments of self that had amassed over time.

Under the cottonwood tree, I unlaced my shoes and fell into the past.

When my father walks down the rolling lawn toward me, I unlace my roller skates and step onto the driveway. We are visiting from *abroad*—the word my parents use, which must mean that where we live is foreign to us even though this place, my grandparents' house on the Chesapeake Bay, feels more foreign to me. The air here smells of salt, of heat, of mowed grass. Everyone else is lounging up the hill by the house, probably eating Triscuits and cheese. That's what we do when we come here, and we also play with the Russian dolls and page through all the old maps. My father puts a hand on my shoulder, crouches down to eye level, and asks if he can talk to me. Before I say Yes, I test my almost double digits self and wait a few long seconds just to feel what would happen if I said No. It's about a new job, he explains. Oh, that's familiar. It's the next line that throws me. In a few months, we will be moving to America. Because I don't know how to absorb this information, I scream at him.

I hate America!

I run away hard, my feet, still in white socks, slapping across the black asphalt. At the old dock, I collapse onto rough planks. Even though I like moving, moving to America is going to ruin everything. I don't know exactly why. I just know it's true. Hot tears run down my already flushed cheeks. But the humid air eventually pulls me upright and my legs dangle out over the green water and I am watchful. The peninsula spreads out to nowhere, but I don't know that word *peninsula* yet, or that the long bird coasting by is a blue heron or that the capital of America, which people really call the United States of America, is forty-five minutes away or that there is a state with the same name as the capital, only it's on the other coast, the rainy one. My grandparents, the ones who live here now, aren't even from here. They grew up as Americans in Chile and raised my father while moving from Hawaii to Japan to Germany to Montreal to Belgium to England. And so far, my father has chosen for us the same wandering life: from Australia to the Dominican Republic to Spain to Mexico and, now, to America.

The crab cage stares at me. It hangs over the water. Piled on top of one another, the crabs are oblivious to chaos and also to their future. This afternoon, when my cousins and second cousins come over, while ears of corn boil in pots, we will paint black numbers on the crabs' shells, line them up like prisoners, and make them race down the scalding driveway. My two younger brothers can't wait for the awesome event. I end up chewing my fingernails.

Reaching into the cage, I dodge the clacking of claws and feel brave.

One by one, I pull crabs out and fling them into the still water.

Plunk. Plunk. Plunk.

I agree with the sound of freeing crabs. They splash. They descend into the murk. Into the seaweed and sand. Float on their backs. Legs splayed out. Bellies white as ghosts. As the crabs go back to their element, my pigtails feel too tight and, suddenly, I'm not sure where I am from and it feels like the most urgent question of my life. Soon I'll be sitting in a classroom where a teacher will hand me the crisp white sheets of an entrance test. I will learn how to fill in ovals with a number 2 pencil and also that I need to repeat a grade because I have no answer for the question of how many coins get dropped into a tollbooth. I don't know what a tollbooth is. I don't know about American quarters or nickels, even though, by lineage, I am American.

We moved to Dallas, Texas, of all places. On the first day of school, I noticed a clan of girls who, after a long summer apart, shrieked and clutched each other under a magnolia tree. After we all walked single-file inside, I sat next to the chubby boy everyone else avoided. He pushed his glasses up a sweaty nose, smiled at me, ripped a page out of the dictionary, stuck it in his mouth, and chewed. Then he actually swallowed. He continued to eat the dictionary during the entire class period. I smiled back like a co-conspirator because something about him made me sad. He was doomed. He was doomed to be an outcast forever. I didn't know whether I was doomed, but the thought of anyone being doomed was too much emotion to handle. Even then, I knew that everyone wants to belong to something, somewhere.

At recess, the girls who had known each other since something called pre-K approached me as I kicked up dust by the soccer goal. They didn't understand why I had been to so many schools in so many places. How can you not know where you are from? they asked. As they questioned me, I began to learn that when people asked where I was from, I would list the countries, and when they asked why I had moved so often, I would say that my dad worked for Colgate Palmolive, and when kids asked what that was, I would tell them it was a soap company, and when they shrugged, I would say that my family was known for moving a lot. When our teacher blew the whistle, we ran back. As we huffed and puffed, one girl commented that I had a strange accent and everyone agreed. Later, my accent would turn so flat and nondescript that no one would be able to connect it to any one place. The girls continued to stare at me. So I ran faster and remembered my old friends from other places— Nader from Vietnam, Maria from Mexico, Fabian from Germany, Anna from Korea, Tabitha from England. They went to international schools like me; they moved every two years or so, like me. We all understood how to be new. We lived in a transient culture. We didn't have to explain ourselves to each other. But these American girls were a different beast altogether. We spoke the same language. I didn't look unlike them. But we had no true common denominator.

Once we made it back inside, they surrounded and studied me as if they were making a decision. Backed up against my cubby, I glanced around and told them that I once had a pet koala.

Small. White. Lie.

Really? they asked, moving closer.

Yeah.

And there, right there, something clicked. My arms shivered with the power of it. Suddenly, they were fascinated by me, by the accumulation of all the information about me. Wait, what are all the places you've lived again? one girl asked. Yeah, tell us, they echoed. Another girl leaned against me and locked her arm in mine. It was unlike anything I had ever experienced. I was exotic in a way that pleased them. At the day's end, my homeroom teacher corralled us outside to snap a photo of each student. I stood against a warm concrete wall and stared into the camera. For the first time, I saw myself from a distance and became aware of two things: the world of definitions and me as the global girl from many places.

A few years later, after I dodged cliques, made a point of making friends with everyone, including the outcasts, and stumbled into my teens, my grandparents invited their sons and families on a trip to celebrate their fiftieth wedding anniversary. My parents kept repeating that it would be "a trip of a lifetime." Though we had lived abroad, we had never traveled abroad per se, certainly not on a wooden boat sailing along the Mediterranean coast of Turkey for two weeks. My father had trained us to know that the boat was called a *gulet*, because when you go to a new country you use its language as often as possible. At first, we had problems—not enough drinking water, an extra stowaway crew member with a broken arm, no rigging, and a partially working toilet. Nothing went according to plan. Nothing was as smooth as it had sounded with the travel agent. But my grandparents had been all over the globe and they adjusted easily.

As I leaned on the cord railing, a warm breeze plucked at my frizzy brown hair, and water the color of turquoise sprayed up at my feet. We had just reboarded after roasting and sweating our way through ancient ruins. I was glad that I had done my seventy pushups, a new regime, in the cool morning. At each crumbled structure, I had bent down, picked up rubble, and wondered who had been there and why and what they had felt. My mind mulled over history and how strange it was that humans existed at all and how I had always wanted to live in cultures and places unfamiliar to me. Now the sea pulled us with its tidal current. My brothers and cousins were stomping around the deck like pirates. The adults relaxed in plastic deck chairs and ate bowls of yogurt and honey for lunch. Laughter bubbled continuously. I caught a glimpse of my grandparents on the bow, shoulder to shoulder, gazing out to the arid shore and sipping from cans of Coca-Cola. It occurred to me that I was sitting on a vessel with the exact people who had passed down movement from their blood to mine. Had they ever thought about how they had created lives of going from here to there? So many *to*'s. To here. To there.

I tried it on my tongue.

But there was no such verb as *to-ing*.

My father, in his short Euro shorts and leather sandals, had once gathered my brothers and me into a huddle to explain that we came from a lineage that goes "a mile wide." If he had been given to dramatic gestures, which he wasn't, he might have swept his arm out over the horizon and let us pause at the enormity of his statement. Instead, he planted the thought, and we each took it as we would. Being the eldest, I would take it the furthest. As the *gulet* cruised, I decided that I wanted to be known as a nomad. *That* was me. I would be as free as a colt and impossible to catch, someone who knew about geography and wore flowy scarves. Like this, I would float from foreign place to foreign place and carry the phrases *global citizen, crossing bridges, gravitas,* with a long *a.* People would come to know me as someone who pored over world maps, obsessed with where I had been and where I would go.

Come *on,* urged my brothers, yanking at my arms, yanking me out of contemplation. The *gulet* had anchored and now we could swim. With one quick step, I transformed into a girl leaping into midair, cannonballing into cool water, scissoring my legs fast up from the depths, wondering about normal things, like whether my blue bathing suit looked good on me and whether I had any chance of becoming as tan and pretty as my blonde best friend. And how could I, the girl who dove down to grab her brothers' ankles like a sea monster, have known that soon after our tour in Turkey we would relocate to Florida, a different state, though we would never again move abroad as a family?

In college, I met a woman from Alaska. We stood on the sidewalk together and talked. When her father had dropped her off in New England, he advised, If you ever get down or insecure, just remember that you are from Alaska. He meant it as insurance. As she bobbed her head and told me this story, I could practically see the root ball attached to her feet.

How about you, where are you from?

Oh, nowhere really, I laughed.

What do you mean, nowhere? she asked, confused.

Not one place. I moved a lot. Let's just put it this way: the mantra in my family is, What's next, what's next, what's next?

Whoa, she smiled back.

I think it's amazing that you can say you are from one place, that you know one place so well, I said.

Well, back at you, she said. I can't imagine knowing so many places.

After we hugged, after we vowed to meet up at the dining hall soon, I suspect we parted ways feeling distinguished by our differences, yet connected. As I skipped down the sidewalk, late for a class, the cycle couldn't help but further ingrain itself. Nowhere gave me a somewhere to be from.

We were all coming of age at the brink of the twenty-first century. Few of us had email accounts; fewer had gargantuan cell/car phones. But soon, the Internet would shoot through town like a freight train, connecting everyone to everyplace without anyone ever having to travel. And yet, we wanted to go places. There were suddenly so many places to explore, so many organizations to work for, so many possibilities for "a life." At least for the entitled, which, by class or education, we were. Even those who had declared themselves desert people or city people or island people yearned for many different deserts, many different cities, many different islands. Sure, wanderlust had been the trademark of every young generation newly released into the world, but, for us, digital technology amped it up. We were steeped in choices. We might go crazy with the options. We were intoxicated by what could be.

For me, already made of transient stock, already infatuated

by my ancestry of movement, the situation steamrolled all my urges together until I could not distinguish the layers. Everyone else would probably settle down into respectable lives eventually, probably in towns they knew well, and I would still be the metallic placeless one, standing barefoot in grass, and when it was time to go, I would leave to remake myself somewhere else: Amsterdam, Peru, another adventure—the kind of woman with all her jets on high, the kind of woman who smelled of wind. I careened toward adulthood. I became ravenous.

As I circulated and held many jobs in many places—some abroad, some not—I got antsy at exactly the one-and-a-half-year mark into a place. My legs twitched with anticipation as I imagined something brand-new, the *what's next* mantra rubbed so smooth now it was a trusty stone in my pocket. Do you think it's an addiction? I joked with my best friend. No, it's just your way, she offered. Sometimes it appeared irresponsible for someone who tended toward responsibility. In New Mexico, I woke up one normal morning, stuffed all my belongings into my car, tied my rent cash with a green bow, placed it on the kitchen counter for my landlords, and left months before I had intended. This sort of thing happened often. When it was time to go, it was time to go. I liked not feeling hooked down; in fact, I didn't know anything different.

And whenever I felt ashamed or unworthy or weak—there were plenty of those moments—when someone was thinner, more ravishing, more accomplished than me, my line about being from nowhere, about being placeless, was my go-to. I blew and blew and blew the image up into a balloon so glittery and gold it led the way, pulling me behind it, its dutiful follower with a tight grip.

But I couldn't have organized any of those thoughts until recently.

This is the woman I brought with me when I arrived on 107 acres in Montana. She was so willing to detach from all but one thing. A few years earlier, my parents had called to share that they had invested in a place for all of us to congregate, since we had no home base. They had sunk their retirement savings into the land. I didn't question then why they felt this was necessary. I simply thanked them, as you do, but remained unaware of what it actually meant. Would I ever spend any time on that western land, I wondered, or even like it? Liking it was likely, since I was known, more than anyone in my family, to sniff soil and seek out rivers. I visited briefly twice, and one autumn came around a stand of cottonwoods and found a deer carcass ripped in half, presumably by a mountain lion.

It's wild out there, I reported back.

No one had any intention of actually living on the land until, one day, I did.

PART ONE

1

HERE I AM

Grass scratched up against my hips. Grass, it seemed, was the way here, even as dark rushed around me: miles of grass, tall and dense and stretching back to black clumps of trees, slumbering mountains, and who knows what else on this warm July night. I sealed my back against the only thing I could—my old gallant Jeep still warm from having rattled up the long dirt driveway. No sound but the babble of flowing water. Someone had grown a hot handful of stars and tossed them up into a black sky. I scanned the perimeter for mountain lions, squinting, as if my looking would actually protect me. I could see very little. Not my hands. Not my feet. And certainly not what would unfold for me here.

I was not alone.

Chris stood somewhere, probably on the other side of the car, doing the same thing I was doing. Taking it all in, as wild grasses bent into open windows to check out our seven stunned tropical houseplants, clothes jammed in every available spot, and cardboard boxes of books. The maw of the East had released us a few days ago and we had drifted ahead of the clutter and mess of it, past lonely gas stations and tumbleweeds, into the openness, to yet another beginning in another place.

You there?

Yup.

Let's go, I announced into the night. Let's walk together.

We slung on our backpacks. The cabin, about fifty feet away, stared at us like an outlier with a corrugated steel roof. My father liked to tease about "the death walk" from car to cabin at night—this from a man who knew nothing more about predators than any of us did. We swished into the grassy gulf, my hands reaching out to feel the cool tips and then retracting back to clap loudly and call out, Hellooooo, here we are. It felt wrong to disturb the great dark, but I did it anyway. I wanted to identify us. The sweet dry smell pulled my chin up to that sensory moment of entrance to a new home. As we shuffled, I imagined the mosquito-snake-rabbit-deer-lion-bear message radiating out: *They are here, they are here, they are here.*

Or maybe, more likely, we humans weren't that interesting at all.

No one had been on this porch in months, or was it years? I reached up to a window ledge for the key. Covered in cobwebs. As my shoulder propped the screen door, I fiddled with the lock and soon swung myself into an immaculate space: two leather chairs, a copper table, red rug, claw-foot bathtub, big white bed, and even a telephone landline. Despite the décor, one swipe against the reclaimed lumber wall could give splinters to pick at for weeks. I barreled in, unloaded my backpack with a thump, and turned on the lights.

Where are you? I whispered, craning my neck out the door.

Over here.

I knew the sound of his trickle. Legs akimbo, his black silhouette was arcing a stream onto the grass. Not self-satisfied, but just acknowledging that, on this land, you could pee outside.

Instead of dropping trou with him, I did what I do best and made an observation.

Beb? I said, using a name shaved down over years from babe to bebe to beb.

Yeah?

You're also marking our territory.

Territory is an odd word, and when I used it, I knew that. I wanted to erase it and apologize to the mountain lions and everything else. This was not our territory, or even the territory of my parents, who technically owned it. Because humans like to name places, my family had named this one, though it was mostly unused and unknown by us until Chris and I arrived. I don't remember how it happened, only that the name, despite the obvious social and historical complexity of calling a place The Land, took hold immediately. It became such a pleasure to say aloud that we actually called it that, swapping information about how The Land was doing, hearing that the knapweed had gotten out of hand, even though we didn't know one thing about knapweed, or about knowing a place.

The next morning, in the daylight, I rolled out of bed and went to see about the sea of green grass surrounding us. It vibrated. Grasshoppers launched themselves. I had never seen so many at once, arcing high, clicking legs together with all the faith that, somewhere, a safe landing awaited them. Blocking the sun with my hand, I stood in the same spot as the night before, wearing nothing but white cotton underwear. They buzzed and pinged against me like little arrows. The grasshopper bombardment didn't hurt. It simply matched my volcanic impulse for new experiences.

And here, right here, a new one awaited me.

I would be strong here. My biceps would get tan and toned. When I scaled trees, dunked in the cold creek, and howled with the wind, a deeper sense of self would seep into me, and that would stay with me when I left for elsewhere. Put me somewhere where nothing stands between the elements and me. Maybe then I could see myself in plain light.

After a few years living in one of New York's many fifth-floor walk-ups, after working in midtown publishing, after one thousand tiny paper cuts, it had been time to go. It had been a good stint. I had done the city. I had done the desk job. But I didn't need to do it again. I needed the complete opposite. My whole life I had stood in front of bathroom mirrors pulling my cheeks up and down and repeating *I'm chill*, a phrase learned from some film, a phrase so instructive of what I wanted to be and was not. Most people would have noted my calm presence and how my curiosity kept me asking questions, real questions, of them. They would have said, You're already strong. But a subterranean discontent had always gnawed at me. Not discontent with the world, but discontent with myself. There had been no great shattering event. It was simply a state of being, my modus operandi, revealed only to those who knew me well. Recently, a close friend had straight-talked me: You change circumstances all the time, but you're still hitting your head against a brick wall.

Nice.

I hadn't wanted to hear it, but she said it anyway.

Now that I was almost thirty, it was time to survey the

landscape of my life and grow up. What that meant exactly I wasn't sure. To nature I would go. Though every new place offered a chance, nature didn't let a person back down. Nature was also an organic extension of our lives together. It had been part of Chris and me coming together. We owned cross-country skis. For presents, we gave each other rocks. I'd lived in a dilapidated trailer surrounded by wild dogs; I'd hiked and slept in a tent for two solid months; I'd practiced my sea kayak roll, even though doing it scared the shit out of me. There were no distractions in the wilderness. I wanted mountains and creeks and quiet to calibrate this new phase of life. We want what we want, even when we don't fully understand the complexity of that want.

Choosing this place had happened quickly.

Cross-legged on the linoleum floor of our apartment, crammed between slot kitchen and rattan chair, Chris and I had narrowed down our options. He was tired of building boats in the Bronx. I was eager for a change—had turned down the conflict-resolution graduate school that accepted me, had stopped taking prerequisites for medical school. Where could we go? Especially when we left our paying jobs. We wouldn't silo ourselves. No. Agreed. So, we ping-ponged some possibilities around. Within minutes, we had it.

What about Montana? I asked.

We shot each other a look, the one you give when you know you've just made a decision that works. I knew I could convince my parents to let us caretake The Land in exchange for not paying rent. When people asked what we would *do* there, I would give the most honest answer I had. I had most certainly not moved here to be a cowboy. Or to prove anything to anyone.

Chris planned to finish the shed garage next to the cabin in order to start his furniture studio. I would write, get to know the place, ride out my minimal savings, and find part-time work when that became necessary. All in all, we would stay for about a year, maybe a bit longer.

Not a retreat but a launching point.

Like these grasshoppers, launching themselves.

I stretched up and satisfaction flooded down through me.

Hey you, Chris called from behind me on the porch. I turned to see him holding a mug of steaming coffee. He moved into scenes like an acrobat, silent and graceful and muscled. Under a mop of black hair, his eyelashes always wafted up and down. I called them delicate fans—so long they had caught my attention immediately in a college class, along with the fact that there was something in him that was not in me and that seems to be how it always starts. Like him, the gray river rock chimney stood out against the cabin's dark wood.

Look! I said, pointing down to the grass.

He nodded and smiled.

You think they'll let us do it? I shouted back, because, on top of our general plans, there was something else we hoped to do here.

Probably, he shouted back. Your parents tend to be visionary.

I just don't want them to feel like we are mooching, I said, moving through the grass back toward him. We have to wait a few weeks so it doesn't sound like we assumed it would be okay.

You're the boss, he said, leaning against a post.

You know, he added, it isn't going to be easy.

I know.

Seriously, Molly, it's going to require patience to build it.

I *know*, I said, knowing also that, with me, he had made an art of managing expectations.

Okay, let's go explore, but you've got to put some clothes on first, he laughed, reaching for me as I snuck past him and sank down to lace up my boots. When I turned back, the landscape had shifted. So focused on grasshoppers, I had not noticed the small white puffs, millions of them, floating down and across the green grass fields, replenishing themselves rapidly under a massive, and I mean massive, sky. I traced them back to the gnarled cottonwood trees along the creek. With branches askew, green leaves fluttered and shook off cotton. It looked to me like a great migration. Eventually I would learn that it was called the yearly cottonwood dispersion. But then, in those early months, I only saw the idea of things, instead of the actual *it* of things.

Underneath that sky, a sky so expansive the corners touched down everywhere, we wanted to build a yurt, actually, a traditional Mongolian *ger*. We had dreamed about the structure ever since learning how to touch each other in our tiny dorm rooms. Pared down had always appealed to us. Chris appreciated the architectural brilliance of a yurt. It was different and refused normality. It would be homemade of a few pieces of wood and canvas. Eventually, we could pack it up and take it with us. That concept seduced me. I could imagine us using our hands to shape wood, growing even closer to each other as we did so, putting all the pieces together on some stunning autumn day, and standing there in front of a home, our home, made by us, together. To build one didn't seem that outlandish to us. Because the cabin was not ours to inhabit full bore, the yurt had now evolved into a real solution.

I wasn't sure whether my parents or brothers would agree to it.

I planned to create a document that outlined all the reasons it made sense.

Because location matters, we took two weeks to explore The Land for a yurt spot. And, in that way, it was a slow beginning. We watched purple thunderstorms roll over mountains and wore wide-brimmed hats under the sun. Leaves unfolded. Everything around us continued to move ahead with the objective of summer. The wheat fields nearby swayed golden. Hummingbirds hovered. Dry air chapped our lips, a reminder of what it means to move to a dry place. At dusk, after long evenings lounging outside, I went to bed without swollen mosquito bites because bugs didn't seem to live here. We made a rule to not walk alone and to always carry bear spray. When the screen door slammed shut at 2 AM, we learned to recognize it as wind, not a predator clawing through to eat us.

Stripes, I had said to describe The Land.

Um, no. Chris shook his head. Stripes are for animals or wallpaper; this place is made up of corridors.

Because he grew up running through a maple and beech forest in western Maine, because he studied geology and understood topography in a way that I didn't, I relinquished the authority on land formations to him. And he was right. From the country road, past the jackleg fence, a meadow with three ponds formed the first corridor of The Land. Beyond that, a creek wound through with its own corridor of cottonwood trees. Beyond that, the cabin stood smack in the middle of the grassy corridor. Beyond that, the topography changed and rose up as steep as a tidal wave, a hill as imposing and long as the great wall of somewhere, the darkest black of the black, home to the only forest on The Land, a forest of evergreen trees called, I had learned, Douglas fir. They grew straight, even at that angle. Beyond that, the flat top or river terrace, what we first called the plateau.

The plateau knocked me to my knees. I had no deep connection to it yet, but when we climbed up the hill, our breath labored, we knew something awaited us each time. I would flop down on the ground like a doll. How could you not, in the middle of a basin surrounded by five snowy mountain ranges? The Land spread flat and south until it reached someone else's wheat field and then swept up to the Gallatin Range, which rolled hundreds of untouched, green, forested miles back to Yellowstone. Like pilgrims, we made a point of going up there every afternoon, even when it rained, which wasn't often.

At a moderate clip, you could loop from one end of The Land to the other in thirty minutes. When we weren't exploring, I read books about yurts and Chris finished the garage: insulate, hang drywall, seal the floor, spend his life savings on large tools, and transform it into a cozy woodshop for his personal studio and, conveniently, for the yurt making. We occasionally hiked from a trailhead down the road that could lead us through a canyon to the creek's origin twenty miles back. One day, Chris installed a black mailbox at the start of the driveway, down by the country road.

Now we're open for correspondence, I said, as if our shaky Internet connection was more unreliable than it really was.

↯

It's true that I had not been in touch with anyone. I hid my silence behind the excuse of transition chaos—not that anything was all that chaotic yet. I just wanted to savor the start instead of immediately having to recount everything to people.

But when Katinka called, I answered.

In many ways, she was my opposite—raven-haired, willowy, gentle, a trickster very in touch with her Italian and German heritage. We had met seven years ago in the high desert of the Southwest. She was studying cranial sacral therapy, and I had volunteered to be her guinea pig. Riding a tandem bike through cactus-infested arroyos knit us even closer together. By chance, we later ended up in New York at the same time.

You're there!

I know, I squealed into the phone. I told her about how the faint animal trails switchbacked up the hill; that our lungs threatened to burst after each climb, maybe equivalent to twelve flights of stairs; that from up there so many mountains, just layers and layers of them, and also the rusty metal roof of the cabin glimmered; and oh yeah, lime green moss clumped at the base of fir trees.

That's amazing, Molls, she said.

And the yurt, well, that's hopefully going to happen, I said. I just feel so grateful.

Sounds like it's just what you needed.

Yeah, the grass is epic, so tall.

I want to lie in that grass, she sighed.

Well, come visit, I said.

↓

It was all feeling so good—and my exuberance for the start of things poured over into finally connecting with people, finally reaching out before the month escaped.

Oh, darling Molly May! Susan cooed over the telephone.

We're here! I tried to chirp back, but it was a sound unnatural to me.

Welcome to Montanaaaa.

Thanks, Susan. Can't believe we're here, I said, descending my voice to its normal range. Susan had been like a second mother ever since our arrival in Texas. Her daughter and I had befriended each other and reeled our parents together. When both families moved away, we all stayed close. She had salivated over The Land for many years and when it went on the market and my parents were looking, she led them to it like horses to water. I admired Susan as the ultimate badass—a painter, outdoorswoman, and fearless creative. She was the sturdiest of supporters, a pear-shaped woman with a long blonde braid who would grab my face and sigh, *When I first saw your big beautiful blue eyes.* . . . When our two families had camped in Chaco Canyon, my first true exposure to a western landscape, she and I walked alongside red rock and I revealed my very serious plan to turn over a new leaf, to become a better person before sixth grade. She had always reassured me that having an inquisitive mind was a gift, even when that mind led me into quicksand.

Come over for a dinner party! Bring that darling Chris of yours, she urged. It'll be a great big group for you to meet.

She lived in Bozeman, a decent-sized university town twenty minutes away from us. It was known as a "mountain town." Though I had logged some decent time in towns over the years, I had never officially lived in one before.

If it had been the 1930s, the word *gay* would have described it best, because there was much merriment, much getting drunk on Old Fashioneds, much laughing around the colorful picnic table, under the plum tree, and near the gorgeous pots of flowers. Susan knew how to have fun. So did these other sixty-plus-year-olds.

Someone casually asked us what we were up to here. We shared that we were living sandwiched between the two canyons, that if you pulled off the main road at the lone strip joint with the neon pink sign of a buffalo, you'd find our road. Everyone knew the area.

We actually just drew up plans for our yurt, I explained.

The yurt immediately redirected the conversation. Everyone fed us an opinion, dangled them out like a bunch of little rafts until we were surrounded—the old pattern of indoctrinating someone into a harsh landscape. One man smirked that young people will do foolish things during a recession. Then someone suggested that a yurt was little more than a tent and that led to the whole gang telling us that we'd never seen a Montana winter and that we could freeze to death in a tent, so we better be careful, not stupid.

It all happened before anyone had forked salads into mouths.

You folks ever been to Mongolia? croaked an older gentleman, eyeing each one of his peers.

Everyone's faces dropped.

Those people been living in yurts for thousands of years, he explained. It's much colder there than it is here. These two'll do just fine.

We were glad for the authority. Coming from us youngsters, it seemed dreamy, but we knew the yurt had been perfected to waft out smoke, hold up against extreme climates, and disassemble in less than an hour to be packed on the back of a horse or yak-driven cart headed for the next grazing land. That was part of its allure. So few homes were simple. This one was. It fit our time frame and our aesthetic. It had evolved over centuries in Central Asia with nomadic cultures—the perfect dwelling for a people on the move. New arrivals to the modern capital of Ulaanbaatar even set up *ger* districts.

Calm settled over the table and soon regular chitchat resumed. Someone asked me where I was from.

Nowhere, really.

What do you mean?

When I explained that I'd grown up all over the world, they asked for the list and I gave it to them, and a few *Ooos* and *Ahhs* came toward me, and the earlier heat dissipated with this new information and they became captivated that a woman from nowhere was building a yurt. I let the praise wash over me like warm waves.

Navigating out of the grid-streets and onto a dark straight road pointing at the mountains, we watched for deer and I slowly shed the skin of justifying myself about the yurt. Was it practical to spend our savings and time building a home that had no bathroom or shower or running water or electricity, a home that was sixteen feet in diameter, when we weren't completely sure how we would earn money yet, or how long we would be here, despite our belief that things always do work out? Not one bit. I had even suggested early on that we lock the cabin and never use it—let's tough it out, sleep in the shop, and cook on a camp stove while building. Chris had smiled, taken my hands in his, and said, Easy, killer.

As July tapered to a close, we decided to choose a spot for the yurt and send the proposal to my family before they got word from Susan. On the plateau, we moved along a sagging barbed-wire fence that separated wild grass from a cultivated square field. A local farmer had asked my parents if he could grow on it: peas, maybe.

Chris wandered into the peas with his straight-backed walk, hands clasped behind him like a monk. I, on the other hand, leaned forward, tilting to get places. Sometimes we walked together; sometimes we didn't. We had become skilled at stretching apart, pulling back in to exchange notes and then stretching apart again. And building the yurt together seemed a fitting prelude to our wedding next June. It seemed like something people should do before saying Yes, yes, and yes again. Though we could now call each other fiancé, I preferred to call him my man, a better term for a relationship that had accumulated so many layers over ten years. I had stalked him, the shy one, and found a man who wrote literary quotes on masking tape with a black Sharpie and stuck them around his room, a man so good and tender I felt I didn't deserve his attention. When he first said he loved me, I parted my hands in disbelief and cried. He was grounded, grown in one house in one state. But he was also willing to roam. We made plans to sail across the Pacific, live in northern Japan, bike down the length of Chile. People called him quiet. He was. Raised by stoic people, he had been unfamiliar with the art of intimate verbal communication. When we hurt each other, my women friends usually took his side. It was hard not to. He forgave my impatience. I could barely forgive myself, let alone him. Though I lusted after other places, I never lusted after other men. Whenever we had left each other in pursuit of a job or opportunity, for long periods of time

—months, even a year—he buried his face in my shoulder and sobbed the hardest. We spoke different languages, and somewhere they overlapped.

Sagebrush stuck up everywhere, stuck up silver. Crushing a twig in my palm, rubbing each individual leaf into wet mash, the scent rose up: campfires and rattlesnakes and open sky. Leaving Chris to the peas, I squinted under my old straw hat and turned back toward the edge of the plateau, where it met the forest tumbling back down, a cascade of fallen branches and rocks, to the cabin. The trees created a visual end, or beginning, depending on how you saw it. From this perch, the valley below ran and ran for miles of wheat fields until it swooped up against another set of distant mountains.

What part of me would emerge here? I greeted the scene with the kind of intention we reserve for something we know might make an impact on us. You say Hello and pause.

Behind me, a warm breeze tossed at my hat.

Behind me, arms suddenly around my waist.

Hey, milkmaid, Chris whispered into my ear.

Err, I growled. Someone had recently told me that I had the face of a milkmaid. I had taken that to mean demure. Now those big red cheeks were slathered in two white stripes of sunscreen.

Definitely arriba, I announced, wrapping his arms farther around me.

Yep, I like the plateau too.

That hill is brutal, though.

Yep, creek makes more practical sense for a dwelling.

But it just *has* to be the top.

You like the juniper bush up here.

I also like the complexion of the sky. You like the clouds.

It's the top, then.

It's the top.

And that's how the plateau became known as the top. We chose a spot tucked against the firs, surrounded by sagebrush, where we could build a platform hanging out over the hillside. That way the yurt could be as low as possible from what we anticipated would be strong winds.

Once we got the okay from my family, once we decided on a meticulous budget of $6,000, an elemental force took over. It put a calendar flipping toward winter in front of us and barked. Time wasn't slowing down, and if there was one thing we were good at, it was getting shit done.

Our shoulders found direction.

We hauled a bright orange ladder up to the top to make sure we did not ruin the vista of our neighbors across the grassy corridor. As Chris ran down the hill and across the dirt road, I climbed to the last rung of the ladder and waved my whole body to reach what would be the yurt's height. In the eight minutes it took him to return, white cotton puffs floated through the air below and I talked myself down from imagining him mauled by a mountain lion. He arrived safely, panting. And he had not seen my arms waving.

We were invisible from all directions—with one exception. The green house behind us, far enough across the plateau to be barely noticeable, was our only wild card. I didn't know who our neighbors were, but I was worried we would represent the passers-through and they would all be old-timers who didn't like change. By default, we would participate in a sad western narrative of the unaware newcomers destroying a way of life that had been. They would think we were asses who couldn't chop wood.

Well, asked Chris, when I shared my concern, can you split wood?

Yeaaaaaaa, hello, I scoffed, knowing that I'd done it well at least a few times, even for a girl who grew up in warm places.

We decided on a low-roof *ger*. Friends didn't understand why we still called it a yurt then. Well, I explained, for one, we are not Mongolian. We have never been to Mongolia. We know very little about Mongolia. Montana may share climate and landscape features with Mongolia, but it is not Mongolia. We are simply borrowing a design and amending it to our situation and, most importantly, it's a respect thing.

To get started, Chris plugged away at trigonometry and drew a scaled sketch on graph paper—an interesting exercise for a circular structure made of nothing but lattice and roof poles. My yurt drawing involved an outdoor scene of lanterns dangling from a rope, a hammock, and if time permitted, a garden of native plants that required no watering. I also drafted our budget on a spreadsheet. Soon, we slipped into collective contemplation and I wrote lists:

1. Can I eat juniper berries raw?

2. Build a garden, when . . .

3. Source canvas material for yurt.

4. Lie in grass to meditate for one hour a day (at least).

5. Foundation?! Let Chris deal with that.

Mongolians traditionally set their yurts directly on grass. Unlike most Americans, they consider it taboo to disturb the earth. Despite the fact that yurts weather seventy mile-per-hour winds on the open steppes, we wanted an anchor. Perched on the edge of our massive hill, we felt no need to wake up crashing through the fir trees all the way down to the creek.

We can*not* afford to be purists, we repeated to one another.

And wanting dry floors, we had capitulated. All of which meant we had to move the yurt's future foundation, a simple one, from the shop to the top. Right now, it looked like a pile of wood.

For three days, we worked like mules and it became a sort of song. Dirt wafted up with each clomp; sweat dripped from our elbows and slid down our ribs. For every two planks of wood I carried, Chris carried three, despite the fact that we measured in at the same height. We could lift each other up and rest heads on shoulders at the same time: eye to eye, literally. Bruises on our shoulders turned purple. The repetition of our movement up and down the hill matted down the grass so decidedly that the faint animal trail became ours.

When we had begun, I predicted it would only take a few hours.

As he lumbered up ahead of me, locked into a rhythm on this vertical angle, I paused on the hill, eased the planks down for a break against a tree. I valued the dignity of manual labor. But sometimes, it just sucked. And that was okay. We shouldered them up plank by plank. Finally, our relocated stack rested inert and ordered in the grass—thirty-eight heavy planks of Doug fir and seventeen concrete piers. It was the only sign of human life on the top. I blew out a happy sigh.

We're almost there, beb, I said, standing in wild grass at

our yurt site, the satisfied ache of accomplishment pulsing in my legs.

Getting there, Chris tempered, which shows just how little I knew about how long it would actually take us to build a home.

Drinking tea the following morning, watching Chris squeeze honey over his toast, I decided that we must formally introduce ourselves to our closest neighbors before they noticed our strange antics. It had been almost a month. I wondered who they were. They lived in a log cabin across the grass corridor. The creek spilled down from us, underneath a bridge across the country road, and then down behind them.

Let's clean ourselves up and walk over, I suggested.

Now? Chris griped.

Yes, now. It's been too long already.

Diane was kneeling in her garden, head down in the succulents, so focused that she didn't hear our footsteps crunch up the dirt driveway.

Hello? I said, and her small gray head arced around.

Oh, hi, she said, as if she'd been expecting us, as if she were picking up a conversation we'd started ages ago.

She stood up and we got to the business of shaking hands and the back and forth that initiates a friendship. In one long sentence, she told us that they had lived here for twenty-three years—that she was a potter, her Dutch husband Willem an artist; the man across the road in a collapsing red barn kept to himself; the family that originally ranched all this land sold their last parcel not that long ago; the dirt road to the west was scattered with various artist or farming types; and the isolated hill among wheat fields, a defining feature of our neighborhood, was named after Harry, the old man who had once lived in a little white house at the base of it.

My response was paltry in comparison: Well, we moved here from New York, but neither one of us is from there.

We insisted on a future dinner together. And that was that. Introduction complete. Hand in hand, Chris and I walked back toward our black mailbox and the fluttering cottonwoods.

Oh, she called out, you should know there's a female mountain lion around here.

Oh, yeah? I turned around, spinning Chris with me.

Yeah, you shouldn't worry about it, but this is her territory. We hear her killing the deer at night in the creek. She waits for the exact moment when they step into the water, and *Snap!* it's over. The sound of a dying deer is an awful sound. And we used to have grizzly bears too. We never saw them, only sign of them. But not recently.

Then she giggled at the memory.

Diane didn't seem out to scare us. She was bird-like, flitting from one thought to the next, enthusiastic about the wildness of this place we all inhabited.

Um, so does that mean we shouldn't walk around alone? I tried to clarify.

Oh no, like I said, you can't worry about these things. You won't ever see the mountain lion, she explained. You just have to know that she's here.

We took Diane seriously. She would soon become our oracle on the history and animal patterns of this area. Do as locals do, I knew. The bottom of our green hill was dense, covered in a thick mat of high underbrush. Walking up to the yurt through that, especially at night, would be ignorant.

Let's trim it down.

Good plan. Yes.

The next morning, gathering shears and clippers, we stomped up to the hill. Despite our mission to clear away the bush to "save" ourselves, I was intoxicated by the fact that neighbor-speak around here actually involved predators at all. Occasionally, a branch whipped me across the face—plants I would later identify as chokecherry, wild rose, hawthorn, and serviceberry. I got used to the sound of little crashes, branches hitting the ground, a bush down. Weeding, in its essence, was good, but that didn't prevent me from bending down to whisper "Sorry" with each snip. As Chris dragged piles of brush away, I clipped away at one section, pious in my dedication, until hours later I had uncovered the trunks of three fir trees. They towered above me now, evergreen boughs fanning out to create a shade shelter.

It's hard, under the wide limbs of a tree, not to be pulled into a daydream, not to flash back to the willow tree in Spain, to hear out of nowhere a phrase from that girl who was me, retelling the details of her story: *One thing I like about myself is the willow tree. But I won't go around declaring that to people.*

Underneath my willow tree, I sit and wait for a message. Its long green branches reach to the ground like hair. It feels like a dome. A few lone ants crawl over my jelly sandals. This is the last time I will ever feel the rough bark, so I lean back into it. My family is moving away from Spain to another country, one called Mexico, and I have come to say goodbye. It is complicated to try to make a list of all the good times in my head, but I try anyway: when the iguanas followed me in here and I swallowed my scream; my afternoon prayers for the dead crows; pulling my scrawny body so high the willow grew extra branches to keep me from falling; when I dragged all of Mom's pots and pans out here for a feast; when I dragged my brothers down here and assigned them other nearby willows, keeping this one, the most regal, for myself; and trimming the willow's hair with shears and immediately regretting it.

I pick at a scab on my knee and then the willow speaks to me.

You are flexible, it says. You have a vision beyond us.

I don't know whether to respond out loud.

No, I am too shy to do that.

Instead, I press my cheek against the bark so the willow will know that I know. What I don't know is that the thing behind my ribcage, a thing I won't name for many years, is fattening up on phrases like that one. Because *beyond* appeals to me greatly, I squint through my hands like a telescope, trying to see past the branches, out past the driveway where we will soon drag suitcases across gravel to cars, beyond the rolling hills of Spain, out to an ocean somewhere, and eventually into a future, unaware that one day I will be a grown-up woman on a hill in southwestern Montana noticing a silence take the place of her man pushing through the woods, and when she can no longer sense him, she will call out, You there?

Yup, I'm here, Chris yelled back.

Come look at these firs, I yelled to him.

After two days, the underbrush was gone. Now a smooth green carpet unfolded down from the forest. What had been scary to us was now inviting, and it took no great mental leap on my part to understand that what had been inviting to animals might now seem scary to them. Though relieved, I was sorry, especially for the lion. She had become the background to our every move. We left one lone serviceberry curving over our tamped-down trail, its longest branch unfolding to signal the top, where, after weeks of preparation, our yurt building would finally commence.

August stampeded in and crisped the grass to a pale yellow. We were finally doing it. Day one of breaking ground. Earlier that week, a farmer had bulldozed open an irrigation ditch that ran part of its course along the base of our hill. Because water rights in Montana are often grandfathered in, what had been a grassy hump became a small muddy ravine. Chris had tossed an extra plank of wood across the four-foot-wide ditch. We crossed it like a bridge to get to our trail. Soon, the earth would start to grow over and fasten it in place.

On our way up, water bottle dangling from my thumb, I stopped on the plank. The routine of "walking the plank" every day to get to the yurt, well, now *that* was poetry, a sort of conscious step into our living situation. Beneath my dirty sneakers, clods of soil smelled aerated and fresh from upheaval. I cocked my head left and then right, as if glancing down a train track, and marveled at this new scar. The Land, of course, like any land, had no say about what was done to it: first, the mini-deforestation of ours; second, the slit opened in its belly; and third, the seventeen holes we were about to dig for our yurt foundation. When shoved into a corner, I shed all decorum and chop my way out. But this place couldn't do that. Places can't leave.

We ambled up the path, through the moist shade of fir trees, fallen needles, pine cones, lichen, damp and then crested the hill, curving around until our faces met the sun, a white orb, beating down on us. Across the pale yellow, heat waves like a mirage pulsed low to the ground. Barren hills rolled back on the western horizon to what we called the badlands. One lone juniper somewhere whispered: desert.

We organized the site quickly.

Let's do this thang, I said.

I leaned my shovel against my calf, warm.

See the heat waves?

Mmm, Chris responded, already prying his shovel down into the soil, focused on our task. To mark the occasion, I had braided my hair, slipped into my trusty lime-colored shorts, and ditched my unraveling straw hat for a more reliable fabric one. Lined up like cubes in the sagebrush, the concrete piers were animated in their togetherness, waiting patiently for these large holes, their homes, to appear. Once buried in the ground, we could attach a wooden framework to them and secure our yurt to The Land. I had never even seen a foundation. Chris described it as sticks with lots of heavy feet.

I pierced the earth, wiggled the edge of my shovel deeper, and tolerated the screech of metal on rock. As we worked, that western smell wafted up: dry, perfumed, gauzy, wind-washed. I muscled out small rocks, wrenching them up with black clay. At least we were not pouring a concrete foundation. Sweat pooled at the end of my nose and one lone bead dripped into the sad start of my first hole, to where a boulder sat in my way: a big old watermelon shrugging at me as if to say, *What'cha gonna do about it?*

Because we had measured the foundation layout down to a quarter of an inch, the hole had to be in this spot. I jabbed around a bit, trying to avoid the inevitable dig around and around and around until it moved. As I wiped my forehead, making a dramatic gesture of swooping my hand up to fling the sweat, I saw Chris. He was drenched, slicked back like a seal, and bent over his three perfectly dug holes, about to start a fourth.

I'm taking a break, I grumbled.

I tossed my shovel and stomped out into the open where I could make an effort at being pleasant again.

After a few minutes, Chris gently placed his shovel down, slugged back some water, and inched toward me. He joined me, cross-legged on that prickly yellow grass. The faint sound of a wing flap pulled our gazes up to the sky. An owl coasted over the fir trees, catching an updraft and then circling. We knew this particular great horned owl. Well, *knew* isn't fair, because how can you actually know an owl? We had seen it fly, perch, and even stand on the ground nearby. It lived somewhere on this land and I watched for it every afternoon. Maybe it had been watching us too, and that thought, of the eagles, deer, and elk doing the same, brought me some ease.

There he is, pointed Chris.

She, I corrected.

Our heads lolled back to follow the owl.

He, Chris sparred back in a brave move. He assumed the rebel in me was looking for something to bite. I didn't. Something inside me was irritated and I didn't know why. Which translated into me wanting the owl to be female. I wanted her to be hunting and I wanted her to be female. I just needed that to be true.

She, I repeated.

Chris poked me. Then he threw his arm over my shoulders and laughed.

My tension dissolved.

I just don't want us to have traditional male/female roles, I sighed.

And as it came out of my mouth, we both recognized it as a throwaway sentence, one trying to take up the space of the right sentence I was unable to form yet.

You know, he said, I don't like digging holes either, but I do it.

That's the thing, I articulated. Nomads don't do foundations. It's taking me a moment to get comfy with the fact that we *are* doing one. But, hello . . . I chose this. I want this. That is what people do. They build a house and a house sits on top of a support. But suddenly, it feels like this is going to take forever.

Molly, whoa, he whispered, no stranger to my monologues.

I gestured out to the stack of wood and shovels, and then let my head drop.

I am not wired to dig into anything for longer than three seconds, I said.

Chris offered one clean sentence.

Just be what you are then.

So I talked it out. It helped me—always—to make a narrative of a moment. My parents' friends emailed me with questions: What's this about a yurt I hear? What is a yurt, anyway? Oh, a round structure, I typed, explaining the mechanics of it in a way I couldn't have even a month ago. But my responses were limited to the basics.

For reveals, I called family mostly.

Oh, whatever, said my cousin about the digging. That isn't bad behavior. You two always work it out. You do the craziest things together anyway. This yurt thing, I mean, kerosene lanterns, mountain lions, seriously, what? It's right up there with the sea lions.

The sea lions felt distant. On a rickety dock in New Zealand a few years ago, Chris and I had spent an entire afternoon on our stomachs watching three of them roll in the waves, roll so close we could smell musk and saltwater and see right down their open red mouths and he had said Marry me and I said Yes.

My brothers responded to yurt talk exactly as I expected. Like me, they moved often, out of habit, perhaps—but neither one of them had intentions to create a life of perpetual uprooting, and neither one of them felt attached to our childhood abroad. They had been young then. We had been each other's reliable. Are you close to your brothers? people asked. In an unspoken way, yes. They were my extra limbs.

You'll have to get Persian carpets, said my youngest brother, the artist and fashionista, a man so sensitive to design he could get "visually assaulted" by certain setups.

Just cover the whole thing in Persian carpets, he repeated. Then everything will be fine.

When I called my middle brother, the former military paratrooper, he listened to me tell him that we would be living in it by the start of November. I explained the general logistics of events, the amount of work that awaited us, and my plan to really get into the experience of living in a yurt and learning whatever this land could teach me.

He gave me one thought.

All I can say is that's so you, he said.

I didn't mention to him, or many others, that I was also trying to locate a self who didn't bang her head against brick walls.

We would cobble the yurt up, find joy in the act of creating something together, and get clear on life. When winter blew its first breath onto our necks, I would already be sitting by a fire in our cozy yurt to ask questions and do what I had come here to do. I couldn't wait for it. I wanted it to happen now, now, now.

The foundation had to go in well before a frost. Our work schedule became relentless. At the end of each day, we slumped into nylon camp chairs, noticed crisp air arriving on the winds, pulled sweaters over our heads, listened to sandhill cranes croak at dusk, watched those prehistoric birds stretch necks out and fly toward a southern destination, and followed paths where deer and elk had parted the tall peas. The peas were actually alfalfa, but we didn't know that yet. We dug some more. We drilled screws and I learned to stop calling them nails. Our arms ached from sawing. We finally finished the foundation. Chris suggested I take on the role of spiritual director.

Why? I asked.

Because, he said, we're going to need one.

When the farmer cut the field, removed the blanket of green, it lost its flatness and we could see how it rolled up and descended, made a shape like a human tongue caught mid-sentence. Those contours inspired me to build a medicine wheel. I had never built one before, had only seen them—and though the tradition wasn't mine, something had to be done. I needed to place rocks in a large circle outside. There I could sit and consider the north, south, east, and west: what they had meant to me in the past, what they meant to me now, and what they would mean to me in the future.

That next morning, light poured into the bedroom, spreading across the plaster ceiling and wooden vigas of the cabin. I followed its movement for a while and then slipped out from the embrace of Chris's warm body. I left a note on the counter: *Building medicine wheel. Down by creek and then up.*

It was my first solo walk on The Land.

I was scared but I did it anyway.

Sun streamed down through the cottonwood's lace canopy. The creek below glimmered copper. Hello to the creek, I sang to greet everything in and out of sight, hello to the creek, and to the rocks and to the bushes and to the liiiiion. I edged along the high banks, glancing behind me at every step, and found rocks the size of my head: rust orange, deep red, blue-green, alabaster, rawhide, mustard yellow. Later, my pile would dry into bland gray shapes, but I wouldn't mind the transformation.

With rocks loaded into my pack, I practically ran up the hill twice. It's easy to feel invigorated by small accomplishments. Behind the yurt site, behind the two ragged hawthorns, I tugged long sleeves over cold hands and reached into the pile. I settled north, west, east, south in the proper locations on a flat grassy spot. I leapt from side to side, back and forth, placing smaller rocks, wondering about the dried-up wildflowers, deciding I would learn their names in spring.

It was okay that I was winging it, right? Because I didn't know much about this act.

For two reasons.

1. On our second date, Chris led me up Snake Mountain in Vermont and reminded me about the cardinal directions. Oriented by the mountains as a child, he always knew what direction he faced. I had never met someone like that. I had never

known how to do that, so I told him that my first sentence in letters was always *Here I am*. Even if I only brushed shoulders with a place, I needed someone to know where I was.

2. My family didn't do this sort of thing. I had grown up half-Catholic, but we had no ritual, at least no ritual I agreed with. We had no ceremony. We had no land knowledge. But, from the time my mother told me that my pacifier had gone bye-bye on the airplane, I was pawing at symbols, even the plebeian ones, and later praying in my bed. Which was also part of why I wanted to build a medicine wheel, as a way to communicate to this place. *Knock, knock, thank you so much for having us.*

Once all the small rocks filled in the wheel, one rock remained: bone-colored and as long as my forearm. It would be the pointer rock, the moving piece in a static form. In the center, I faced it east toward the direction I'd recently come from. A prayer. I needed a prayer for this place. Squatting with my eyes closed, I asked for one.

Please. Help me. Remember. To be patient.

Thank you.

The valley had bleached itself out to an eggshell-white glow. The air smelled of fresh-cut hay. Watching over it all was our foundation. No floors yet, but a framework of sturdy wood beams. It was a thing, an entity accomplished before the ground had frozen.

Not knowing what to do next, I slipped off my sneakers and socks. The soles of my feet were peeling. It happened every time I moved to a new place. The breeze caught some of my dead skin—flick, flick—and deposited it nearby, in the crooks of parched plants, on the matted-down spongy areas of grass. When I stood back up, my feet scrunched with cold. Later, when Chris and Susan crested the hill, I would posture my body to pretend that what I was doing, after all, was stretching. But for now, I reached palms up to the dark green boughs of The Land, to the wide sky, to the Gallatin, Tobacco Roots, Bridger, and Crazy Mountains that I could name now and to everything I didn't know about yet.

Here I am, I whispered.

2

THE WALLS GO UP
AND DOWN
AND EVENTUALLY UP

October 2009

We flew back to New York for three weeks to tie up loose ends. In the corners of dark bars and on busy sidewalks strewn with fallen leaves, I answered questions about our soon-to-be yurt and described the wild savannah grass. There's a penetrating silence. There's a plateau surrounded by mountains. But friends could not stop with the same maddening refrain.

Wait, so you actually live there now?

Wait, so you actually live there now?

As if *there* were a place that people did not inhabit, as if *there* were the moon.

Perhaps I had been vague about it when we left, made Montana sound like a very brief stopover on the way to somewhere else. I laughed and told them, Yes, yes, we do live there. They blinked at me with visions of what they probably imagined that wilderness to be. I realized then, and would continue to realize, that I tended toward being an isolationist. Not in a hermit or serial killer way. But the urge to put myself in hard solitary situations persisted—knocking on a stranger's door simply to goad my own courage, avoiding moving in with or anywhere near college friends because that would have lacked challenge, picking fruit and hauling kelp and farming for two seasons while others plowed toward success in graduate school, building a tent while others bought proper houses and apartments, never choosing whatever seemed easy or obvious. We all have ways of testing ourselves, and this was mine.

I didn't know whether that was good or bad.

The more my words about our new life trailed out of me, the more I wanted to jerk away from the masses and get back to it. I just wanted to be there. I was ready to live in our yurt on The Land, but continued to skip over the fact that we had yet to build it and that about 2,492 unknowns lay ahead of us.

Like, for example, the snow.

When we returned to Montana in early October, the cotton-wood trees looked as stunned as we were. Leaves hung like green glass ornaments on branches of ice. Beneath them, the ground stretched white and pillowy for acres and acres of snow. The air did not move. Nothing moved. Fall was no more. The whole white glittering landscape had been frozen in the act of transformation.

Look, I said to Chris and snapped two icicles from the cabin's metal roof. I hit them together and they shattered over my winter boots, a sound breaking the spell of quiet. An owl, maybe *the* owl, coasted silently from firs to cottonwoods. Our breath steamed out into the cold air, and that cold air returned to chap my cheeks.

Chris walked to the shop to shovel an entrance to the doors. I decided to edge along what had been the grassy corridor. The snow now made a blank canvas on the land. Animals had been traveling here all along, perhaps at night, tracks left behind: the plod of black bear, skitter of vole, and steady slink of fox. It was a map of stealthy movement. In great S-shapes, paths spread for hundreds of feet, thousands of feet, in every direction. Not one of those creatures had taken a perfectly straight line. I wanted to frame it on the wall: white on white on white. Who had been where and why? I tromped over to the yurt path to find out.

How laden with snow, how low to the ground the dark green boughs had become.

How strange, these markings beneath me.

I wondered, for a moment, if a large dog had prowled around while we were gone.

Four toe pads and no claw marks.

Oh my god, oh my god, oh my god, I repeated into my hands until my gloves smelled of warm leather and Chris yelled up, What?

She *was* real. The elusive was real. Her recent presence here pushed me down to place one hand in the print. I imagined her muscular shoulders moving slowly, deliberately. The way her nose might push at the snow to scent deer. Electricity coursed through me. I could taste metal in my mouth, could smell the cold. Few people in Montana ever saw sign of a lion. Our absence had allowed her to draw a trajectory through The Land. Would our return make her flee? I didn't want that to be the case. But I didn't want to come face to face with her either. As I lifted my head to the trees, light stabbed down through and sparkled up the snow.

Later that night, we gathered around the dinner table and

chattered on about the lion with Chris's parents, who were visiting for a long weekend. We wondered where she slept, whether deer scattered on intuition, whether she would be back.

And, as fortune goes, the next morning, as the rest of us poured orange juice, his father, a quiet man adverse to excitability, looked out the window and watched the lion sprint up our driveway and across the snow.

There's your cat, he said.

By the time I registered what he meant, she was gone.

I had missed it. So had everyone else.

Long tail, he explained, holding his arms out in wingspan.

Boots on, I led the march out to the spot. We measured a ten-foot distance between her bounds. It had to be the same lion —the one that claimed this land within what I'd read was usually a hundred-mile radius. If I had been standing there when she darted across, would she have balked, leapt for my neck, or moved swiftly by, her coarse tawny hair brushing against my leg? I wanted to know whether, as she made her dash, she had sensed us behind the safety of our walls. She, of course, built no permanent walls of her own, only slipped through the wide wise landscape.

Winter would clamp its jaws down soon. Diane had told us so in the same breath she'd explained, Yeah, that lion hid behind her car to track deer in the yard. This first snow dump, she said, was a solid month early. It would probably melt, but it did mean that we were in for a big winter. The yurt needed to be up and closed in by official winter, right around Halloween. Just three weeks away. Not for any other reason than we didn't want to wait until summer to live out this experience. We wanted out of the cabin and into the yurt. We also needed to find jobs eventually. And putting a yurt up in winter would just be much harder.

Before assembling the pieces, we had to construct them in the woodshop.

But I knew nothing about carpentry. Had sawed the legs off a desk, once; had banged a plank onto an old wood shed, once. Building the foundation had been basic. Now I was joining Chris in his art. I did my form of due diligence by researching and reading some poems about wood and work. He gathered materials.

It almost goes without saying that none of this would have been possible without Chris or without the cabin. He held the practical vision in his head. He problem-solved the design. He was the mastermind. We also had running water. We had heat. We had a shower. We even had Internet, though it, along with the landline, relied on a tower in the far far distance. If clouds rolled in or weather pummeled us, both shut down. When people shared awe or concern about our yurt-building process, I was quick to set the scene. No, we hadn't locked the cabin as I had once suggested. No, we weren't camping in the snow. By our standards—maybe not everyone else's—life was plush.

We woke at 7:30, ate bland oatmeal, and crunched across the snow to the shop.

Not bad for a commute, Chris said, coffee mug in hand.

Not bad at all, I said, and threw my arm over his shoulder.

Chris had created a true craftsman's studio. It was bright and organized: workbenches, wood slabs, and chiseling tools. Stacked books reminded him of the mentors I had watched him collect over the years—Calder, Noguchi, Nakashima, Krenov

—and how they, and indigenous boat building along with Japanese joinery, had taught him what they knew, even across the span of history. He had had no living teacher, only his own discipline and the yearning to make. Even when he drove me insane, when his stubborn silence monopolized us, I knew that no transient woman could resist a man who works with his hands.

Five large gray machines took up most of the space. They were ready to create a hazardous dust environment and make this a modern-day enterprise. The grunters, I called them. Building the yurt would be no act of whittling in the forest.

It went like this.

I suited up with a dust mask, goggles, and bright yellow earplugs. I accepted that this outfit was antithetical to the life we were trying to create here. I accepted the irony of being inside now so that later we could be out.

I feel like a scuba diver, I laughed, sort of thrilled by it all, as Chris trained me to use those gray machines, ones like the flat table saw, whose spinning blade rose from beneath like a monster.

I worked hard to pay attention. During that initial week, wood dust coated the air. I became astonished by the simple details of this world. At night, before showering, we stood naked in front of the mirror and stared at the tiny wood particles that had accumulated on our hair like dandruff, on my earlobes, his earlobes, the same ears that had begun to assimilate to the drone of being inside the aluminum reverberations of a cruising jet. Our life smelled of fresh-cut wood and, for now, I was way into it.

↙

The wall(s) came first. We would make four wall sections because a yurt, being circular, traditionally required accordion-like lattice wall sections tied together to make the one wall. Many folks first experience yurts as accommodations at a ski resort or alternative retreat center. But those yurts come as kits: all the pieces ready to go. We needed to start from scratch —with the long slats that would eventually make a lattice that would eventually make four separate walls that would eventually make one wall. They weren't going to appear out of thin air. Not out of this thin air. The air outside was cold as a sheet of metal. The shop offered warmth, as much warmth as a place with machinery and tools can.

I'll cut them, said Chris, and you can sand them.

Got it.

From a slab of red oak, he cut them into rough shape and tossed them into a collapsing pile for me. The whine of metal chewing through wood harmonized with my electric sander. My job: to smooth them down. As I manhandled the seven-and-a-half-foot-long slats that late afternoon, I thought of them as ribs because every structure must have ribs to contain what lives inside. My sander vibrated over one *khar mod* and I repeated the word over and over again to imprint it in my mind. We fell easily into using Mongolian words, though some were harder than others. *The Complete Yurt Handbook* had graced the back of our toilet for months.

To avoid cramping, I learned to alternate arms over a few days. It was also a reminder that expectation mars the goods. After getting to 84 *khar mod*, I celebrated with a *Whoop!* until we realized that our math had been off and we actually needed 155. If numbness moved from my fingers up to my elbows, especially on my left hand, the sander would jump out from my grip, once, twice, and skip across the table like a frog, kicking dust up at my face.

What I wanted to say aloud but didn't: Repetition can be a bitch.

Neck aching, I swayed my hips back and forth, as my hands, in garden gloves, went about their work. Nearby, small black spiders moved across the concrete floor, unbothered by the roar of machines, happy to be in from the cold. It was an assembly line. It was metallic car parts. It was sorting through fresh apples on a conveyer belt, something I had actually been paid for once. It was muscle memory. It was all-consuming. It was a groove. Groove. Groove. Groove. And depending on what you think of grooves, that situation could stagnate you or enlighten you. I breathed in the plastic of my mask and told myself that the stack was almost done, a few more, a few more before bed, try it with eyes closed, a few more.

My best friend Nader and I are sitting cross-legged underneath the white jungle gym. His French mother has adopted him from Vietnam, and I'm pretty sure I'm American, but those distinctions aren't distinctions for us yet, at least not in first grade. I tell him I have a secret. I've just discovered what I want to be. What does he want to be? Oh, maybe a train driver. I lean in, cup my hand over his ear, and whisper that I plan to be a dolphin trainer. He pulls away to grin at me, but I grab his head and pull it back to say, But mostly, I'm going to be a traveling translator of languages. The confused scrunch on his face doesn't bug me. My father has just told me about translators and how they get to live in a brand-new place every single year. When Mrs. Barbaro rings the bell, everyone scrambles around, detaching from swings and each other to race back inside. Holding Nader's hand, I snap him back up to standing. And then we run. I run fast with the lightness of being so sure of myself.

Beb, beb, hey, beb?

What? I said, yanking at my mask, pulling it off my face.

It's midnight, Chris said, placing his hand on my shoulder. At my feet, the *khar mod* had smoothed themselves out.

The snow melted almost as quickly as it had fallen. Where white had buried everything, the matted-down yellow grass now tried to spring back up. Mud sucked at my boots. One afternoon, *hoo hoo*-ing to make my presence known, I walked the long walk down to the mailbox and made note of what the freeze had done.

Cottonwood leaves had gone purple—mottled and mauve. They no longer fluttered in the wind. I didn't have the history with The Land to feel sadness, but I did have enough instinct to peg an abnormality. I picked a leaf off. It was the size of my palm. Pressed to my nose, it cracked and released the scent of forest decay. So much had happened out here, and elsewhere, in the short time we'd made our long slats, the *khar mod*.

But I had barely noticed.

I returned to the shop, bear spray jammed in my back pocket, trying to imagine a world where purple was the color of growth.

Framed by the garage door, Chris wrestled with a bundle of *khar mod*.

Look, I said, thrusting my brittle purple leaf at him.

Whoa.

We stared at it together, as if it were a newborn. I had a habit of always saying—Look—and wanting someone to see what I was seeing. My family teased me for being that person who first observes that we are having fun and then announces that we are having fun, instead of just having the fun. So far, the yurt building had been fun, but it was all a preamble to the final product. As much as I hated what it meant to be someone who only wants the product, I wanted it like a lightbulb wants a lamp. Let me start my living here. I couldn't start to do what I had come here to do until the yurt was up, or so thought the me intent on her plans. And that maniacal approach, along with the real deadline of winter, created a mission of complete, complete, complete. Our fourteen-hour workdays had begun to elbow in too far. We had failed to notice the change in leaves.

In the past, when monotony had taken hold, I usually got in my car and drove—either away or just out long enough to experience something brand-new, a place of worship on a Wednesday morning, a cow giving birth on the roadside, even a conversation with a gas attendant. It was an easy out. We'd been tied to these particular 107 acres since July, actually more to the shop space, and we would be for a long while yet, even at this pace. Yurt construction, turned out, might not be a simple one-month ordeal. It wasn't like us, or like me, to not acknowledge all the purple leaves in the rest of the valley, in other towns.

Beb, I said, pointing to the *khar mod*, it's been, what, seven days of work on these?

Something like that.

We have got to take breaks, or get out, or go out, or something.

Yeah, he agreed, but first we've got to soak these things.

I tossed the leaf parts into the grass and bent down to help slip the webbing rope under this stack. In the beginning, we had often called them *khana* by mistake, trying to remember whether *khana* meant complete walls and *khar mod* meant slats of the wall, or vise versa. *Khana. Khar mod.* Kha-what?

Together, the *khar mod* could have been the pickup sticks of some great god. We needed to soak them for a few days in the ponds so that their cells could absorb water. That moisture would then allow us to steam-bend them into a curved shape. That shape would give the yurt its waist.

Well, Chris suggested, cinching the stack together, we can probably just carry them across the creek.

Sometimes this man liked to rub a physical possibility raw, or at least until dark when everyone else was ready to give up. Unlike him, my perseverance worked best when moving through the waters of a hard conversation for hours. We could exhaust each other with our respective ways and now knew when to request a *Halt*. That summer we had rolled boulders across the creek for a makeshift bridge. But there was no way I wanted to drag this heavy load, lift it, and balance over cold water like a prima ballerina. Please. Especially when there was another way across the creek.

Nope, I insisted, we're driving.

It felt revolutionary to be in a car going somewhere else. Even if that somewhere else was right across the creek. Mud splattered up into the wheel wells until we turned right onto the paved country road and across the paved bridge. We pulled up against the jackleg fence, one that framed the cabin across the creek and gave The Land an aura of the old ranch homestead it wasn't. I had entered this way once with my parents and knew to slide three logs across and down to open the fence. From here, we gazed at a wide-angle view of cottonwoods stretching up the creek and eventually into the mountains.

We are so lucky, I said, reaching for Chris's hand, delighted by this minute shift in perspective. On this side of the creek, The Land lost some of its wildness—a meadow so bucolic it was only interrupted by a faraway stand of aspens collected together like whispering friends. Their frostbitten leaves had gone purple too. Yellow ground, purple trees, gray sky.

Like American Gothic.

We drove straight back over the matted grass to the farthest pond, one long enough for a decent swim, but not at this point, not with my brown sweater and brown pants and brown boots. I sniffed at the marshy smell of ponds, pushed the *khar mod* bundle into the water, and tied it off to a flat rock on the edge. Because geese had perched here in the summer and shat, we called it poop rock. The ribs floated. Chris ran out to the meadow to find heavy rocks. When he returned, teetering toward me, I received the handoffs and heaved them onto the bundles. Splashes of clear cold water disturbed the silence. But it worked.

The ribs sank.

The sun began to lower itself behind the hill. I squatted on poop rock and Chris stood behind me, pressing his knees into my back so that I could lean into him as we paused in the evening chill. Magpies flitted from aspen to aspen, where the last spot of golden day held its ground among the fade.

Almost there, I said.

Getting there, Chris corrected, repeating our refrain, one that would last through the whole process and beyond.

I decided, right then and there, that while Chris worked on the roof poles, I would take on these walls. I would build them. I gave the two bundles a pat, as if patting them to sleep: Be good, dream well, we'll be back in the morning. Only we'd be back in about a week, and by then, Katinka would be here.

When I picked her up from the airport, we caved into a long hug. My sturdy always felt so pronounced against her lithe. She pulled back, looked around, and clapped her hands in quick little claps.

It's so tiny and friendly here, she said about the one baggage carousel, the one carpeted stairway, the one flock of bronze geese flying overhead. Katinka had come to get the hell out of the city and to meditate, a practice she had developed along with zooming around on her Vespa, frequenting tiny liquor bars, and buying illegal raw milk from the Amish. But before going into her silent meditation, she wanted to contribute to our yurt building. She had always dreamed of making her own.

I'm so glad you're here, I said, hooking my arm into hers as we walked out to the one parking lot underneath a bluebird sky. We sped down the road, our arms out the window making waves in the cold air, the mountains drawing us toward them.

So how's the yurting it? she asked.

Yurting it had been our phrase for what we were doing, or at least the phrase we offered to people and the one they spoke back to us on our answering machine.

It's going really well, I began, and then described how we had started planing the roof poles and these were called *uni* and looked like jousting sticks and there were sixty of them; that we'd decided against the $150 electric planer, so we were hand-planing them; that we'd also been digging a foundation for a cedar porch, which was a little late, but the ground hadn't completely frozen yet; that curlicue wood shavings and the idea of stripping something down were great but hand-planing the *uni* was so grueling, especially because the only way it worked was by moving with the grain, instead of against it; that we chomped way too many bags of salt and vinegar potato chips from the Exxon station, but oh well; that I had asked Chris to embrace the uncertainty of our dwindling cash; that he had asked me to start being "rational for a change"; that this actually wasn't, to our collective disappointment, the love-make-all-day venture that everyone assumed it was; and that, actually, getting a shelter up before winter was starting to feel like an acute impossibility.

Ooo sorry for the litany, I sighed, surprised by myself. You know how I get unimpressed with my behavior sometimes.

Yes, yes, she laughed, go easy on yourself. No one else we know is building a yurt.

It's just taking longer than I thought and we haven't even been at it that long.

Hmm.

You know I'm not the most patient bird on earth, I said, smiling.

You *are* patient in a lot of ways, Molls, but it sounds like you're being asked to sit back for this one, she offered.

The dreaded words! I sang out to the window.

Girl, she said, just let it unfold.

For the first few days, Katinka helped us hand-plane our roof poles. She learned to call them *uni*. She learned to smooth them out and shave off excess wood. We kept the door open to a fall landscape where purple leaves cartwheeled across the driveway and collected inside. Without snow, the world rewound, backstroke by backstroke, tried to get the season right this time. Katinka wore safety glasses, though we didn't require it, because she wanted to play the part.

We've got you at forced labor, Chris teased.

She was slow, meticulous, and intentional. Had I been missing something by rushing this experience? I assured myself, in the way we do when we compare, that she had the advantage of engaging in the process for a few hours, instead of months, instead of under the sudden pressure of winter. My parents had told us that we could chill out, quit, and just live in the cabin until summer, when we could resume building the yurt. I had responded, Thank you, but no, absolutely not.

The last evening before her meditation, we whirled around the kitchen, chopping ginger and carrots and whatever else we could find for chicken soup simmering on the stove. Making time to brew up a soup had not been on the agenda so far and it felt good, especially with winter approaching. Chris volunteered to chop more wood for the fire. He pushed the side door open to go out and then sprang back.

Something's out there, he whispered.

Hushing each other, we stuck our three heads out into the dusk. A big black bear sat on its haunches staring at us. It was twenty feet from the porch, off in the bush underneath the firs, out toward the edge of what I called no-man's-land. Katinka had arrived wanting to see a black bear—and there it was, musky flesh and all.

Hello, bear, I said aloud.

It stayed long enough to become a shadow in the night.

When the bear eventually scampered off, I followed Chris

out to the chopping block. As he swung the mallet down in the dark, I blew sounds into my harmonica. It echoed out into the dark bushes, punctuated only by the *chop, chop*. I spun in slow circles to make sure a black bear wasn't about to tear out of the woods at us, a potential so implausible that later, much later, we would joke that we had ever been so concerned.

We barely saw Katinka during her meditation. In the shop, as we waited for the *khar mod* to fully soak in the pond, we exhausted our forearms and worked to plane the *uni* out over and over again. I left bowls of salad and soup outside the door of her small room, the tiny bedroom in the cabin. Occasionally, I caught a glimpse of her disappearing into the muted landscape like a ghost in her long white down coat. I had warned her about predators. You walk differently in a land with predators. When she brushed it off, I gave her the facts: Remove the word *mountain* and you get *lion*.

Four days later, she left a note asking us to join her for her final meditation. We did. Then she broke her silence. She had felt the presence of predators, and of all creatures, eyes watching her as she walked in silence—horses turned heads, dog ears perked, noticing her, the one human, the one moving object, from a mile away.

What she left me with was: This land wants you to listen to it.

Allow yourself to slow down and invest a little bit, she suggested, in *all* of it.

Will do, that's my plan, I said, and wrapped her into a hug before she walked through the doors of the tiny airport. Maybe investing part of your heart in a place was made easier when you had an old tie to it. My parents had recently shared that a few of my ancestors had passed through Montana. I liked knowing that detail, as if my time here now somehow made more sense. My great-grandfather Ovid had lived for a few years in Butte, a mining town an hour or so west of us, sometime between selling his coronet for food in Mexico and deciding to make a business from copper tailings in Chile. When I was four and he was over ninety, we met at a reunion. It was he and his spectacles that I associated with my bloodline of vagabonds and expats, the wide-eyed ones who believed that bolting equaled progress. Nothing tethered them to a predetermined life. And they spun and spun and spun this long thread of belief. They pursued otherness and that led to great tolerance for others and intolerance for the now, because something better lay ahead, some better version of life, some better version of themselves. They, most likely, had never built walls.

When Katinka left, I felt left behind. Not that I wanted to follow her. It was simply the sensation of staying while someone else left; so, without much thought, I took to the highway. I didn't feel proud of myself for wasting the gas, but there I was anyway, responding to a reflex, gunning my Jeep down an empty highway with no real purpose other than heading toward Butte. I wouldn't get there but wanted to pretend that I might. On a dirty man-made road, orange willows lined underpasses against a gray autumn sky. My face settled into a perfect calm because I was trying to receive a feeling, like a junkie. It had been far too long. The pavement zipped by, or maybe I was still and it moved beneath me, a conveyer belt pushing me far, far, and farther. Images of steamships, passports, lines drawn on old maps, blood branching out into my veins. Leaf veins. Moving. Wheels. My heart smacked in my chest. I started to lean forward, to lean so forward that I pressed on my seatbelt as if I were a ship's maidenhead. I glanced at other drivers to see if they were doing the same thing. No one but an eighteen-wheeler was on the road.

Maidenhead woman.

Ten minutes later, the whole feeling blew right out of me. This was absurd. Woman drives three exits on I-90 to feel like she's going somewhere. She must need it bad, that woman. True nomads don't do it to feel it; they do it to do it, woman. They migrate with the grasses. They move from necessity. They know no other way.

Once, in Mexico City, I asked my mother whether we were real nomads, because I had taken great care to educate all my classmates that some people think all nomads wear turbans, which shows how much *some people* know about the world.

No, we aren't nomads, she says as we sit on our red brick porch.

Why?

I don't know, Molly, we just aren't, she shushes me and walks inside.

That isn't the answer I want. If we aren't nomads, I'm not sure what we are. So that's when I convince my brothers to run away with me. It won't be the last time because that's what nomads do. We pack a few chocolate cookies, one corn tortilla for each of us, and no water because carrying water isn't a thing then. When I unlatch the heavy iron gate, we suck in a group breath to acknowledge that we are breaking a huge rule by going into the *barranca*, where rats live and trash blows and who knows who hides out.

Don't worry, I say, just follow me.

And we descend the broken concrete steps until we are pulling our way through weeds and a gross water smell that makes us all hold our noses. I don't know where we are going, just that we are going away and it's important to be someone who goes away. I like the feeling. I like being defiant. I also like being an adventurer. But soon, my youngest brother is limping from some undisclosed injury and the air feels cold and we see the rats scurrying down below and in one united move, we turn around and head home and older sister feels both relieved and restless.

There had been so many small escapes like that one. But this place, with mountains ascending to my right, was radically different from the *barranca*. On the other side of the highway, to the south, the land flattened. Yellow plains extended like waves, swallowing houses and pinprick trailers, spreading far across the wide valley for miles until they swept up to another set of distant blue mountains, where rivers poured out from canyons, where wolves prowled at night, where, in the elevated land between two canyons, a little cabin nestled on a creek, and next to it a woodworking shop, and in that shop, bent over our yurt wood, stood Chris, the man whose name I had changed to Cristobal when we first met so that I could infuse some allure into a name so common, so American, I felt it didn't do him justice.

I once notified him: You just have to know that I will never move to the middle of the woods with you. The phrase went down in history, catalogued by friends who laughed that I was severe and that I did actually like the woods and that he hadn't even asked me to do such a thing—to which I responded that this was me setting the clear boundary that I craved movement, not the humdrum I associated with people living permanently in one cabin in one forest. This was just who I was. Made of the stuff restless people are made of. Made of a rhythm that takes leaps, like fish, from one thing to the next.

But here I was in the middle of the woods with him.

I wanted to laugh at myself, but how do you do that if you aren't good at it?

Looping around the exit and redirecting toward The Land, I rubbed my temples and blew out of my mouth. I knew it would happen again. I would come back to the highway.

As late October compressed wind into a steady cold, I drove down that highway a few more times as a self-soothing measure. We were nowhere near done and winter was supposedly around the corner and that was just the way it might have to be. The Land and the yurt process had already begun to prime me for whatever learning I wanted.

It was hard to see it that way, though.

You do whatever you need to do, Chris would say when I returned from driving.

His version of that was making pancakes for breakfast and dinner, as his family had.

Together, during short breaks, we took turns to swing arms and have the other keep pushing them like swings, like blood flowing, like progress.

Sometimes, when I couldn't will myself into a cold car, I stood in the warm steam of the cabin's shower instead. Both actions made me feel pliable. When the hot downpour soaked my head, turning my hair to seaweed, coyotes howled outside, a sound so contrasted to the warm shower it elevated the experience.

But often, I found a few moths—wet and dying at my feet.

Aiyyyy, I would squeal and shut off the water, crouching down, cooing and coaxing each papery moth, with its limp wings, onto a square of toilet paper. *I'm sorry, so sorry.* When we had first arrived and opened the cabin, whole colonies of brown moths had fluttered to life beneath the screen doors. I didn't know where they'd all gone since then, but some had found refuge in our bathroom. I called them peasant moths because the glamorous moths were few and white and furry and usually plastered in the middle of a wall, sure of their placement. These little brown ones were unsure. I liked them more for that.

Balancing the toilet paper square like an important document, I would tiptoe through the dark cabin and onto the porch to set them free. As my wet body twitched in the cold air, I forced myself to linger with the satisfaction of freeing something that had been doomed. Not that being released into the frigid outside wouldn't lead to death. But it would be a more noble death. That was my reasoning. It would be a transformation. Let go. Let go. Let go. Move on. What a lovely thing. It felt as familiar to me as the angle of my flat feet. This scene unfolded so often that Chris came to expect my squeals, and the sight of me, steaming and partially shampooed, running around naked trying to save insects.

At last, the *khar mod*, soaked down to the last fiber by the pond and softened to a rich dark brown, were ready to bend. But we needed a steam box. Chris, drawing on his boat-building knowledge, replicated the steam of our shower by making a rectangular box, about the size of a single bed, from pink insulation, duct tape, two dishtowels, and an old gas canister. His ingenuity turned me on to him, over and over again. It always had. I was more fascinated by what the box, propped up in the shop, could have been. Perhaps a time machine, one to crawl into and beam yourself back to 1640 or, better, 5 BC.

We pulled on our leather gloves, loaded up the box with five long *khar mod,* and shut the dishtowel door. Steam pumped inside in an effort to move the ribs toward elasticity. After sliding them out, we would bend each one around a wooden scaffolding nearby in order to permanently mold its shape as it cooled. Then later, we could remove them from the scaffolding and tie them together at intervals to form the lattice.

Prying one hot *khar mod* out, I rose into awe.

I just can*not* believe that our walls will be made of this!

That was the last sentence anyone uttered because what followed deserved silence. Hand it to Chris. He wedged it into the scaffolding. Repeat. Switch roles. Switch again. When the box started to leak big clouds of steam, clouds that enveloped us, that filled the entire shop, we paused to take photos of us in the mist, and somehow the whole steamy scene made me think we were beautiful, that I was beautiful. It had taken me so long to feel beautiful. Everything smelled of water, a peculiar smell against my heavy fleece and down vest.

During our two days of steam bending, sandhill cranes gathered in great numbers and flew south. Inside at work, we had missed the migration. Willem and Diane emailed us a photo of a V-formation flying right over the shop. Hunters were also sighting in nearby. Gunshots started to ring out at least twice a day. The sudden *pow-pow* always startled me, and I had to trust that those shots banked into a hill somewhere. Hunting didn't bother me, at least not responsible hunting for food. But I was a vegetarian and had been my whole life, unable to stomach the thought of meat. When my mother had demanded that we eat the chicken on our dinner plates, I picked at it with my fork to remove all the little blue veins and red dots and anything that looked like flesh. Only then could I manage one small bite.

Birds leaving. Hunters planning. Everyone, and every animal, was focusing on what needed to be done before the arctic descended.

When we were finished, our final product dominated the shop like an art piece. On the scaffolding, the *khar mod* now became the ribs of a dinosaur. I leaned back into Chris's warm hug. He tucked his nose under my wool hat and we studied the symmetry together. One part of the yurt was almost complete. Over the weekend, we would pry them from the scaffolding and finally, finally make the walls. But for now, it was stunning —wood bending into those shapes.

You know that phrase *bend like a reed in the wind*? I asked.

Yeah.

Not sure I believe in it.

Well, you aren't someone who bends unless *you* want to, he teased.

With that, we closed the garage door, turned off the lights, and headed toward bed. As I washed my face and rubbed coconut oil into the cracks by my eyes, a changing woman stared back at me. She looked weathered, a word that had engrossed me with its power as a child. Maybe bending was a question of saturation. If a person saturated herself with enough water or wisdom, then she might bend, but only ever for the right reasons.

↓

Though our plan was ordered, everything happened all at
once. While the *khar mod* dried into shape, we returned to the
uni roof poles. We still had thirty-six to finish. The shop took
on the radiance of effort, as our wrists turned sore, as heaping
mounds of curly shavings gathered and, in a nod to beauty, we
left them. Each individual shaving had a unique flecked pattern,
the story of a tree within it.

One day, in the middle of it all, a brown UPS truck drove up
the driveway. Because the cabin was invisible from the road, few
people stopped by. But people probably knew we were here. I
always felt sheepish explaining that we didn't actually own this
place, as if I shouldn't be allowed to be here.

I watched the UPS man slide down from his truck onto two
long legs.

He loped over.

Hello there. Good afternoon, he said, sticking out a hand to
greet us with the best combination of shy and friendly.

I'm Brooks.

It's nice to meet you, Chris and I responded in unison,
shocked at the introduction at all, now understanding that this
must be his route and that we would probably see him often.
After he handed us a small box of parachute cord, we exchanged
pleasantries for a while. He reminded me of someone plucked
from another era: genuine, kind, and probably just a bit younger
than my parents as he scratched at a graying sideburn. He was
the kind of man you immediately trusted. Noticing the wood
shavings and lumber, Brooks raised an eyebrow.

We're building a yurt, Chris explained.

You plan to live in that? Brooks asked.

Yep, I inserted quickly, but it's only going to be sixteen feet
in diameter, so it'll be tight living.

I wanted him to know that I knew how to talk shop.

Cozy, he smiled.

I might have been projecting, but I was pretty sure he liked us. We had just put in a few big orders for yurt materials, so I knew we'd see him again.

The distinction between Sunday or Wednesday or Tuesday started to blur. We talked and slept yurt. All day in the wood-shop. All night thinking through what the next day held. With that focus, a patina spread over every fissure in our lives, so that even brushing our teeth somehow related back to the yurt. At some point, walking to the shop bleary-eyed in my same old brown jeans, I understood that I had no skill for what we were doing—the building part, at least. In the evenings, when dark cabin windows stared at me, I snuck onto my laptop to calculate and compare what I was doing to what others were doing. Classic mistake. Most of my friends were kicking ass in something, some job, some life, which made them shine. They probably thought the same of me.

Sometimes I think you've got it all right, Molly, one writer friend, successful and prolific beyond her age, wrote to me.

Really? I wanted to ask back. Like hamsters, we were all running that loop of wondering whether what any of us was doing was enough.

And so then my maybe's began: maybe I should be, maybe I should be, maybe I should be doing *that* instead. Oh, but you like this yurt thing, I told myself. It makes you feel powerful. It makes you feel odd in a way that you like. Still, something about building this home continued to frighten me in small doses. Were we building a particular life in a particular place?

It no longer felt like an isolated experience, as if tethers hitched to the trees had begun to creep out toward me.

But I would buck up. Buck up. Pull. It. Together.

One regular morning, I patted my cheeks and said, C'mon.

So much hugging, Chris laughed, as I held him tight in the kitchen.

What's up? he asked, pulling back from me.

Nothing, I said, just turning over a new leaf about the building.

Perhaps in an effort at self-preservation—and who could blame him—Chris had stopped paying attention to my fitful sighs during the past few weeks. His blank stares were the worst indifference. Like any woman, I'd been keeping tabs.

He hugged me back.

Oh, good, he said.

On this day, I had an easy task ahead of me: stand, hold piece of wood flat, pull a rotating press down into the wood until it grooves out a wood plug one-half inch long, repeat, and then pop them all out. The drill press was not intimidating. These bungs would fill the drill holes on our cedar porch. And once summer beat out winter, I would lounge on that cedar porch, proud of our accomplishment, and drink whiskey. I—am—going —to—make—eighty, I mouthed to Chris above the screeching of the table saw. He flashed me a thumbs-up and bent back to his work.

As sun beamed into the shop, I concentrated on the bungs. This was great. I could do this. In fact, it was a privilege, a but-ter-on-bread kind of privilege. Just be patient, if not for your own sake, at least for his. The drill press hummed along. I decided that, while making bungs, I could spell out a wooden love note for him to find later: Love You. I needed a gesture and this was it. The pitch smell of cedar wafted up through my dust mask. Cranking through the bungs, counting them one by one, I became methodical. Even calm and content. This was how life could be if you had the right attitude. And for almost an hour, life cruised.

But when the plug cutter jammed in the wood, instead of releasing it, I gritted my teeth and pulled down, which is when the wood got stuck, spun around the press at five hundred revolutions per minute, flew off, and whacked me in the ribs.

I yanked my mask off and bent over, breathless.

Absorbed in his own work, Chris did not notice me leave.

The world outside glared yellow and bright. I punched the air, stumbled toward a stand of cottonwoods, and sank down into a pile of leaves. How do you grow into someone you like? A great force pressed my shoulders into a hunch and walls closed in on me. My mutters dissolved into heaves and then into sobs.

Clearly, some feelings had come to a head.

But the cottonwoods stood like saints around me. They were quiet. Even when their leaves turned purple and died, they never complained. They had no need for discontent. Unlike other trees, they knew how to grow back from a stump. I groped at the ground. My other hand wiped snot from my face. I didn't rage with the thought of what the hell I'd gotten myself into. I had chosen this. But the messy process of change had started its mess without my approval. I wanted to be *in* the yurt for that, not in the middle of building it. This place, meant to bring happiness, had not done so yet. If trees could walk, I wondered, if they could walk across the plains, what then? But these trees had no need for walking. They were here and they were tall.

⌄

When a herd of at least one hundred elk descended from the mountains into our neighborhood, Diane told us they would be here for the winter. The brown clumps were easy to identify against the yellow fields of the valley. But when nestled in the trees, they were hard to pick out. I got better at scanning for antlers, wide and upturned and mythical.

Because my eyes had begun to accustom themselves to the textures of this place, it was strange that I had yet to dream of it. I didn't trust those who didn't trust their dreams. Dreams set my bearings. As a girl, dreams had allowed me to practice the adult feelings I knew I would have to feel one day.

After my cottonwoods meltdown, I dreamt hard, the kind of hard that leaves a face swollen. My family was floating down a muddy river in a lavender-colored home. Eaves had collapsed. No one seemed particularly alarmed. As the river took us, the house shed more layers, until it became a raft on which the five of us sprawled. When it landed, I walked alone through a wilderness. Thick kudzu vines wrapped up columns on an ornate house with no walls. My arms floated up to feel around.

Then a voice whispered, You have no accent.

So what? I yelled back.

You have no accent at all. Ha ha ha. You are accentless. Ha ha ha.

Then my first dream about The Land made itself known. I was measuring and drilling holes at 2, 9, 16, 30, 37, 51, 58, 72, 79, and 86 inches down the long spine of each *khar mod*. Over the past several days, I had already drilled those holes. My brain was repeating reality. My lineage lived inside me. The walls also lived inside me.

When I rubbed an oil-soaked rag up all 155 of them one morning, twisting the rag around until deep reds and purple flecks emerged from the wood grain, I speculated on whether this action too would slip into my dreams. My hands smelled of linseed and my thumb felt arthritic. Lined up against the outside of the shop, the *khar mod* dried in the cool breeze. Each one had been cut, sanded, steamed, hole-poked, and now greased up. But the collective whole, in that moment, presented itself as if it were a bamboo stand transplanted to the backdrop of a harsh mountain landscape.

I was starting to be able to see the yurt.

On my outdoors day, I woke up exuberant and relieved to be free from the dust and machinery of the shop. Just put me on a lawn in autumn. There would be satisfaction in tying our *khar mod* together to form the four wall sections, or *khana*, that would create our lattice wall.

It's *bungtonokhana* day, I sang to Chris. He had become deeply involved with making our skylight, the *tono*, what Mongolians call the wheel of heaven. It rolled like a massive carriage wheel. With the outside covered in clear vinyl, it would eventually serve as a window to the sky. Through it, we would watch the night pass over and occasionally a full moon beam down. And to that, I said, Yes, yes, yes. Making it involved complex woodcuts and design. Often, I would slink from the shop back to the cabin after midnight, even though Chris couldn't break his trance. Sometime later, the walkie-talkie would beep to tell me he was ready to come in. Swaddled in a heavy coat, I would stand on the porch, flashing him in with the flashlight, one hand on hip, eyes scanning for predators.

But now, in bed, I was singing at his tired face.

You are so strange, he mumbled, squishing a white pillow over me.

Yeah, but you like it.

We wrestled and then talked about the night's bellowing winds.

Early November now, past our expected finish date, our momentum sped like a horse in sight of its destination. We had confidence that we'd get the job done before the anticipated snowfall because no snow had fallen yet, not after that initial dump. But the grass had dried to a sharp brown and the temperature dropped more each day.

I hauled my stack out to the lawn between cabin and shop: crisp air, shivers, smells that reminded me of college schoolwork and falling leaves. Purple cottonwood leaves blew about, here and there, decaying, sweet smell of decay, trees bare. A few hawks coasted above, in a white-blue sky, making shadows, dipping and diving. Being in the presence of them, and of the wind, and the trees, and even the brown grass, relaxed me. Autumn happened on the ground here, in red bushes, not red trees. I took great care to peg down the tattered graph paper instructions with two nails—not screws, now I knew the difference—and lay out each *khar mod*. To visualize the spatial orientation of the whole mass required a map, at least for me. I sat down, pulled the wood up into my lap, and began to thread parachute cord through the holes, joining two *khar mod*, slowly, grateful that the sun warmed my bare hands. Though traditional leather strips would have been my preference, we had opted for a synthetic material that would last longer. With one foot pressing down on the wood, I yanked up the cords and tied each one off as tightly as possible, as if tying my own fingers into a knot.

I was well into a decent rhythm when Brooks drove up in his UPS truck.

He hopped out and started to roll a heavy log-shaped package up to the shop.

As he and Chris dawdled in conversation at the shop's garage door, I watched Chris scoot the huge roll of white canvas out of the box. It had finally arrived—tipi material thick enough to withstand prolonged exposure at this high altitude. The canvas would shape out like a circus tent. It wasn't traditional felt, but there was no felt to be had around here, certainly none that we could afford. To sew the canvas together, we had also bought a bright blue industrial sewing machine.

Brooks and Chris walked over.

Hey, Brooks.

Heya, he said, handing me a Styrofoam cooler. This here is from me and Marcie. It's just some elk jerky I made, a couple tenderloins, and some of those dried tomatoes from her garden.

That's amazing, I smiled, squinting up from underneath a half-assembled *khana*. Thank you. I just can't believe you went to that trouble. Seriously. So kind of you.

You guys almost done? he asked, nodding down to the *khana*.

Not quite, but once we finish, we'll have you and Marcie over for dinner in this big old canvas tent. Do you all live around here?

Yep, we're the green house up there, out back. You can probably see it when you're up in the field.

Oh, man, I quickly said, catching eyes with Chris, *you* are the green house. Yours was the one house we were worried about when we decided to build our yurt up there, and we measured the height to make sure, but we aren't totally sure, you might be able to see the tip of our stovepipe.

Don't even worry, he laughed, waving it away. We don't mind looking at a stovepipe; we love the idea of the yurt.

You sure?

Absolutely.

Thank you so much for this elk jerky, I said, unsure of what to say next.

You know, I added, I've never had elk before, or deer.

Well, see if you like it, he smiled.

Then he turned back toward the UPS truck. Watching him leave, I decided that Brooks was the kind of neighbor you'd want to grow old with, if there was such a thing.

I cannot believe he's the green house, Chris said.

I know, I said.

Chris walked back to the shop. When I refocused with fresh eyes, I saw that my partial wall was wrong. I had tied forty *khar mod* together backward, incorrectly. In traditional Mongolian custom, it was critical that each *khar mod* start at the bottom left and rise up and right, instead of bottom right and rising up and left. This wasn't an architectural problem. It was an energy problem. They believed that if the orientation was off, then everything was off.

So much for following my map.

Other rules were less important to me: Do not step on the threshold; do not point your feet at the hearth; do not whistle; do not step over anyone (especially old people); do not put water on the fire. But I was a sucker for superstition. Changing it was my only option. I needed to undo each one of the knots I had tightened hard.

Three hours of work—gone.

If I grit my teeth any harder, they would crumble. Chill out.

Using needle-nose pliers, I dug under the knots and pried them apart. It was work for patient, delicate hands, not these hands. The lowering orange sun cast tree shadows across the lawn. A bumblebee appeared and buzzed its way to each piece of burned tip p-cord that stuck up, nosing at it as if it were a stamen. Painful to watch something get rejected over and over again without knowing why. It was not going to find the true thing here. But it moved systematically across the *khar mod*, determined.

Go on, I urged, waving it away.

The sun eventually slipped behind our hill and I pulled the half-made *khana* into the shop and prepared to hunker down for the long slow tick of night. On the cold concrete floor, I knotted until a callus formed where my thumb pushed against my forefinger and then I kept going. And because repetition lulls us, so the trance of my fingers lulled me.

My brothers and I each have a blue placemat printed with a world map. Our fingers move all over it. My hopes live among the colorful countries. At lunchtime, we start our ritual. I say, Let's do it. My narrow shoulders shake with excitement. We trace the path between all the places we've lived. Our shape, so far, looks like a strange star. We've lived a lot of places, says my youngest brother, on cue, and I recognize it as the voice of belonging. On my count of three, we close our eyes. Go! We each drop a fork over the placemat. Wherever the first prong lands will be our next place. I push my hair behind my ears and get ready to foresee the blueprint of our future.

Falling in and out of memory, I worked with the pieces flopped over my legs. The *khana* grew larger and larger, filling the space like an organism growing and multiplying, pushing toward more life, more breath, until it knows it has reached its own capacity, and then further still when it understands that there is actually no limit to its growth. With each knot, I grew smaller in its presence.

Done! I sang, fastening my last knot.

Chris skipped over from his workbench. We heaved it up together and pulled it out to its length of fifteen feet. *Lattice* is not a word I like. It reminds me of ladies, doilies, quaint window boxes, and all things fragile. But *this* was a structure, a screen. This was our wall. Nothing about it looked frail. I stuck my face through one of the rhombus shapes, then through another one, and another and another. Each hole became a place. Each place connected to other places. Each blank space something protean.

I flung my arm around Chris and kissed him, inhaled his wood smell. Under the flood of shop lights, our heads leaned together and we gazed at the first complete part of our yurt.

Even a repetitive pattern can be nuanced, I said.

This is true, he responded. We had little time to applaud and congratulate ourselves. Must push on—three more *khana* to go and a long night and tomorrow ahead of us. Unaware of what the weather had in store for us, we folded it back in on itself, like an accordion, snug and secure against the shop wall.

3

ANIMALS AND ACCELERATION

November 2009

Two days later, we stuck a yardstick into thirty-four inches of fresh powder. Chris held up a camera. Snowflakes salted his eyelashes, scruff, and green wool jacket. Creek rocks, now white-capped, looked like teeth poking out of the flowing water. He watched me watching him and smiled.

Winter was his beloved season.

There was nothing left to do but surrender. When plans changed suddenly, with a shock, I was usually good at those first moments of disbelief, of *Isn't this crazy*, of *Oh, well, here we go anyway*. Carrying shovels, we trudged the unsteady trudge through snow toward our unstacked firewood pile. It had transformed into an albino whale. The night before, I had pulled a big blue tarp over it because I swore I could smell the snow coming. As we pinned it down with logs, Chris had bent his chin down, teased me for being cautious, and insisted that there would be no need to cover it so fully.

Glad I covered it, I said, and shot him a sly smile.

I had also pulled any scattered tools into the shop.

We continued up, pushing snow off our plank, now a mere indentation over the filled-in ditch. The white illuminated the ground, softened the contours, and opened the space for seeing. It was a relief to see so much. This would be the snow Diane had mentioned, the snow that would stay until June. One look up our hill and I wasn't convinced that we'd be able to pull our yurt's woodstove up it now. We pulled ourselves up first. Cold air burned my lungs. Fir boughs dropped heavy with snow. Nothing stirred. Because it was probably a weekday, I couldn't stop thinking about my friends sitting at desks in offices. This place had started to feel like my office.

At the top, the flat field had been frosted with whipped cream, as if a spatula had shaped the snow into tiny peaks and valleys, creating an effect I would later learn by name: *sastrugi*. Under a white spread of sky, Chris stepped in up to his thigh and then plied one leg up and in front of the other. I used his trail and tried not to fall over. We could have been trekking across Antarctica with sleds, dogs, and the comforting knowledge that another warm body was nearby, somewhere.

Snow slid easily off our new cedar porch. But the yurt foundation was completely buried by snowdrifts. We dug and dug and dug and launched snow, trying to find the outline of where our floor would soon be hammered down, of where our walls would straighten up, of where a structure would form. My lower back ached. Shovel right. Shovel left. Switch sides. So many people had dug themselves out of hurricanes or earthquakes, with no forecast of the *how long* or *how hard*. This was clean. This was nothing. Pushing my pointer finger through a shearling glove, I bent down and wagged it in front of Chris's face.

He snatched it.

At the end of this thing, he laughed, I am going to personally throw away that jacket and those pants and those gloves.

True, my outfit had not changed: powder blue down jacket, brown jeans, and white wool hat. It had just been easier to step into clothes already on the floor. While we dug that morning and cleared the site, others nearby must have been dealing with snow too. No one gets an out with weather.

We finished and slipped back down the hill. I waited for the plow company to show up and clear our driveway. There was no going anywhere until they arrived. But, by late afternoon, they still hadn't come.

Exertion, they explained when I called.

Exertion?

Yeah, both our snowplows broke from exertion.

Like others on the end of the plow route, we would be trapped for two days. All we had was a pantry full of rice and some frozen pumpkin soup. Our grocery shopping habits had not adjusted from city life. I called Susan and asked if she could bring bread and cheese and lettuce to our mailbox once the main roads were clear.

Now this felt more serious.

I paced around in slippers.

Chris seemed less concerned about not being able to leave. As the soup heated, I redirected my thoughts toward field notes. Flies, so many of them, appeared sluggish with cold. I slapped a book down near a fly. Small flinch. No flight. Across the street, through the leafless cottonwoods, I could see horses unmoving behind fences drifted over by snow. Off in the distance, whole forested mountains had melted into winter's combination of white and indigo. Somewhere, some bears had not hibernated yet. They were ramping up the urgency, loping up and down hillsides in search of bark, insects, moths, sustenance.

Other souls were getting out of here, like the geese whose honking sounds at night foretold of other lands and traveling through dark. Willem emailed us:

> Some snow. I left a message on your phone that for-
> mations of snow geese were flying overhead, but
> you must have been somewhere else. Anyway, this is
> one of many images. Believe it or not, this is the
> first time we have seen them here.

We had heard geese, but not these geese, not the snow geese, who flew over town first, luring people out of houses, a phenomenon we would hear about later—enormous white birds in a blue sky, gliding south, toward us, over us, flapping away, which meant that, in mid-November, winter had officially dug its foot in.

I sank into a brown chair, and scalding soup burned the roof of my mouth.

Get into it, beb, Chris said, noticing me watching the white palette broken only by pale brown sticks for trees.

Oh, I'm into it, I said, but these bones don't know about the cold.

That's not completely true, he said.

Still, I said, I have no childhood memory of cold.

My bare feet tiptoe across a tile floor, avoiding cockroaches. We are in the Dominican Republic, where my memory starts to crystallize, and for the first time in my life, I feel a cool breeze slip through an open door. What is that? It only lasts a sec- ond, but I recognize it as an opposite to the constant sweat on my naked body. Someone is yelling something in Spanish and I swerve around the bamboo furniture, hold its rungs with my chubby hands. My mother lies naked on a wooden table. It is massage time. Underneath now, I arrange wooden blocks. As the day heats up, my cheeks will flush and flush and flush to red. I am only old enough to know a few things about myself. I am an older sister. I like pirates. I like when my dad tells me about how he hops around the broken glass on his morning runs. My birthday is in July. We eat orange juice popsicles. I will learn about scorpions soon. Outside, on our concrete patio, the honeysuckles smell sweet. Some children draw back curtains to wait for a snow day, but I don't even know what putting on layers means.

My childhood never had a constant place. But my childhood had constant heat.

Chris had left me to my contemplation and gone to work on emails. I snuggled into my scarf and pressed my nose against the cold window. In Vermont during college, I bought my first wool scarf and learned that with cold comes cozy. Chris had often cupped my cold feet in his warm hands. I always wished they were star runner's feet, that I could dash through a meadow like a gazelle. But they were flat and I had actual hips. You aren't very good at accepting love, he would tell me. You know, I would lob back, maybe there are hot weather people and cold weather people. Like the lizards I grew up around, my blood was lizard blood. That's what happens when your body never needs to heat itself.

When I lived in a few cold cities and one damp maritime place, I made friends with cold. Other days, I would shake my finger, Not today, cold, today I say No to you because my body doesn't know how to greet you, today. You can wake me up another day, but not today.

I rose to put the kettle on.

You want tea, beb? I called into the bedroom to Chris.

No, thanks.

Under the cottonwoods, a flash of movement drew my attention back out the window. A deer rose from sleep, shook snow from its back, pricked its ears up. I had read that the instinct to "shake it off" allows the brain to reprogram. I wanted to train myself toward being present to everything around me. I wanted to train myself toward the long winter, rather than away from it. Not that a dry Montana cold was a foul cold. But in any direction I spun, snow and stillness blinded me.

Back in action, we made a move to install our yurt floor. Our snow camp soon accrued tidy piles of saws, brushes, cans, and bags of screws. The sun beat down on us the whole day. No wind. Just as we had planned, based on the weather report. As I darted around the foundation, my bulky snow pants made me feel bulletproof, as if cold didn't stand a chance. Chris had warned that I would get hot, and sure enough, I did, always inept at matching temperature degrees to the actual physical sensation. Operating like machinists, we fit the awkward pink insulation to the foundation's wooden frame and stapled a plastic vapor barrier over it. I worked fast, eager to move past the artificial construction material, eager to get to the wood.

Our wooden planks snapped together so well.

One by one, down they went, snap, snap, drill, drill.

Only a few hours of work.

We got ourselves a floor, Chris said, and flopped face down on our new Doug fir floor, what had been living trees not very long ago, the same kind of trees that grew on this hill. I crawled next to him and snuffled across the wood like a snail searching for information. What did it mean to have our very own floor? I had never made a floor or even thought about floors, other than hearing my mother talk about "nice wood floors" the one time we moved into a new home without tiles or wall-to-wall carpet.

We stayed there for a while. I eyed the wood grain. It spread for sixteen feet, like a collection of thin rivers charting course. It would be a small space for us. But we would squat on it. Our boots would scratch it up. Our tea might spill onto it. The floor would creak and swell and shrink as it aged. I tickled him under the armpit. He pushed me over and rolled over me and I rolled over him until together we rolled to the edge and up, back to work. The yurt was finally coming alive.

While Chris hand-sawed the floor into a circle—thank you, merci, gracias—I gathered all the tools, reorganizing, consolidating, making myself useful. It didn't take him long. Done and sweating, he slouched up against a snowdrift.

Your turn, he said.

I'm on it, I said back, smiling as I shook the metal can.

My satisfaction spread as quickly as the dark chocolate stain over the floor. Bent over, I slopped it on thick in sections, brushed it smooth, and soon deeper patterns in the wood emerged—great big knots, striated streaks the whole length, waves and swirls. I moved deliberately, remembering how desperate my teenager self had been to dye my walnut bed frame a pale color, because driftwood, wood that knew how to drift along, appealed to me then. Now here I was doing the opposite, altering a pale thing into a dark thing. In the past few months, I had come to prefer dark, as if gravity were making its presence known.

The stain oozed out black.

I imagined the contrast of white against it: deer bone, canvas, snow.

This nontoxic stain required us to mop away the excess goop; otherwise, according to the instructions, it would dry sticky. With old T-shirts, we started rubbing and that's when the dark color started to lift away. Disappointment slipped down my insides.

Oooo, that is not what I expected, I sighed, putting my rag down.

What do you want to do? Chris asked.

No, no, we have to mop it up, I know, I know.

There could be no debate, really. I watched my ebony floor fade and accepted the muted brown. But, surrounded by fields of white, the brown floor still appeared extreme, as extreme as the weather would turn. This floor, our floor, was speaking out. It was the pow in the quiet, the brown on the white, the Hello, this is real.

While the rest of the valley slowed under snow, we finalized our yurt parts, and momentum built. Dark slid over the landscape well before dinner now. Winter had the effect of relocation for me, reminding me that soon our yurt would be done and I could start my living here. I shuffled around inside the cabin and scratched a list of things I wanted to do.

1. Learn to read tracks and scat.

Animals leave behind the story of where they have been. They stomp or slither or scoot this message out. What a thing. I hadn't seen a track other than my own until college. What are those tracks? I asked Chris on our first date tromping through a frozen forest. What do you think? he asked. Furrowing my brow and trying to look beautiful, I recited all the eastern animals I could think of to this eastern man. But disassociated from the place, my search for the right answer did me no good. Finally, I gave up: I don't know, a cow? Maybe you don't know this animal, he smiled. What is it? It's a moose.

2. Shoot a gun.

My Vietnam-vet uncle let me shoot a pistol at a beer can when I was eleven and new to America. On that lake in Wisconsin, he gathered all us young ones around. The kickback made me gasp. Lying to the neighbors when they came around to see about the noise took serious giggle suppression on my part. Later, as a woman, I played target practice with a rifle and a mossy log. But guns still scared me. In this landscape, I felt I should acquaint myself with them. Because it was a *should*, it would take me a long time to actually see to doing it, a long time to learn that I was a cross dominant shooter.

3. Eat the wind.

Diane had warned us that winds ripped on these hills, whistled all night long. What would that mean for yurt living? At least we would be tied down to the foundation, rooted to the ground. And from there, I could poke my neck out and eat big gulps of wind.

After three days brushed by a cold wind, the stain dried. We covered the floor with another blue tarp to protect it. Having a floor was like having one arm wrapped securely around our future here. Nothing was in our way now, other than potential weather. We had finished almost all the wooden components—walls, roof poles, and a skylight. Now we just needed to make a door, sew the canvas, haul everything, plus the woodstove, up the hill, and assemble. The yurt just had to be done before my trip back East for Christmas on December 15. That gave us a few weeks.

We're *so so so* close, I trilled at Chris. Al-most there.

Getting there, he said.

Then my parents arrived to spend ten days with us over Thanksgiving—my worldly, open-minded father with big cheeks, the one who had slept on park benches and led tours in Russia, who either laughed so hard his face turned red or took up residence under the dark cloud of impatience, who refused to condone cultural stereotypes; and my graceful mother, who drove down unmarked roads just because, who would ask any question of any stranger, who chowed down on a bratwurst while recounting her modeling days in Japan, who was always mannered and had accepted that her daughter was opinionated and less willing to please than she had ever been. Without knowing it, they stepped right in front of that barreling force of us and we screeched to a halt.

After a few days of visiting with my parents, I was huffing like a horse.

We've got serious shit to get done, I whispered to Chris, the two of us squeezed into the single bed in the tiny office room. I was unfamiliar with the pace of hanging around, eating meals, and doing virtually nothing.

We'll get it done, he assured me.

But it's the end of November and we can't do any of it while they are here and . . .

Molly, he interrupted, they are your parents and they own this place and they are lovely people.

You're right, I said, cracking a window to hear trees rustle outside. Thank you.

He had always been my tall glass of water.

Instead of stopping completely, we compromised and busied ourselves with side tasks, things that allowed us to play at importance, things that we had avoided. Like getting firewood up to the top. Underneath the albino whale tarp beside the cabin, round logs peeked out at us, some frozen together or frozen to the ground. From leftover two-by-four planks and old jeans, we had built wooden pack boards designed for turning our able bodies into efficient haulers. With the sturdy external frame part of a backpack,we could stack as many logs as possible up a person's back, lash them down, snap the waist belt, and go.

It took a few false starts to learn. The logs smelled alive, of pitch and rough brown bark, the last remnants of summer all collected under that tarp. They tumbled off. We repacked. Tumbled off. Hit our shins. Repacked. But eventually we got it —seven logs for me, nine for Chris.

My parents had bought us red rubber crampon-type things that strapped over our boots. It was an unexpected gift. Over glasses of wine, we had all laughed together about whether metal teeth were actually necessary for tracking up the ice path with heavy loads. But without them, nothing would have been possible. I called them grippers because that's what they did for me. No slipping. We might have looked like every other human on this planet who carries her—because let's be honest, the women do most of the domestic hauling—water, sticks, tea leaves, food to sell at market, or gravel to move from one place to another. Even those who have never burdened their bodies might have cracked open a contemplative book to read that, if you truly wanted to know yourself, you must start with one job: chop wood, carry water. This adage would soon become literal for us.

That first afternoon strapping firewood to our pack boards, I glanced back to the cabin where my father was cocked halfway out the door, pointing a camera at us, trying not to be seen, my mother's face right behind him, conspiratorial. My first thought: Smile. Second thought: They are so curious and I love that. Third thought: My parents, like me, are tourists to everything.

I placed another log—thunk—and paused to stare at the hill of fir trees leaning over me, so stately, so sure, as if they knew something none of us knew, as if their long invisible roots reached out toward me. My head jerked back to my parents. And then back to the trees. And back to my parents. I had grunted a log from the frozen earth, loaded firewood onto a pack board with my fiancé, and failed to notice that a decent part of that felt normal.

Maybe I was no longer a tourist to this life.

And when I understood that, the trees, unsympathetic, shrugged, as if to say, Calm down. Don't hyper-analyze.

I can't deal with onlookers, I explained to my parents a few days later.

They understood why I had banned them from watching us haul our 350-pound woodstove up the hill to our new floor. We had considered many other options: asking Brooks if we could drive the stove to his house and then across the other neighbor's wheat field to the yurt, hiring a four-wheeler to pull it up from the west end of The Land, dragging it for miles up through the dense hawthorns and up a short ditch. But we had managed everything on our backs so far and we had a certain pride about that. No need to stop now. The hill, this tidal wave obstacle of ours, could be overcome. Chris built a sled for the stove. We settled on the shortest distance from down to up, and, with the promise of beer and homemade bread, wrangled seven friends, some we had just met and others we had overlapped with in other places, to help us.

The night before, Chris and I had stayed up late, pressed together in that twin bed, eyes wide all dark night long as we each, independently, panicked about whether what we were doing was just plain stupid. Despite my bravado at times, I was a pro-seatbelt kind of woman, no daredevil with drugs or random sex or woodstoves.

You awake?

You know I am.

If that thing falls down the hill . . .

I know, Molly.

Split melon for anyone in the way.

I *know*.

It'll be okay, I said, placing one hand on his forehead, the other on my chest. Then he turned his back to me and scooted in, so that I could rub his head. His tension had seeped into my tension and my tension had seeped into his so that we held our breath against the severity of the situation. Boxed up in a crate in the shop, the innocent stove meant no harm. We had chosen a rectangular utilitarian stove with a bake oven. Because Chris had grown up hearing his father pad out to the living room at

2 AM to stoke their woodstove, his parents bought us ours as an early wedding present.

Gray clouds hovered the next afternoon when everyone arrived. The light spread flat and muted. One of the guys, Gregg, a broad-shouldered man raised in a valley west of us, offered his retired climbing ropes and expertise on pulley systems. The rest of us, all wool hats and gloves, grabbed a rope and pulled the loaded sled across the irrigation ditch to its starting position. I prayed that our fir trees wouldn't act out, that their deep root system appreciated the challenge of holding onto the weight of something that might eventually, when they died, burn them up to warm the people who honored them.

It was a stretch, but it was true.

What they must have thought of us, these small figures scrambling all over the hillside, engaged in what, to us, was a very serious project. The group energy had galvanized us. People were excited to be involved, to be steady in lunges. To see others enamored of our project reminded me that I too was enamored of it. I heard myself answering questions about the *tono*, canvas as barrier, and where yurts evolved and how, and realized that I actually knew something about it.

I was standing next to a friend of a friend, a woman I had only met once. Both she and her parents had grown up in the valley and were inextricably tied to the landscape of Montana. She could also run close to fifty miles through the mountains in one go and she had gorgeous green eyes and she exuded confidence.

So, where are you from again? she asked.

Oh, nowhere, no one place.

That's right, lots of moving, right?

Yeah, I smiled, loosening my hold on the rope, letting my shoulders pull back.

Ah, hence the nomadic yurt, she said, nodding uphill.

You got it, I said. It's sort of the way my family operates, not the yurt part, but the traveling and relocating.

Hm, she answered. That's cool.

I was pleased to be who I was. We arranged ourselves and I scanned the hillside. But as the anticipation built, as we all waited for the signal, I started to wonder about history and what other people had walked up this exact hill before. Did their descendants still live here in the valley? I wanted to believe that I was touching on an old tradition, that where we would drag this woodstove, someone else once dragged sticks for a home, a dead deer, or her own tired feet toward a vantage point, a place to look out and organize herself in a context.

When Gregg gave the okay, we heaved and ho'd and even shouted *Heave* and *Ho* and two groups worked with each other to yank the thing up. Two hours later, our momentum pulled us over the hill and we didn't stop, just ran like hitched reindeer toward the yurt porch. Once there, blanketed by a dark blue sky, we all erupted in cheers and slapped the kind of high-fives sports teams give each other. Everyone steamed under jackets. And though we may not have been able to name it that night, I suspect everyone felt that adrenaline, the rush of bringing heat to a home, even one that wasn't there yet. In the jumble, Chris and I found each other's eyes. We squinted love at each other, acknowledging, for the first time, that we didn't have to do everything alone.

ꙮ

With fire come animals. Wild and domestic. We wanted a dog, especially for some modicum of protection from the mountain lion. But we planned to find this dog after the yurt building, after our wedding ceremony, after the summer, when cash flow might be more likely, when we had some sense of what was next. I had scooped up dying crows as a girl in Spain, wept over dead hamsters in Texas, shaded dying grasshoppers with leaves in South Africa, and cradled fallen squirrels during a brief stint in Boston. Chris was equally devoted to animals. Once, in Greece, we found a goat stuck in a soccer net. He calmed it with a gentle firm hand and set it free. I envisioned a rescue dog—large, odd-looking, not the standard black lab mix, a mellow and clear-eyed disposition like Chris.

But I would take whatever dog found us.

Generally, elders advise the following: Do not get pregnant or impregnate before you have a partner, do not spend money you don't have, and do not adopt an animal when you aren't on solid ground yourself. And yet my parents persuaded me, because they do know how to have fun, to go with them to an animal shelter—just for a look.

We followed the dog handler down a narrow hallway. As we got closer, the barking got louder. She swung the doors open and we stepped into the full onslaught. Yelps echoed from sterile pale yellow walls, so many sounds with nowhere to settle. It was the sound of emptiness. As far as kennels go, it wasn't a bad place. It smelled of bleach and, somewhere, dried-up pee. My parents coasted ahead of me. Pinned by the question of why I was here right now, I moved slowly.

I floated past a few cages until one big deep bark turned my head. He stretched back into a downward dog. He was a tiger: a short coat of orange and black called brindle. Sinewy and tall. Pacing in a small space. His expression pleaded, I need a home and I need to run. I am *not* in my element here. I squatted and stared at him. He approached and stared back at me through the cage. The other dogs barked and barked, but his eyes just held my gaze.

There you are, I said.

All I remember the dog handler saying is this: Bruno is ready to be with his people. He just needs to know who they are. He needs to settle. He's one and a half years old. He's a loyal breed. Great Dane mixes always are.

It took me one evening to convince Chris that the dog he had not met yet was the dog for us, despite the one billion impracticalities. He knew I could be impulsive, but he also knew that I had a gut like a house has a roof.

The next day, we met Bruno in the chained-off outside area. He was neither engaged nor disengaged. Just watching us as we stroked his back. It was clear he'd been homeless for a while. We signed the papers and loaded him into our Jeep. As we drove away, he stuck his broad face between us to peer out the windshield. I wondered where he had come from. We were just another set of dog handlers to him. He didn't know where he was going and that is what he was trying to figure out. His eyes were black-rimmed, like Cleopatra's. He surveyed everything —the barns we passed, hawks flying overhead, cars passing us, snowbanks, even dead wheat stalks blowing in the wind. That he didn't know whether someone would feed him that night was hard to feel. We had already decided to shorten his name to

Bru. But observing him that moment, I decided that my covert name for him would be *Brujo*, the Spanish word for wizard.

Driving down our long driveway, I watched him and wondered whether he would soon whine with eagerness at this familiar approach. The Land deserved the joy of a roaming dog as much as a dog deserved the joy of it. But he had no attachment yet. He just stared. Out of the car, he marked his spot and then sniffed the perimeter. He circled the cabin. He circled the shop. He circled my happy parents. He cruised along part of the creek. He sniffed every room. He slurped food from a metal bowl. He sipped some water.

That night, Bru curled up on a stack of gray Army blankets. I wanted to soothe him, to reassure him that he could stop the search, that we would never abandon him, that he belonged with us and here and wherever we moved next.

Chris spooned me.

We now have a dependent, he breathed into my ear.

My parents left on the early flight out of Bozeman. I dropped them at the airport under a half moon and pulled away into the dark with the confused feelings that come with a goodbye. Night made shadows of houses, hardware stores, and even the bright Exxon station. The world slept. I drove home slowly as snow glided like water across the road. Rounding the last corner, my headlights shone out over a massive herd of elk sitting in a snowy field. Yellow eyes. Collective hot breath steaming. I expected them to be there because they had lingered, intermittently, for the past few weeks, in this field across the street from us. They gravitated there, somehow aware that it was off-limits to hunters. Protected. Like shelter.

The yurt would become a shelter for us soon, our very own shelter.

Just as winter leaned forward, we accelerated.

Not yet knowing whether our yurt would fit together, we had to practice by putting the whole structure up in the shop, like an assembly kit. We couldn't risk frozen fingers and a mistake on the top. We also needed to cut the shiny insulation and canvas to size by testing it over the yurt framework. Raising the yurt twice was necessary.

When we stretched out the *khana* lattice, anticipation tingled up my arms. We were going to see our home. It formed a circle and each end lashed to the square door Chris had built of hickory. The door had a large wooden handle for opening and a lock, the only way to keep the door shut without a doorknob. The wall barely fit inside; we had to squeeze by on the sides. But it was our wall and I was pleased to see it. One hundred and fifty-five slats made this ribcage. I pressed my palms against my own ribcage.

Hey, dreamer, Chris yapped at me.

Coming, coming.

We cinched a wire tension band around the top of the *khana*. The theory: a tension band would create a boundary that upheld the framework. Boundaries, of course, set a person free, but it would take the cells of my body a long while to even begin to understand that concept. Our *tono* skylight would float above in the center and distribute its heavy weight to sixty *uni* roof poles that pushed down into that wire tension band. It was ancient *ger* design; it was pure engineering genius.

Next, we stood on either side of the *tono*, which had been strapped to a makeshift scaffolding.

How about one of us holds the feet and the other hoists it up? I suggested.

Nice, I like that, Chris said.

It was a little chapeau on stilts. We got it up. I climbed a ladder and greeted it suspended up there.

Hello, *tono*.

Chris fed the *uni* up to me one at a time and I inserted them, like pegs, into the respective holes around the *tono*'s circumference, like rays into a sun, or, for the anatomically inclined, male parts into female parts. Below, Chris worked his sailing knot magic and tied them off to the wall. According to our books, these few could hold the *tono* up; the additional fifty-two functioned as extra support. How little we actually need.

So we tested it.

The moment of truth, I declared.

I stroked one of the *uni* and asked it not to break. We unscrewed the scaffolding, piece by piece, waiting, at each turn, for the yurt to collapse on us. But it didn't. With one slow oomph sound, that *tono* sank its weight onto the few *uni* and hovered above us as if it had always meant to be there.

Chris leapt up the ladder, gripped the *tono*, and let his legs go like a monkey.

It's a living structure, he said, bouncing and then doing pulls-ups, one, two.

Bru, who had been snoozing inside the yurt walls, started to pace the circle. Was he nervous about being closed in? Our vet had told us that separation anxiety was common for abandoned animals. So far, not having thought through a training plan, we just kept him with us at all times. I babbled at him as we tied the other roof poles.

The tiger and the tent, the tiger and the tent . . .

One tent. One dog. Two humans. This was his life, and ours now. The yurt wood glowed in the otherwise gray shop. So orange you might duck under the door to find a roving clan gathered together with small bowls of spices and hummus. For now, here, an empty space for us to fill. One day, to pack and take with us.

The yurt didn't add up to much bulk material. I ran my hand along the *uni*, bump bump bump bump, to welcome a structure that would hold us, a structure that would nurture my nomad story, my nomad urge, my nomad self. I didn't want to leave that incubator to step back outside, where I could hear the wind howling, where I knew that a ledge of snow sagged over the roof's edge, where temperatures had started to plummet.

During that week, as December unfolded, we woke to −16 degrees and a ground so frozen that brown leaves skittered, audibly, along the surface. Our car didn't start. Eventually, we would swaddle it with the only thing we could find, our big roll of shiny insulation, and set a heat blower under it. Eventually, the frozen door handle would open. Eventually, it would start. We pulled scarves tighter around our faces. The little hairs in our noses froze. But at least we could hole up in the cabin. We still had to sew the white canvas strips into one shape that, like a circus tent, would fit over the wooden yurt structure.

By we, I mean Chris, the steady man, the boy who had focused on making a balsam fir airplane model or architectural drawing or snow cave for so long his parents had to check in on him. He cared about his sewing machine. He could visualize patterns backward.

You are a reincarnated tailor, I told him.

And you are the Queen Bee herself, he slung back, repeating what he knew my grandmother and mother always called me. A fair enough statement. Because while we set to work, and the cabin transformed into white waves of canvas piled so high that Bru slipped into them and slept, I clacked on the computer to finalize our yurt payments instead of turning to the wedding planning that needed attention. It was only six months away. The whole wedding thing riled me up. Not that I didn't want to be married, though we had considered a civil union or something that felt less steeped in old laws. I just loathed that people in general fluttered their hands and cheeped desperately for information about the inane details of the wedding. Oh, tell me about the napkins. Why not ask instead how about the actual marriage-to-be, the complexity of writing vows, the surge of loving someone completely, the bravery of saying Yes, yes to that person? Some thought that seriousness made me the worst bride ever. Which was probably true. I had always been wary of effervescent chatter, especially the kind that avoided the real issue at hand. But I was particular about how our ceremony would unfold. There would be no walking down the aisle *to* my man. I wanted us to walk toward each other from the sides. So did Chris. When friends asked whether I was nervous to commit, I said No because that was my truth. Any doubts had shaken out early on in our togetherness. This was the man I wanted to love with, grow with, struggle with. The napkins wouldn't shake or support that feeling.

Beb, I've got the number, I said, after an hour or so.

What is it? he asked.

I mean down to the oil for our lanterns, the last screw, the dollar. Guess.

Eight grand. Total.

It's $4,149 for each of us . . . so just over eight, a little over our budget.

Not bad, he smiled, not bad at all.

In my organizing, I had copied down the weather forecast for that week of what we called *raising the great white tent*: 15, −2, 4, −16, 0, −22, 1, −16. It seemed significant to document these details, to remind ourselves that what we had done was real.

Ah, it's like sewing a raincoat for an elephant, Chris explained, carefully feeding the canvas through.

From the well of his silence came the best metaphors, the most succinct straight-and-narrows. The sewing required tedious concentration. So, without much deliberation, we did something we had never done. We snuck the television from its hiding spot behind a Chinese chest and turned it on to watch the international soccer playoffs. Little sweaty men ran all over the green. Hello, world. Hello, other people living lives out there. Right now. It may well have been the most important moment of the twenty-first century for those men. And it was. It was as important to them as erecting the yurt was to us. Knees tucked to chest, I curled in on myself and let the contents of my brain settle. We, these men and I, would never know about each other. I would never be a soccer player. I could never be everything everywhere. I could never be part of all the important moments. I could only tend to my own, even the ones that felt unremarkable.

↓

The night before what I thought was our final day, we had smoothed every last piece of the yurt: wood, canvas, insulation. It was all arranged in a neat pile on the shop floor.

Already stripped down to my underwear, eyelids heavy, I opened the heavy door to let Bru out for his late-night pee, a usual reluctant swagger out into the cold.

Instead, he bolted.

For a moment, my mind hung in the thick liquid of disbelief.

He was gone.

Oy! I yelled into the dark. But there is nothing you can do in this situation. Your dog has caught a scent or heard a rustle and he's off. You are a human with two clumsy legs. You haven't even closed the door to the cold air now frosting the windows. You are practically naked and he's surely past the hawthorns a mile or two away by now. Chris and I didn't even have to exchange words. For two hours, we stood on that dark porch in our down jackets and called out to Bru. We took turns: one of us watching from the warm lit inside, one of us yelling from the cold dark outside. I assumed that if we stopped yelling, he would never be able to track his way back to a home that he might not know well enough to find again. It had only been three weeks.

I imagined awful things: a failed leap across a barbed-wire fence that would snag his collar and freeze him into the snow, an exploration through a horse barn that would end in an angry farmer with a shotgun, a sudden realization that he was hungry and cold and lost in a porous world.

Stop.

A sprint into the woods, even at night, was natural for an animal. Maybe he was exploring, enjoying the long stretch of his legs. Why not run out into the dead of winter like that, why not follow excitement right back into the wild we came from, why not feel the hot rush of my own blood?

Bru did not come back. We gave up when night shed to a dawn rising over the hill. As we slouched back to regroup in bed, I coached myself through a pre-grieving sorrow. I had only known him long enough to know that one day his presence in our family would be something inseparable from the rest of my life. But we weren't there yet. Familiarity had not set in. He was still the shelter dog figuring out his situation; we were still the adoptive parents working on *sit* commands.

Just in case, we left the door ajar.

Then, as if allowing for the possibility that actually beckons the thing, something clopped onto the porch. He appeared outside, panting, dusted with snow, wagging his whole body up at us, looking mighty pleased with himself. His eyes darted from me to Chris, trying to figure out where he stood, what he was to expect.

We growled at him, a discipline method we had learned in a library book. Once he slunk inside, once he slurped back a whole bowl of water, I gave him a rubdown, checking his paws and making sure that all parts of him were intact. He was alive, more alive and vital than I'd seen him. It had been part of his education.

To know his place, he had had to run away from it first.

Is that true? I asked him.

Pant, pant.

The coming back was the glue.

🡇

Morning materialized too quickly. It was the day for getting all materials to the top. We trekked up the hill eight times—with heavy stacks of *uni*, *khana*, canvas, a *tono* that had made Chris look like a turtle, and a fat role of silver insulation that had made me look like a rocket about to take off. With wind chill, the temperature was below 10 degrees. The grogginess of an emotional hangover pulled down at my face. I noticed Chris searching that face.

I'm cool, I reassured him.

Down at the base, the door was our last item. It was massive in girth and made of solid wood. To call it a hobbit's door would make it sound more cute than it was. But it was almost square and we would have to duck to enter the yurt. Chris decided to strap it to his pack board.

I'll just lean over. You can make sure I don't fall over.

That sounds ridiculous.

It'll work.

We had no other option—it was too heavy for two people to carry in their hands. We got the pack board loaded and started to move, slowly, barely. Under a wool hat, his eyes changed and I knew it as strain because he wasn't one to reveal strain.

Don't pop, please.

He simply nodded up the hill. I took the cue and danced in front of him with my hands up and ready. Ready to be a pillar he could fall into, I guess. Bru was attached to a long leash tied around my waist. His thick tail curled up in a permanent arc. He wagged hard enough to slap my legs, happy being right under-foot. About a third of the way up the hill, Chris bent over more.

I tried to uphold the flat board of him, but he finally gave in.

Going down, he wheezed.

He collapsed on top of me, on top of Bru, and the three of us, trapped under the door and tangled up, slid downhill long enough to have backtracked the distance we had come. There goes a door, sliding, with legs and arms sticking out of it. We were all fine: palms padded by gloves, snow down our pants. I was relieved. I didn't want Chris crunching his vertebrae. Formulating Plan B took seconds.

We'll just carry it up old-fashioned style, I said.

Yup.

We gripped it like a table, elbows cocked, biceps fuming. Though we had believed it impossible before, we managed to do it. Every ten steps, we paused under the fir trees to rest the door on our thighs, where later, in a hot bath, as water beaded on my skin, I would find two purple bruise bands.

Once on top, we caught our breath. We propped it in the snow, short and squat against a white backdrop. It became a mystical door in the wilderness. Chris rested his elbow on the frame. My chest swelled.

It's so stunning, beb, I breathed, just there alone in the snow.

I had been starved for that image—the doors we had entered in new homes, the doors we left, and the knowing that one door would never be the last. This door led somewhere. Open the latch and step through.

Our fixed deadline had arrived. I would hop on a plane the following afternoon. Chris had agreed to stay with Bru over the holiday—one of us had to—because I hadn't seen my brothers in a year. He would visit his family a few weeks later.

In the dim light, we stood at the counter and ate pancakes and yogurt. The wind whooshed and whined. Our firs seemed to be swaying wildly to some underground beat we couldn't hear. The top's climate, by any guess, was not peaceful this morning.

Well, the book says it should only take about an hour, I said.

Yeah, but people in Mongolia don't erect yurts in the winter, Chris reminded me.

Okay, I said, here we go anyway.

Dishes clanged into the sink. We headed out. We could have paused to acknowledge the moment, the near end of this project, but we didn't. We were workers in motion. I sucked lips over teeth, away from cold. A few yards into the snow, Bru lifted a frozen foot and stopped. Was this a protest? He had chewed off his sled dog boots when we first bought them and so now he would have to suck it up. We still couldn't leave him in the cabin alone because he would howl and howl and scratch to get out.

Come here, I beckoned and squatted to blow hot breath into his paws.

Then up we trudged.

Dark gray clouds moved over us. Occasionally, a pinhole of light broke through and shiny snow flecks drifted north into the valley. At the crest of the hill, we met the wind. Heaps of snow had spread over the yurt platform. I shoveled it off, set Bru up on a wool mat, and tucked a red down jacket around him so that only his square snout stuck out. My eyes burned and watered. I twisted and knotted my scarf over my hat like a headscarf. It wasn't a violent wind, just as consistent and loud as crashing ocean waves. We couldn't hear each other. Nearby, Chris was hunched over to push the sled up for what I assumed was a windbreak. I crawled over to him. We secured it as best we could.

What do you think? he yelled.

I think we are not going to be able to do this right now, I yelled back.

When we stood up, the wind slammed the sled down. I turned around to go. Chris and Bru followed. The wind snaked in front of me, covering over our footsteps from half an hour ago. No birds in the sky. They knew best to wait this out, and so should we. Down the path, we slid and gripped, slid and gripped, slid and gripped.

Back in the cabin, as tea water boiled and Bru stole off into a warm corner, I remembered my naïve suggestion that we lock the cabin and not use it at all during our yurt building. *That* would have been a scene. To get him to laugh, I snuck up behind Chris and slid my frozen hands up his shirt, into his armpits, and then down his pants. He wiggled away and told me to back off.

Those are my warmest bits, he laughed, pushing at me.

When our faces finally thawed, we peeled off layers and sipped on hot liquid.

He checked the weather on his laptop. I pressed my forehead to a cold window and watched cottonwoods flop around in the wind. To me, wind was folklore. It blew seeds to new places. It transported messages. It relocated dust particles, leaves, and people. It lifted running girls off the ground. No element could squelch it. But someone once told me that wind could also strip a person of her identity, "just strip it right off of her" so that she is more naked than she's ever been, so that she becomes the essence.

I know nothing about the science of the wind, I said.

Nope, precision is definitely *not* your thing, Chris said, smiling at me.

I jabbed him, squeezed his shoulders hard until he turned his head away from tracking weather. The wind had been clear in its message: You cannot rush the final moments of a process you have rushed since the beginning.

Let's go driving, I said.

As we bumped down a long, empty back road, I scraped at the ice on the inside windshield. Though wind rolled down from the mountains, picking up and swirling snow in the fields, the weak sun spread around here, away from the shadow of our hill. Cold seeped in through cracks in the car doors. Horses stood still, their nostrils wet from hot breath. We commented on how the Gallatin River braided, its quiet houses, whether we liked them or not, whether the placement would have suited us. Which house would you live in? What horse would you choose? Palomino, definitely. Do you see those elk? Yep. Their racks curled up like basins that caught the wind before it swirled out. What does that mean? You tell me. I thought about my highway drives, the few of them, and wondered whether they would happen again. When a situation went static, like the impossibility of getting the yurt up today, my only answer, always, was movement. The car heater finally kicked in and we slipped off our gloves to hold hands by the gearshift. We stole glances at each other. He took my wrist pulse with his thumb, a ritual he started when we had first fallen in love, falling asleep, taking my pulse, just to feel, he said, the beat beat beat of me. Bru fogged up the windows in the back.

It was the first time we had relaxed in three months.

On our return, as we drove back up the snow-packed driveway, the white tugged me back to our first dark night on The Land about half a year ago. How distant the wild green grass seemed now, how distant that woman standing in the wild green grass seemed, like an old tattered photograph our great-great-grandchildren would find in a closet one day and know nothing about, how more distant she would become even to the woman wondering about her now.

There was no time for daydreaming, though. We hopped out of the car and the barely swaying trees told us that the wind had died down just enough. Man, the weather changed fast around here. We had to continue. We had to use whatever time we could get. We hustled up to the yurt site with what remaining daylight we had. Working from the ground up, we hitched the *khana* and door, then the tension band and *tono* and all sixty *uni*, and tied each one off. I jammed two fingers. But everything fit well, as if an invisible force had pulled tiny strings and lifted the wood into place. As we worked, I shook myself to keep warm on the ladder. Roof poles closed in around me, closed out the barren landscape beyond. Strange to gaze *out from*, as opposed to *at*.

Almost there, Chris said.

You finally said it, beb, I hollered. You finally said, *Almost there!*

He grinned up at me with those dark squinted eyes.

By the end, stiff and grateful for the now calm gray sky, we walked back a ways. Under the down jacket, Bru did not budge to join us. We stood and stared at a new presence—the brown skeleton against a white landscape. My younger self who planned to translate languages had never found Montana on a map, never conceived that this parcel of land would be anything to her, that it even might be a translation for her.

No need to speak.

We held hands and watched.

Couldn't pause for too long. We needed to prep our canvas. Just then, the wind somersaulted out of the mountains and made its way across the field toward us. Canvas fluttered up like a flag. We chased rogue pieces of p-cord. I plunked firewood, one, two, four, onto insulation and canvas to hold it down. Chris gathered backpacks. Snow blustered at our faces. Our plan to finish that day scattered right along with all our leftover materials.

We trotted away. I glanced back as we moved fast toward the dense firs. Goodbye, brown skeleton. The hardship of this project started to fade, as it always does with time. I skipped ahead of Chris and thought not once about mountain lions. We would deal with the canvas in the morning. Only a few hours of work left. Bru sprinted down barking to greet a stranger pulling up. But it was Brooks and his UPS truck. Like water spilling over an edge, we told him our story.

The grand finale wasn't fetching. We began early. My flight took off in four hours. As wind whacked at our ears, we yanked at a flapping canvas, yelled at each other to hear, moved around the stove still boxed up in cardboard and plastic on the porch, and a few gratuitous *Fucks* flew out of my mouth. Then, only then, was the yurt complete. It was that quick. It was that unceremonious.

But when we stepped through the door, into a cocoon of relative silence, our sixty wooden roof poles pointed up like golden spokes to the circular *tono*, where light poured down through and lit up mounds of snow that had blown in and collected at the base of the lattice walls. The canvas blocked the wind.

It's like being in a cave with light, I said.

It's done, said Chris, as he tucked one hand into the back of my jeans.

On our race to the airport, we were too stunned to speak. Perseverance had become a great emptiness at completion. Anti-climactic. I felt like a blown-out egg. I didn't want to leave. I didn't want to go somewhere else. To do what? Eat candy canes and exchange presents with people who had no idea what we had done? I didn't want to leave this man, this experience, or this moment. I wanted to sit in a bath with Chris, sip white wine, and talk over our bruises.

We did it, beb, Chris said, covering my glove with his glove.

Yeah, we raised the great white tent.

At the terminal, late for my plane, I looked down at my feet, for once unsure of what to say. Clean black shoes had replaced my metal grippers. But my hair was still matted down with sweat. He leaned on me. I hooked my chin on his shoulder and smelled him, smelled the cold of him, the fir of him, the snow of him, all of him and of us. Two weeks from now, I would fly back here and we would begin our yurt life—a life where we would take turns stoking the fire, where we would enter a great hibernation, where I could now, finally, just be.

PART TWO

4

HAWTHORNS, ICE, OTHERS

January 2010

I t might be for evolution's sake that a woman returning to a place feels expectant. The old minerals have been swept away in one broad stroke and she gets to go at it again. Perhaps because she is built to grow many seeds, if she chooses, in the same womb over and over again. Her biology reminds her of this and the new radiant start, whatever it is, calls out to her, Hello, hello. She can remake herself as she intends. At least she thinks she can. And this innate belief is what keeps her breathing.

Without wood dust lodged in my pores, I could now move into this life. I had not been good at building. But I *was* good at roughing it. I could hike up a huge hill in winter to sleep in a yurt. I could learn how to tend a wood-burning stove. I could write with cold fingers. I was ready to be present and do what I had come to do—explore The Land, get strong, and become contented with myself. It's a total luxury, I admitted to friends, who reminded me that I had chosen it and not everyone chooses it, so don't feel guilty because all people inch toward wanting to know what will make them feel full. Chris gently suggested that not everything in life needs to be a self-improvement project. But I didn't know how not to be geared that way.

Nothing but me, a man, a dog, a yurt, and wide open space. Perfect. From now until June, when we would go East for our wedding, nothing would take me away from that intention.

As late afternoon unfolded, I balled up newspaper and stuffed it into the woodstove, just left of the door, a few feet in past our stash of firewood. While I was away, Chris had built a basic futon frame for our mattress and pushed it to the opposite side of the yurt for fire hazard reasons. It was under one of the three small vinyl windows. We would be able to sit up and stare out to the field from our bed. The remaining space wasn't much—not in 200 square feet with no corners—though I hoped to work a desk into the curve to the right of the door. Along the far wall between stove and bed, a pile of bowls and mugs would become our kitchen. Kneeling on the floor, he was chopping sweet potatoes with ski gloves on. Bru coiled up on a wool mat right by the unlit stove. This would soon become a familiar scene, the warming before we could undress even a little. Arranging a pyramid of sticks over the newspaper, I blew the word *topophilia* on my bare hands. To love a place. Knowing that a French philosopher and a Chinese American geographer had coined the term raked the cliché right from the meaning for me.

Our small dwelling, and our small clan, made me love this place.

I feel like I've landed here and it's new, I said.

Good, he smiled.

I lit the match.

The fire hissed, quieted, started up again, and dwindled to a quiet point, as cold as the rest of us. I wanted to be good at this stove and its particulars: what to do when it was being stubborn, where it liked airflow, how to manage when it died a small death, how to lure it into being. Other than tossing a match on a gasoline-soaked bonfire, I had never made my own fire. I fiddled and the damper clanked. Chris let me work at it, let me stay squatted and focused for a solid fifteen minutes. He didn't offer pointers. He watched me figure it out.

So I did.

Eventually, my nothing crackled up to a little bright flame. Voila! I said.

Because it would take an hour to warm up the yurt, we dipped out for an evening ski. The sky—how could anyone get over the immense sky here? Cauliflower clouds streamed over a gray expanse and over us. We, so small in our surroundings, skimmed over snow and avoided hard patches of blond ice. He and Bru burst ahead. I sprinted after him, spraying snow behind me. Like this, we began the flirting that comes from even two weeks of distance.

The expression *get the lay of the land* had crept into our language, so that Mark Twain, and everyone, used it. How did a person get such a thing? Much about The Land was the same. The field gleamed white. Dark green firs broke snow monotony. Where the slope plunged, they towered up like telephone poles in a hundred years' stance. Gliding with poles in one hand, I yanked my hat farther over my ears and then stopped to do a proper job of it. As my layers jumbled, cold slithered up my nostrils, spread itself red across my cheeks, tried to sneak through the neck of my down jacket. For once, I didn't race away to get blood pumping. Faraway silhouettes now, my two men played tag along the fence line: Chris hunching over like a monster, Bru stretching down submissively, curled-up tail unmistakably his. Our yurt life had finally begun. And when I knew that to be true, I dashed out across the distance, careening over the starched laundry newness of it all.

That night, we cranked the stove up.

Let's see what this baby can do, Chris grinned, stoking it with another log. As it did what it could do, as the lanterns shed minimal light, we ate, got drunk on whiskey, and shared New Year's resolutions that made us both cry a little with thanks.

Without yurt tasks, the blank space of what to *do* with our lives actually lay before us. As intended, but still. Lying on the bed, elbows propped, we discussed creative time: could we find it, what if we didn't, how long could we live off our savings, there was a reason artists usually paired off with lawyers or doctors, but we believed our way was possible, were we naïve, was it selfish, what were we doing, what was art anyway—maybe it was a tornado, if I believe in you then I should believe in myself, yes, agreed, you too, yes, hold my face, we can do it then, you're right, it isn't even a choice, it just is, I agree.

After our conversation, things had changed. In the warm orange light, the yurt beat like a heart. Bru had retreated from the stove to our pile of boots. He was panting. We had unclothed and sprawled out on the bed like starfish. I rolled over to glance at our thermometer gauge: 95 degrees inside and −5 degrees outside.

Now that's fucking hot, I said.

I knew it could crank, Chris agreed and pulled me back toward him.

I didn't drift away into my usual dreams. Flames pulsed at the stove window and transfixed me from beneath the covers. One of us needed to stoke the fire every four hours and we had not drawn straws. Wind whooshed and the stovepipe *tink, tink,*

tink, tink, tinked like a tinker in a wagon approaching from some distant place on a cold snowy night. I was as alert as a mouse to the new sounds.

Hours later, I slipped out from under Chris's slumbering dead weight, stepped into my boots, and pushed the heavy door open.

Cold wind blew my loose hair up. In the blackness, I caught faint outlines of grass poking up from snow, a collapsing fence, the curve of our hill, and the strange disorientation of night. I held myself in a hug for a while, a hug responding to meat locker cold, then stomped off the porch to crouch. My pee steamed into the snow. The firs seemed to breathe with the breath of animals. Wind rushed down my back and in between my legs, and goose bumps spread like a rash. Just stay. Stay longer. Dare yourself. My hands covered my face to no knowing of what was around me. I wanted to be liberated back into a skin that was mine, yours, ours, liberated to be alive, feral.

It wasn't as if I hadn't peed outside before.

But this was new. At my back, the yurt throbbed heat outward. I scraped a compass into the snow and stood up.

In the morning, I snuggled deeper under the covers, away from a chill left by a fire now turned to coals. Last up at 3:08 to stoke the fire, I had not woken again to tend it. That internal clock would come with repetition. I stared at our ceiling, where our carbon monoxide detector was tucked between two *uni*. It was necessary but stood out like an ugly white bug. Over the mound of Chris's freckled back, through the vinyl window, an eggshell cast lit up the snow. Hard to pry away from a warm body, but I forced my feet to the cold wood floor even as they shrank from it.

It was the first of January and I craved the solo hour or two that important days warranted. Bru shook his collar and roused himself to come along. On our second lap circumnavigating the field, the sky began to release light powdery snow, the kind of snow that makes distinct snowflakes. It sifted down over me and muffled all earth sounds, with the exception of my boot squeaking out into the whole valley like a small hurt animal.

Hello! Hello! Hello! broke the silence. I ignored it at first, assumed it a crow or wind gust or engine screeching far away. Some say that if you have never encountered a thing—like another person up on the top here—then your brain has trouble allowing the possibility. You cannot see, hear, smell, or taste it until it literally presses up against you. The sound repeated itself, continued to yell until it finally reached a crescendo. Gray mountains dominated the view in front of me. To my left, the field spread like tundra. Only a red fox in the distance inched across the white expanse. When I craned my neck behind, a small figure charged along the fence line toward me, waving one hand wildly and using the other to hold a leash attached to a yanking hound dog.

I steadied Bru with a firm hand on his back.

You stay, you heel in.

We met at the fence.

Hi, she breathed.

Hi, I breathed.

No one is ever up here, we said at the same time.

She was another neighbor. Her place abutted ours at the west end of the field, which, like a true plateau, dropped steeply down to a dirt road and to the farmhouse she lived in with her husband and son. What began as a shy encounter turned into story swapping. When her mules had trailed along the fence, we had taken the liberty of petting them. She had spotted our yurt and wondered about it. They were also newcomers, as of eight or so years ago. When they found this place, she just *knew*; she stopped the car and told her husband, This is it. Then she learned that it had been the original farmhouse for all this land, the hundreds of acres of this land that was now split into separate parcels. We ruminated together on who else had once frolicked up here long ago, appealed to the heavens, hunted. Those people had been the real people of winter.

You guys here for good? she asked.

Nah, maybe another year, but we love it for now.

I liked this woman. We would eventually meet her husband and son, but we wouldn't see them a whole lot, or anyone, at least not for a long while. Lives get busy. Unless we walked to the furthest point of The Land, we never saw their farmhouse. And it's easy to forget about places you cannot see.

People on my periphery—my friend Eric's suburban aunt, a long-lost friend of my mother's, my father's conservative old boss—had responded to our yurt photo slideshow as if we'd given birth to quadruplets. Complete awe. They wanted to know more: why and what it felt like to have accomplished the *dream* of building our own home, because everyone dreamt of building a home, but few actually did it, and a yurt at that. Many people didn't understand why we would deliberately leave a warm cabin for a tent with a stove. Desperate for the scoop, they asked, How is it?

I've got one word for you: *elemental*. *Elementary* would

have been just as accurate. Nomadic tent dwellers understood an uninsulated life as the only life, shepherding camels, yaks, horses to other pastures, understood it in their bones, in a way that requires no articulating. I had not. Without a window cracked, the thick cabin walls had insulated us from even the sound of the creek four steps away.

But, in only a few days of yurt life, we understood that this living would be living with a thin membrane. Owls started hooting, or perhaps we started hearing the lone *hoo hoo* as she distinguished herself from the dark. Wind rattled against our canvas walls. Somewhere in the distance, coyotes yipped at the start of evening. Smaller animals scurried by, brushing occasionally against the walls. No sensory event was kept out. No layer between *this* and *that*. I could have opened a pickle jar, stuck it outside, stepped back inside, and still smelled it. No such thing as battening down the hatches. Already, cells within me were waking up, absorbing more. It was exactly what I had wanted —to be awoken this way—though I had not expected sitting inside the yurt to feel almost as raw as walking on The Land. I could foresee a summer where the wild mood of a thunderstorm drumming on the roof would course right into me.

The yurt didn't allow me to envision that I was anywhere else but here.

Here you are, take it or leave it.

At first, enthusiastic, we squeezed our days short in order to get up to the top before dusk. We became masters at long evenings of quiet. No electricity. Just cooking on the woodstove, reading by the fire, the smell of kerosene lanterns, and the flickering shadows and light of them.

To bed?

Yup.

And one of us would snuff out the flame.

The tranquility of a circular home stunned us. Occasionally, one of our cell phones rang. They actually worked better on the top than down by the cabin. But not much else jarred us out of our trance. I felt undeserving of the calm. Each morning, we peeled our grippers from the icy cedar porch, stretched them over our boots, and started down the hill for the day. Back to a toilet, shower, running water, refrigerated food, Internet, and the woodshop nearby. These amenities were critical. Otherwise, we would have had to sponge-bathe and depend upon the root cellar we thought about digging but never did. Was it cheating our original vision? No, we had never intended to be home-steaders, and I'd gotten over any need to make it harder for us about four months ago. Sometimes, as evening approached, our work below, often on the computer, lasted longer than we hoped and our departure from the bottom was late. When the world south of latitude 45 degrees poured a gin for cocktail hour, our sky had long turned dark. The nightly commute up was daunting.

Step out the door of a warm cabin and zip your jacket higher. Notice the black hill looming over you. You can't see anything, but you can hear the occasional snap of a stick or just silence. You pause. You strain your ears. Nothing detect-able. Now, walk into it, walk up it. You are forced into brav-ery. It's a good thing that you've trained your large dog to fol-low on your heels because the lion hunts at night. You don't know yet that, most likely, a lion wants nothing to do with you. You beam your flashlight into dark woods to distinguish your-self from a deer. The crescent moon pokes out above the trees' fringe and you plod up with a pack board slung with bags full of food, bowls, cups, and spoons; and don't forget the olive oil, or the two-gallon jug of water, or the bear spray; and don't forget to sing, even if you feel like an idiot. When your trail turns to sheet ice, scamper up a different way, because even those metal spikes won't do in some situations.

This happened every night.

Sounds like you're pulling security, joked my ex-military brother.

As we established patterns, figured out how, moved through the night, the world abandoned its creamy façade and took on a new luster. Surely, during that period, my eyes had the clear look of someone immersed in the unfamiliar. On big moon evenings, everything turned placid. Blue light cast itself around, seeping into any shadowy place, any nook so that we could all see. We could get our bearings. Moon shadows from the gnarly cottonwoods stretched far and black across fresh snow. I would loiter on the edges, trying to make sense of this midnight art, a careful etching made with the blackest of inks. When we moved by them, sucking in cold sharp air, our long shadows disturbed, only for a moment, the image.

Though I had lugged my two large bundles of clothes up to the yurt, it quickly became apparent that they actually needed to be in the cabin near the shower, unless I wanted to double back on a task. We stored rice and beans in the yurt. Vegetables lived in the cabin where they wouldn't freeze during the day. My books divided themselves between both places, often based on subject matter. We dashed around asking each other, have you see my headlamp, what about my black bra, where is the ketchup bottle, where is the knife?

I started to call us The Bag People.

We carried everything up and down in old canvas bags.

So began our back-and-forth.

One afternoon I stuck my head into the shop to ask whether Chris was ready to go upstairs. He nodded Yeah and neither of us realized what I had named until we crested the hill. With that, the yurt became *upstairs* and the cabin *downstairs* and we learned to move between them like liquid, as if they were parts of the same lone dwelling, connected by an ice staircase scuffed by our grippers, one that echoed with my constant *Helloooo to the forest*, a phrase so common now that, to keep it interesting, I pinched the *oooo* sound as if I were someone's bespectacled great aunt showing up for afternoon tea.

The morning Chris got up the way a fisherman does, I knew it was time, in mid-January, for me to snap into gear. He high-stepped into stiff pants, pulled his fleece and then a jacket over his head until he emerged focused and handsome and ready to start work down in the woodshop by 8 AM. He had a few furniture commissions on tap. From the bed, I watched his routine take hold. I needed a routine.

You coming?

Nope, gonna write, I said, spying my laptop on the floor. I could skip breakfast this morning and work for the three hours my battery would allow up here. Away from our unreliable but still present Internet, I might be able to drop into myself faster and avoid worrying about what other writers had accomplished that I had yet to.

I'll just call you when I need Bru, I said.

You sure?

Yeah, that'll work.

That was how we decided to manage the lion situation. When I was ready to go downstairs, I would call Chris on my cell phone and walk out to the snowy edge. Bru would appear at the bottom of the hill. I would call him. He would run up and together, owner and protector, we would descend through the forest.

I sat on the bed with my laptop on a pillow. No desk yet. The yurt was spare, but it felt like a temple. Because it seemed deserving of respect, I tried not to hunch. Every few minutes, my gaze moved up to the *tono* and a matte white snow sky hovering above. I noticed a small black spider dangling on thread. It lowered itself onto our white bedspread and crawled away from me.

Back to the screen. I refocused on two essay drafts. For a long while, I typed away and made progress until my stomach complained. We had snacks somewhere; where, though? I found a stash nearby, poured some sunflower seeds into a cup, and kept words gathering on the page. Snow collected too and blew against the vinyl windows, only to melt in streaks because of the warmth from our stove. I wanted a bowl of warm oatmeal, but the seeds, those pale salty seeds, would do for now, especially because they reminded me of being young.

My brothers and I can sit on our outdoor terracotta steps in Mexico City for hours, teasing our big old St. Bernard dog below, spitting sunflower seeds like our life depends on it, trying to spit far enough to plant a seed. I rip open another package with my teeth and hand them out, one by one. My middle brother asks, Are we gonna stay here? and I respond, Nah, and rub his back. Remember, we go a mile wide, I say, and both brothers lean in so close to listen that what I say had better be good. The sun beats down on our knobby knees as we sing "La Cucaracha." How will other places feel on my skin? No one in my whole family cares about nature, at least not outwardly. My parents do not kneel down to introduce me to specific plants with specific names. I won't be a name knower either. But nature is my opal and it always will be. Later, when sadness or anger socks over as an adult, I will lie down on grass and watch ants marching along with purpose, or in circles, and that zoom in will allow me to zoom out and breathe. As I grow, my mother will say, You've always needed nature, much more than your brothers. It calms down that fire in you.

The fire had petered out in the woodstove. No more wood neatly stacked by the stove. I grabbed my coat-hat-gloves trio and stepped outside to practice my chopping. Chris had done me the favor of re-teaching me how to split wood and then letting me practice on my own without being watched.

He couldn't believe I called it chopping instead of splitting. But I figured that, until I was graceful at it, I would call it by what my actions appeared to be. Outside, sun shone through falling snow. The seven-pound maul swung behind me and up to the apex place where its dead weight took over and followed the arc down hard to the exact center. Chop. Sometimes two chops. Wood pieces collapsed to either side. I had organized myself like a center linebacker—feet spread, good grip, focus. A few times, the maul bit the wood partway or bounced right off a knot, sending the worst reverberations up my arm, and a little fear too. I didn't want to hack into my own leg.

I was training myself into a life that required firewood.

People in the North Country don't glorify this basic act, so I didn't want to glorify it either, especially because, later, I would meet eleven-year-old girls in this town who split wood to earn extra pocket money. But with silver earrings in my cold ears and hair loose, standing on a snow plateau surrounded by silence, I felt powerful. Not that I was willing to admit that to anyone. It was about as adult as I had felt when I signed my first W-2 form. The great exception to being an adult, of course, was the fact that The Land we were being adults on was actually owned by my family. That was about as adult as fish sticks.

Soon, my task was complete: seven logs split into quarters.

For the kindling, I had to hold the maul at its neck and use its sharp end to hit a hunk of wood that my other hand was holding. Making chopsticks was fine work I had not been born to do. If you didn't move your fingers quickly enough, well, *sayonara*. My left arm sprang away. I tried again. I tried again. Before lumbering back to my laptop, I was able, for a moment, to see myself as a strange bird performing a spastic dance.

I could make this a routine. But, no, my routine needed to be writing and exploring The Land. I needed to approach it all systematically. I couldn't just let this place wash over me. I couldn't just fade into the oblivion of daily mundane tasks. That couldn't be.

When Chris found me kneeling on the bathroom floor with my journal open, he washed his hands in the sink for longer than was necessary. Like a clever spy. He knew what it meant when I started making lists. Some people had no need for lists; others could fill a weekly trash bag with lists. They helped me in chaos. Not that I felt chaos. I just needed a productive structure.

I'm fine, I reassured him, waving him away. Just organizing myself.

1. Explore hawthorns.

2. Draw parts of The Land in detail (ice, cottonwoods, creek, firs).

3. Read about snow and symbolism of color white.

4. Make money to go to Japan, three months at least, honeymoon?

5. Finish book on literature from the "Axis of Evil."

6. Deal with health insurance and vet visit for Bru.

The hawthorn area scared me the most. Diane once mentioned that if the lion made a den anywhere, it would be in there, in the thicket of black bushes dense enough to be a mangrove. Oh, yeah? I had asked. I think so, she said. You might need a machete to get through there.

I'm off, I announced to Chris later that afternoon.

Tackling the list, right? he said, leaning on the kitchen counter with a smile.

Yes I am, I barked back, and then he pranced toward me like an elf, a conciliatory move he had inherited from me and taken on as his own.

We held each other in a long hug.

If I'm not back in two hours, I said, come find me in the hawthorns.

The two-inch long red thorns ripped at my jacket. Scooting on my stomach, I crawled under tight spots and then widened my knees like a toad pushing its way through muck, stretched

arms forward to find a branch and pull into the next movement, enjoying the work of my triceps, checking to make sure
the bear spray didn't leap out of my back pocket and that Bru
was still with me in this maze. Getting through here in the summer would have been impossible, but snow had tamped down
the small bushes. Occasionally, my head dropped to rest on
that soft snow and first I heard blunt silence and then my own
blood pounding.

There is a tuft of hair. There is a track. Sasquatch. Every
fallen limb shaped like the horn of a rhinoceros, or the snout
of an alligator, beautiful, a place untraveled down here, a place
of ducking and getting snagged, eyes in wood, eyes in snow
watching me. Such beauty; it would be hard to lose interest in
it. There is a fence, the end of The Land. There is my armpit,
and whoa there is my smell. I like my smell. I always told friends
that anyone who says they don't like their own smell is lying.
Electric-car-racetrack was the way Chris described the smell of
me when I came on to him. He smelled of crayons.

Oy, Bru, come, I growled.

He had found another passageway. His tiger coat flashed
behind a mat of branches. It stopped at the sound of my voice.
In the ways only dogs can, he contorted his body through the
hawthorns to find his way back to me.

I told myself to relax. Remember the tussock cliff you almost
fell from, the lightning that just missed you on the bridge, the
canoe flip that almost drowned you, all the other moments.
So relax about the lion and your fear of it. You know deep in
your soul that it is out there somewhere, but you don't want
to see it; you don't want to encounter it. That's normal. Worst
case: It gets you. The chance of any predator encounter was

a minuscule .000009. But still, some part of me, of all of us maybe, was not okay with the potential of being what most other animals are—prey. It never felt good to not see the big things coming.

When we finally found the edge, where the hawthorns thinned out, the sun was low in the sky. Almost there. I stood upright, pirouetted to check my perimeter, and tucked sweaty curls back underneath my hat.

We made it, I said to Bru, who was busy sniffing around the snow.

With a thick forest of thorn bushes at my back and a treeless snow hill in front of me, the cousin sensations of relief and bravery mingled. I could go back in there, no problem, I thought, now that I was free of it. Even the smallest distance from it made it seem doable now, made me shrug a little at why I had been worried at all. But there was pleasure still in being able to know I had done it. I reached out to a thorn and ran my finger along it: sharp tip, spear, spear.

We scampered up to the top. I sank my butt into snow and stuck my gloved hand under my jacket over my heart, as if to pledge allegiance to something. The grain silos stood gaunt against the sky. A truck droned into the quiet; then a snowmobile whirred somewhere. Below, the black mat of what we'd come through was what people never assumed the wide West to be—a tangle.

Bru licked my earlobe.

I welcomed the hot scratch of it.

I came through *that*, I reported to the snow.

But this snow didn't have a message for me. It just was. And here I was, with snow itch, melting in my socks, sliding down my pants, down the back of my jacket, feeling deep satisfaction, the kind that melts everything but love away. My eyes slit serene. These were the moments I lived for, to be on the other side of the tangle, to have emerged to rest on the pristine snow, momentarily. People who always lived with the clean slate of snow, did they lose their knowing of it? Their senses must dull to its routine. If I had eaten an apple every day of my life, I might forget the sweet taste of it.

Or maybe, maybe I could find the whole world in this country of snow.

Or in ice. Now I was on a quest. The next day, I plodded down to the cottonwoods behind the cabin.

What do you hope to find down there? Chris had asked before I left.

I don't know exactly.

But he knew that I was trying to have a conversation with The Land—with its hawthorns, its animals, and now its ice. Ice layered over the creek in long, pale blue sections, like catwalks. Deer had begun to use these passageways to get across, leaving their delicate tracks in the snow skim. They knew not to slip into the dark crevices where water gushed and echoed up its sound. No part of a creek was ever solid and unmoving. On his haunches, Bru sat guard with his floppy ears cocked up and back. I picked a spot on the creek's edge under cottonwood branches dusted with snow. With my coat zipped up over my mouth, I stuffed an extra jacket under my knees and began to draw. In other circumstances, this could have been a real laissez-faire thing to do. Get up. Sit down. Rearrange. Draw. I wasn't one of those people drawn to endless tracts of ice. So trying to communicate with ice was like trying to to put my shoes on the wrong feet.

An artist friend told me that if you really want to know a place you must draw it. More importantly, you must draw what you see, not what you *think* you see. It was a confusing demand —to draw what I saw versus what I wanted to see. Not sure how to distinguish between those. We all wanted to see what we wanted to see, which in turn, would become what we thought we saw. How could you pry yourself away from that impulse? It seemed that when you glared at something hard enough, you eventually burrowed your way through to the other side, where that thing becomes not what it is supposed to be, but what it is for you.

I stared at the blue ice and saw everything but blue ice. There was the lace on my fold-over socks when I was six and living in Spain, or a whale's baleen from a Baltimore museum, or the ice cubes I used to suck on after school, or the slit of a vagina that symbolizes, well, everything, or a basket of sand dollars I touched in a tourist shop and felt sorry for, or adipose tissue beneath my microscope in seventh grade, or the bubbles my brothers and I blew in the pool on scorching days, or striped wallpaper from a house we never moved into, or the gap between being twenty-nine and being thirty; and quickly the shapes I saw told the story of my past.

But no drawing happened on my paper.

I moved toward the ice and pressed my ear down.

I listened for drums. Drums had never entered my childhood, but to listen for them seemed appropriate, as if they cued the approach of every life event for any of us. My cheeks had gone numb. When would these ice slabs crack and release back into the flow?

Without the yurt building as a storytelling anchor, our life had become a mystery to friends. I had slipped away from regular touch with them, so consumed by the living I wanted to do here. But in occasional emails, the same question surfaced: Where do you *go* if have to *go* up there? Outside, in the snow. The benefit of freezing temperatures was a solid shit by morning, easy to bag and haul downstairs. It smelled of nothing because nothing smelled of anything in winter here. Not so easy to soap hands and pour water over them in frigid air, but we did it.

When we pulled the yurt door open each evening, one of us leapt into bed while the other started the fire. We took turns. Unless a fire had been going all day, there was no thermal mass to hold any heat. Ten degrees outside meant ten degrees inside. Usually, after his turn at fire starting, Chris would sneak under the covers to tickle my stomach and neck, forcing me to beg Stop, stop, stop.

But sometimes, he waded toward the bed like a lost soul. I trusted our frugal ways and that we could make a living. Especially with some of my savings left. But he wallowed further in our diminishing finances. After college, I had forced us, against his will, to break up for a year and date other people so that we could truly choose each other. But I love you and you love me, he had said, voice choked. It doesn't matter, I told him, we have to take the risk. Part self-protection and part wanting him to learn to shake up life. Now, when his vacant eyes made me want to grab his shoulders and shake him and demand that we stay optimistic or else, I tried hard to remember what a good friend had once told me: Just because you can't tolerate imperfection in yourself does not mean you shouldn't tolerate it in him; that just isn't fair of you.

It was my turn to rally and be the fallback. The yurt building had not irked or upset him. But the living, the part I loved so far, would open like a black hole beneath him every few days. Even when I wasn't sure, I assured him that starting a business takes time and that the money would come. Let me rub your head, I would say, and then trace the outline of his brow and nose over and over again. Under the stare of our *tono*, in the haven of our yurt, he would release his worry in ways that never happened downstairs. Someone had asked us if we felt like pioneers. No, no, no, real pioneers were people who showed up to a place they had never seen with no resources and no way out. Dealing with sixty mile-per-hour winds potentially ripping the stovepipe off and the presence of a lion was one thing. But I was clear that our situation had been facilitated by the privilege of landownership and choice. It was no Dust Bowl. It was no frontier. We could go out and get paying jobs when we had to.

I still wanted to feel like the pioneer of something.

We all want to be the bushwhacker.

When I woke to a fire that needed tending, I would step out of bed and put on our gray pigskin gloves. The moon often shone down through the *tono* and lit me up like a firefly. Dry heat waves radiated at my bare quads and stomach. I would unlatch the stove door. The flames would adjust to a new pressure before I could open the door completely. If the door hung open too long, smoke would puff into the yurt. Speedy wood placement was not always my forte. And when a log lost balance and fell back out, lengthening the whole process, allowing smoke to make its escape, I would squeal, slam the door shut, and vault over a pile of clothes and into bed. But the smoke always found us. Our throats burned raw. We could not hide from it, not even in the palms of our own hands.

Gotta open, Chris would breathe, as we stumbled from bed to push the yurt door wide open. We would hold onto the doorframe and arc our necks up to the moon. To let the smoke out, we had to let the cold in.

Quiet is a sly creature. You barely notice its arrival. As the end of January drew near, my hours filled with snow and essays, and my days did the same, and a white snow palette burned into me so that abstraction became familiar. Like light reflecting off a shard of glass. The only person I saw, with few exceptions, was Chris. Body language even replaced our conversations. We spoke in gestures. Days could pass without me having uttered anything aloud but, Dinner? My voice, when I heard it, was strange to me, gravelly even. The trees said nothing, of course, and stillness, even the impossibility of stillness, wrapped me into a bundle.

I liked not having to respond to anything or anyone. It was the muffled sound of swimming underwater and knowing that the loud sounds live on the surface somewhere else, but you are under the surface, safe and unbothered and allowed to wonder. So despite my tendency to want talk, I became as quiet as ether. When someone knocked on the cabin door, I asked Chris to get it or hid in the bathroom. When emails flooded my inbox, I didn't answer them. When the landline rang, I covered my ears to the shrill and only ever answered for the worst reason: obligation. It's all part of the experience of this place, I told myself. My moments of alarm about the change in me were infrequent.

One afternoon, as we skied around the field, I asked Chris, the man who operates on quiet, if he felt he had become more quiet living here.

What kind of question is that? he laughed.

Well, feels like I can barely form a sentence, I explained.

Yeah, actually, you *have* gone shy.

Shy might be the wrong word.

Quiet, then.

Yes.

We moved along the barbed-wire fence and I came to a marking in the snow. Someone had written HELLO!! in block letters on our side. The person had done it without any guarantee of us seeing the letters past the approaching snowstorm.

Look, I pointed down.

Maybe that's all anyone needed—I see you and you see me. It was a call across winter. The green house stared at us across the distance.

Must have been Brooks, said Chris.

Maybe it's a skill, I said.

What? Chris asked.

Learning silence in order to hear your own truth.

You, he teased, and locked onto my arms like a lobster, pushing me as I pushed back, surrounded by mountains, two figures collapsing in on each other until eventually his gravity pushed me down, away from my philosophy and back to the tactile world where cold is cold and snow bunches around your jacket collar.

Had the winter, this place, quieted me? I had always believed that we are shaped by the places we inhabit, that our bones are knit from the essence of our surroundings, that our mannerisms are born from the mood of a place. Grow up surrounded by peach trees and peaches will grow you up. You could almost look into a person's eyes and know hot or cold, vast or lush, rural or urban. In Old English, become is *becuman*, meaning "come to a place, come to be." We be-come our landscape. No way around it. Which left peripatetic people like me not orphaned, but an amalgamation. Each country we passed through had raised me. It was as if I'd been the beneficiary of a whole gang of wild aunts and uncles who had offered me different models for being. Without a home place to reference, I had always shifted like a chameleon. The Land was simply a new member of the clan adding new wires to my awareness.

So don't be shocked, I told myself.

Everything rolled along easily. I continued to meet new parts of The Land: the length of the irrigation ditch, the cluster of cottonwoods down by the mailbox, the top's far edge as it narrowed to a point. Disconnected from the rest of the world, I cared even less than I already had about Facebook and breaking news and social happenings. Everyone else could churn on the important loop and I would lace up my boots and walk through snow. I loved with a capital *L* this place. I had loved other places, but this one felt different somehow. My quiet became a long-awaited friend.

But then, in early February, Chris's older brother Mike arrived from eastern Turkey. He had been living in Erzurum, a town far closer to the Iranian border than Istanbul, on a teaching scholarship. During his one month off, he came to Montana to spend part of that break living in the cabin. I had always adored him—for his obsession with literature, his need to offset that obsession with manual labor, and his tendency to be a tad erratic, like me. Though he was ragged with travel, I could smell the buoyancy on him. He told us about yogurt and almonds and plums, *hamams* "with bacteria crawling around from the Silk Road," people who insisted kindly that he eat goat with them, how male friends held hands or pinkie fingers while walking down the street, and that his Turkish had gotten good enough to get by. I was leaning so far into his stories that my chair pushed back and crashed me to the ground. As he spoke, I glanced out the window at snow. This place existed at the exact same time as *that* place.

But, he said, Coming home is the best part of traveling. I'm a homebody; I just want a house in the woods to take care of.

Really? I asked.

Not so long ago, he had rolled a sleeping bag out on the floor of our New York apartment and talked about how he couldn't wait to move to a foreign country and mix it up. I reminded him of this.

Yep, he said, we're all crazy.

By *we* he meant all of us young-ish people.

At the dinner perch each night, surrounded by the smell of crushed tomatoes and pasta, we sat and debated how best to live this life. We came to no grand conclusion, only the obvious one —that so often we crave the opposite of what we are doing. Or we don't have the stamina to stick to any one thing very long. It wasn't just us. Most of our friends, especially those our age, steered that way.

One night, after we left Mike settled into the cabin,

something unknown howled in the dark and eventually coyotes began to yip until they faded out to the low moan of a truck. The yurt, despite the appearance it gave of warm shelter, was no Grandma Moses painting. That I decided, lying in bed. It was a nomadic structure. It could hike up its skirts and walk. Where would it walk to? Early on, before building, we had envisioned renting a roof space or large balcony in a city, Lisbon, Prague, or Reykjavik, and one day moving our yurt there for a spell. How great would that be? How implausible, but how strange and new, despite the prospect of shipping the whole thing across an ocean. More likely, we would take it with us down to the Southwest or even farther to Central or South America, now that we had Bru for the next ten years or so. I knew the yurt wouldn't last for years and years—at some point you need a second room—but it would do for our next place or two. We would choose a small town, set up the yurt, and live for a while, eating avocado and watermelon, still working, me on a book, Chris on something to do with tropical woods and furniture. He would learn Spanish. I would fine-tune mine. My vision for it was clear. I would feel the addictive feeling that comes with growing new synapses with every new place. We would grow awarenesses we never knew were possible.

But I was in our yurt *here* right now, staring out the window at darkness, and holding, it appeared, my ribcage. The thing behind that ribcage gave a little whimper. I wanted to shush it. Why is it that the second we hear about someone else's grand life, the one we are living loses its value? I would not have been triggered by the news of a marriage or pregnancy or child or new job or new car or boatload of sudden money. No, none of that. Only by adventure and living in a new, usually foreign place.

Pure. Unadulterated. Envy.

I lulled myself to sleep with this thought: Look, it's okay, you just don't like a small radius, but you already knew that about yourself and this place is what is happening now and this place is good, really good.

My silent time faded away. The three of us skied together, talked every night, caught up on what everyone else we knew was doing. Later that week, Mike called one of his closest friends from college, a mutual friend of ours who lived in D.C. and worked for the Department of Defense as a writer/researcher of long manifestos. But he preferred the part of his job that focused on how to improve relations with other countries, specifically those in Africa.

Do you have electricity? he asked me when the phone was placed in my hands. That started a funny exchange, with me explaining that in the cabin, yes, in the yurt, no, but that even in the cabin, the landline didn't always work on foggy nights. Here I was pointing the phone at the radio tower so many hills away in the hope that the scratchy background noise would go away.

Not even Internet at the yurt, he said.

Nope.

And then he laughed this wholesome laugh of utter incomprehension.

Au naturel. That's amazing.

No, *you* are amazing, I said, and walked toward the back of the cabin, away from the brothers already tossing corn chips in a pan for nachos.

Well, Ms. Woman of the World, this is quite a change, isn't it?

I grinned a little before responding, glad that he had called me what he had.

Yeah, I said, but it's no *Little House on the Prairie*, Mr. D.C.

We ate a late dinner with Mike and slept in the cabin. Chris and I sank into the enormous plush bed, a far cry from our hard futon. No woodstove. No ambient sounds. I was, as usual, flat on my back, in order to stare at the space of possibility between the ceiling and me. Before he fell asleep, I needed another human being to listen.

There's a reason people go crazy in caves, I said.

What? He rubbed his eyes awake.

The yurt, The Land, I said. It's not the last thing I want to do with my life.

He rolled toward me. I knew to expect anywhere from a five- to twenty-minute silence from him. He liked to form complete sentences in his head before uttering them. I scratched my forearms, zoned out, and waited for his response.

Then he sat up.

Molly, he said, no one ever said anything about this place being the last thing you will do with your life. Especially not me. Don't even try to pull that "Chris is a homebody" shit with me. If you want to move to Japan tomorrow, or Chile or Nebraska, find a way to get us there and I'll go. And you don't want to go work for the UN in an office without a window, drinking bad coffee and eating donuts and getting depressed because you are overworked and unhappy. You've never wanted that.

I know, I said, surprised by his force, that he, not prone to swearing at all, had used the word *shit*. He flopped back down and flung his leg over mine.

Sometimes, he responded, you need to be reminded that *you* make your own choices.

It was a truth my friend Jen and I had belabored a thousand

times on the phone over the years, reminding each other and ourselves, in down moments, that we were the only ones responsible for every choice we made; so, essentially, get into it or change it. Why did we often assume we were being excluded from a better place; why did our whole generation? She was a self-made climate change lawyer living in a city—a humble human who actually wished she lived in the woods. When her email showed up a few days later, it felt potentially serendipitous and I opened it with happy expectation. How are you? she asked, and she wanted to hear from me and then mentioned, as an aside, that she would likely be going to Denmark and probably Ethiopia next year and maybe even Cambodia for her work.

It didn't take me long to get to the highway. Dirty snow lined the edges, spitting up when trucks passed by, and they did pass me as I hung in the right lane and drove west. Across the white valley, past the same miles and miles of trailers and homes and raw land, our hill stared back at me. I could pick it out and know exactly where the yurt hid behind the fir trees. It was calming. It was inviting. And now, I felt threatened by The Land. I didn't know then that it was offering me something I needed but was scared to take. Was it enough to do my *this* instead of doing her *that*, to be here? I wondered it in the same way someone asks herself whether it's okay that she just read a book for three hours on Sunday instead of being productive and luminous. My soapbox had always gone one way: When you resign yourself to a place, learning stops. You become that stick in the mud, the person who goes somewhere new and can't believe that people dress that way or eat that way. They are "other" than you. It is why wars happen. But if you live *elsewhere*, if you move *away*, especially many times and often, your perspective becomes wide angle, includes more shades than you previously thought possible. You better yourself in the process. You choose evolution over decay, over stagnation. And it's fun. If someone found my bleached skull millennia from now, they would still find the remnants of that belief lodged in the bone. But now, that Molly spent most of her days wandering alone on 107 acres of land. This was good; this was brave. Few people took the chance to quiet themselves. But if I stayed here much longer, I could lose my worldliness.

Who was making me stay?

No one.

Cálmate, I said aloud in the Spanish of my youth, and my car pulled off at an exit to turn back around.

Meanwhile, snow drifted down to the earth, as it does. And this new snow pressed down on any uncovered yellow grass so that even the barbed-wire fence leaned a little more, giving into the southwesterly wind, appeasing it. The creek remained a frozen blue crust. Fewer cars drove by. Horses across the street lined up to face the same direction. They were expressionless and tolerant of the situation because there was no other way to be, because this is the point when you assume winter might start to wane and pack up its bags. But the middle of February here is like the middle of February in any northern place. You are asked to hunker down again.

I, however, was ready to be unfrozen.

I wanted the ice to crack.

I wanted to watch this place change.

The sun reflected a gleaming white world back at me and

I took myself out on walkabout. I didn't like to use that word casually. For one, it didn't belong to me. But I had attached to it like a glop of wet cement ages ago, because *about* had no finality, no certainty, no interpretation, and somehow that felt like kinship.

C'mon, Bru, I called out, as we crested the top. We made our way out to the narrowing place, where both the sun-baked southern slope and the northern slope, corniced with snow, dropped to the dirt road. Even millennia ago, people would have gathered here with fire, to send prayers up. Chris and I had made note of that from the very beginning. It was that kind of spot. I stood and tried to see as far as possible. Bru, it seemed, was doing the same. My hand found his soft ear. The view extended out to low hills and faraway mountains and eventually the ocean and I remembered.

It isn't my first time at the pyramids in Mexico, so I scamper up to meet the dawn of time. The tiny stairs ask me to lean forward again so that I don't fall. People have prayed to the sun god up here since 100 BC. My lips are blue from a raspberry snow cone. Halfway up, I pause to redo my side ponytail. At the top, the earth spreads orange as far as the ocean. Though I'm not sure if there is an ocean near here. My parents and brothers crawl slowly to get up here. They look like ants. Waiting for them, I kneel down on the hard stone to pray, but only for a second so that no one will see. My prayer is simple: Please, may I always be able to see out this far.

On our way down, rounding the cabin, we saw the deer and I grabbed Bru's collar. They ambled along the creek, along the same path, over the same fallen trees at 12:45 every afternoon. Routine, I guess, had never failed them. Maybe they trusted in their own hoofprints, identifiable, marking the spot, so that each time they made that lap, they were finding themselves again.

I was not bred to live like that.

The cold air and I pushed into the wood smell of the cabin to find Chris eating a sandwich and reading one of his books at the kitchen counter. He smiled.

Your grandfather called.

He did? Strange. He never calls.

Yeah, you should listen to the message, but first come over here.

I walked over. He took my gloves off and then slowly kneaded my fists open.

Overtures were unlike my grandfather, the man who lived abroad until retirement, the man who took us on that sailing trip in Turkey, the man with a reserved sense of emotional display. But a few years ago, he had printed out over one hundred entries on my blog and sat down to read each one. He had responded with: I never knew you had these feelings; you were always just a little girl to me; now I see that you know about things; you have feelings about the world.

Maybe age softens us.

I dropped all my gear, pulled my hat off, and pressed the playback button.

> Hullo, Molly. This, this is Frank. Your uncle, or your grandfather. . . . Um, I'm not sure what I am anymore. I wanted to tell you that I think it is spectacular what you have done. I saw the photos of the

kurt. It is just spectacular, just spectacular. Okay. Goodbye for now.

I replayed it. I listened to the scratch of his voice, his lilt, his enunciation of every syllable, every vowel, the *kurt* instead of *yurt*, the admission *I'm not sure what I am anymore.*

Warmth spread up my limbs into my center. The yurt impressed him. That shocked me. The great world had seen me through a telescope, found me out, and made a comment. The great world was him: a man whose job not only relocated them every two years but sent him traveling to places like Afghanistan and India where boys with machine guns stood by as he surveyed new roads. He was a concrete engineer who brought a technology that allowed those people accustomed to dirt roads to move farther and faster than they ever had. My family had made a living building roads—those hard gray strips of nonattachment. Like the highway.

My vagabond grandfather thought I'd done well.

Standing by the refrigerator, chewing on my fingernails, listening to him applaud the yurt, I smiled and stared out the window. I could never lose my worldliness. I came from a lineage of worldliness. I was made of that essence and it would guide me.

5

THE STORY
I TOLD MYSELF

March 2010

Surrounded by low clouds and an early morning chill, we stood at the edge of our medicine wheel and held hands. Chris was leaving for three weeks. It was his turn to visit his family. We couldn't see the wheel because snow had buried it for months. Neither of us had wanted to stomp over there with a broom to brush brush brush until rocks appeared. People didn't go around yanking coyote pups from a hidden den or forcing wildflowers to grow and bloom out of season. The rocks would show up when the snow melted, *if* it did. A concealed thing needed to reveal itself in its own time.

Friends asked whether I was scared to be alone on The Land. It honestly hadn't occurred to me to be. Sure, when you've shared nine months in one place with only one person, his absence is palpable. But we had stopped patrolling like commandos and what had once been unfamiliar was now very familiar. Nights alone in the yurt would lure the kind of contemplation that only comes with true solitude. My days, though, would be the same. Pull a wool hat over my head and romp around with Bru because, along with my list, my urgency had shot up like a bean stalk. After our wedding, after the summer, we would start to plan where to next and when and did we need jobs. This slow alone time here, now, was a rare breed. I had better use it well. I now felt that my reaction to Chris's brother and my two friends had been pathetic. Hearing about the whereabouts of other people always made me desperate for a new set of circumstances. It was the human condition to want more, to seek literal greener pastures, a desire encoded in our DNA to keep us alive, right? But being powered by my need to experience more and more and more seemed now like a vow to remain thirsty. I did not want to be that woman who felt inadequate her whole life. Now I needed only to listen, as Katinka had suggested. Listen. My current geography always pushed me to understand what I was feeling and when I was feeling it. Answers could be locked up in the aspens or rivulets or cottonwood bark. Talk to me. Please.

Let's go, Chris said, and we crunched back across the snow path toward the steep.

Ooooo, ooooo, I called into the forest.

We are here. We are here. Again. Side-stepping down, starting the slow slip, the grip on ice, I stopped.

Oh my god.

What? urged Chris.

Oh my god, I smell it.

What!?

Somewhere down there, somewhere hidden in the trees, a green jungle was bursting out of the snow. Chris scrunched his nose and sniffed.

Water, I said. Don't you smell it?

He sniffed again and then I watched it find his nose, find his eyes, until it spread across his face and sashayed back to me.

We ran down, slipping, catching our balance, arms wide, rushing to see what we had smelled. On flat ground, I traced it like a hound right down to the creek.

The blue ice had let go.

A small gray bird dipped its beak and splashed water back up onto its wings. I had never cared about smelling water before, only known it as a fluid that fell from thunderheads, pooled around gutters, formed chains of lakes, and made my hair frizz. Now in its presence, I realized that it had disappeared for months. Or maybe I hadn't been here long enough to know what winter smells like.

When I ran back to the cabin, we grinned at each other. Chris reached around my waist. It was the middle of February. And today, as we loaded the Jeep with his duffel, our wool hats would not be encrusted in ice.

It was a good thing I had a few solo weeks ahead of me. The spring thaw encouraged a sort of resurrection in all living things. Everything now smelled of horses. Or hay. The snow evaporated in fast little drips. People in town surely poked their pale chins up to the sun. Birds actually chirped. Once, not long ago, Bozeman had been known as a horse town. It had been common for horses to clop down the street with a little girl bareback, her arms wrapped around its neck, a lovely way to get to know yourself at that age. Now it seemed that every front yard nearby had at least two horses standing around. Really, it was the smell of manure. And horseshit is horseshit. I liked the sour rank of it. My appreciation came from its refusal to be anything other than exactly what it was.

Bring on the smells.

But a few days later, a huge snowfall dampened the burst. The great cold silence was back. My parents called and suggested I give myself a break and just sleep in the cabin. No, the yurt was my abode. No part of me wanted to be downstairs. Plus, now I had a desk—a new addition crafted by Chris. It curved along the yurt's wall, with a drawer for papers. He had made it from poplar because I asked him not to use an expensive wood on my account; though he had sanded it and sanded it until the whole thing felt perfect to him. We had carried it up in the snow together. It looked as foreign as the door had in the tundra landscape. There, he had said, when we placed it, *your* writing desk, for you, my beb.

I hiked upstairs, lit lanterns, and watched water boil on the stove. The radiant heat warmed the yurt slowly, deliberately. It was the kind of cozy you learn to make for yourself. As I ate zucchini and buckwheat noodles, Bru spread his body over my feet. The dark chocolate had not made it into my bag and up the hill, probably because I had decided that my alone time would coincide with yet another no-sugar health shift. I wanted it now. I would have stuffed the whole bar into my mouth. I pushed my dinner bowl away and sat at my desk. When other middle school girls had professed allegiance to blue pens and bubble letters, I stuck with black ballpoint because I thought that was the stark color someone with profound thoughts would use. Glancing over teachers' shoulders, I had borrowed styles and practiced until my lean letters moved across the page with a controlled swagger. I grew to love making marks. Even a grocery list brought me a sense of creation.

I didn't feel like serious writing, so I slipped out a blank piece of paper and doodled and wrote words that came to me—woven, blue, erupt—and remembered that once, as a girl, I had begun a creation myth.

It was still unfinished.

Placed on top of a whale, she was a girl given the mission to grow into a warrior. As the big gray whale dove down, she held on, and when the pressure in her ears built, when breathing was impossible, the whale hummed, Trust me. They plunged into the darkest dark she had ever known. I'm scared, she whimpered. Trust me, repeated the whale. They sped faster and deeper to an unknown place. And because the whale had asked her, she let her eyes open wide to take in all that darkness until she saw a light flickering. It shone brighter and brighter and soon, they sped through white light, and soon after that, a great force catapulted her into a forest the color of limes. Her limbs were suddenly long enough to spring from, her feet flat as lily pads, able as planets. As she traveled among trees, night became her companion. She tied her long hair into a knot, with two ends blowing behind her as she ran. Because she had the knowledge of movement, no creature could stop her. She was never scared. She was brave. She roamed and roamed, and word went out that a woman roamed the land. Some feared this woman and her worn feet. Not once did they catch her baying at her own oblivion. Not once did she feel alone. You will die without a home, they cursed her. But she knew what no one else knew. Being out of her element was her element. Limbo was her home.

Evening wore on. The lantern light brightened as the sky turned black. There was no use finishing the myth. I would let it stand as its own story. I would let it play itself out without my meddling. Then, in an instant, as if a hand had pinched my bladder, I needed to pee now or else. I inched like an old woman, legs crossed, over to the door, but Bru got there before I did. He nosed it and his hackles feathered up. Then he growled, low and deep.

I sank down to the floor.

What? I mouthed at him.

He snarled at the door handle. Down on his level, my eyes searched his, trying to understand what he was trying to tell me. Only recently had he begun to make noises—yawns, howls, groans—in what I assumed was the healing process of an animal feeling free to finally take up space. Should I back up to the far end of the yurt? There was no way in hell I was going to open the door. He might bolt into the darkness and leave me to be munched by the unknown out there. I couldn't hear anything. No footsteps. No prowling around.

One day, but not today, this would be funny.

I eyed the ax by the door and made a plan for how to get to it, or use it—god—if I needed to. Bru's growl extended itself long to a rumble. If this was pup behavior testing out how to protect me because alpha man was gone, then his timing was not ideal.

We waited.

We waited some more. For what, I don't know.

What was out there?

The pot. I needed the noodle pot. I scurried over like a crab, stood up long enough to yank my pants down, and squatted over the empty pot to let her rain. My breath let out. And together, the pee, the pot, and I rested under the concave embrace of the *tono*. Stars twinkled through it. My own relief found Bru and he backed away from the door. He turned his head toward me, jowls replacing snarl, bowing in play, coming to check out what strange water had just appeared in the pot.

No tracks in the snow when dawn lit everything pink. Invented by us or not, the thing had come near and left no trace. But it wouldn't stop us from our day of new terrain. In the summer, crossing over the creek to the pond side had been an ordeal. Water gushed over our rock bridge and wet sneakers slowed us down in what I called the sponge grass, layers and layers of thick grass bent over itself. We had soaked the *khar mod* over there, but that's it. Loving the pond side, with its pastoral ease along the road, would be like admitting you preferred weak tea. But now, in winter, it was as stark as the rest of The Land. That really was the description: stark. I had never lived anywhere so stark. It stripped itself down to what it was, bare-ass naked, no plumage to cover the warts.

We stood on the edge ready to cross.

Let's do it, big man, I said to Bru, who had become The Big Man to me because he was so big, so tiger without the heft. The thick layer of blue ice had not melted during the warm spell—cracked in places, yes, but then refrozen. It arced over the creek like a bridge. Bent at the waist over my skis, poles prodding ahead for a thin patch, I traversed. On my heels, Bru stayed low and dug his dewclaws in for the ten seconds it took.

We landed on the other side like astronauts.

The field rolled out before us: white, glistening, untouched for thousands of feet until it hit the jackleg fence. This was the winter scene little children living at the equator could barely fathom—one I had envisioned when my mother spoke about her Wisconsin childhood. All we needed was a horse-drawn carriage and some tingling bells. It was here that the traveler decides whether to make her own mark. I wasn't sure. Bru felt otherwise. He dove in, nose first, somersaulting, flipping back and forth, spraying snow, bounding to a fresh patch, starting over, marking it all up, collapsing for a moment, rested, and then up popped his head to check for me.

Youuuuuuu, I heard my tin voice break the silence . . . are so *so* wild.

We hacked our way through. Ahead of me now, Bru's webbed toes expanded, and I, the clumsy one, leaned into the snow, maneuvering two sticks on my legs I could no longer see, like lifting concrete blocks with the sheer oomph of my quads. When my balance gave and I toppled over, Bru spared no second to pounce on me and lick my face, as if he could lick me up. Holding his snout down in play, I saw our destination—the aspen grove, a clump in a treeless meadow.

Eventually Bru lost his brawn and fell into my wake. My hash marks had left messy human tracks. We passed near a less intrusive track, the *tuk*, *tuk*, *tuk* of a vole. What had she been on the search for then?

The aspen grove moved closer.

In the hallowed space, bare limbs stretched up to the sky. I leaned against a tree. Why had it taken me so long to spend time here? Someone had cut a heart shape into the bark of another tree—A.A.+F.A. 6/23/04—less than two months before my family bought The Land. This would be a good place to consummate something, such a good place. Soon my leaning turned into a slouching sit and then a rustling around to find the right position that wouldn't numb my butt. Drivers on the road might have spotted a distant black figure moving through a calisthenics routine beneath gray trees. My gloves had already frozen into hard shells. My hands closed into warm fists. I squinted up at branches fanned out against a white sky. Squirrels used limbs as bridges to get from one tree to the next. No squirrels around today, though. So many trees going up, so many bridges going across. Closing my eyes to the remarkable sensation of every cell throbbing at the place where exertion meets cold, I knew Bru would keep watch as the fallen bridge entered my mind.

It is Mexico City and I'm starting to feel as grown-up as an eight-year-old can. I convince Ermilo, the man who picks us up from the bus stop when my mother can't, to take us to the bridge. Just for five minutes, please. I'm a pretty good convincer, so, he does. As we stand near the edge of a cliff, toeing at the weeds, I hold my middle brother's hand and gaze out at the two ragged ends of the bridge. They look like open mouths of metal. What captivates me, though, is the whole blank space in the middle, especially because I want to make a map of it. Did it hurt the horses below when it fell? I ask Ermilo. No, he says. Did people die? He says, I don't know. Then I ask him about his daughter, who is probably about my age. Sometimes adults tell me things that only adults tell each other. As he mumbles, I nod and say *Sí, sí* in all the right places. Eventually he realizes that I'm just a girl and silence falls over us. My brother fidgets and I scold, You could fall; hold my hand. We could both fall.

My mother had recently told me, over the holidays, that the bridge never fell. The builders just ran out of money to finish it. What, no way, really? It was a story I had told so many people over the years—about how that fallen bridge had made me wonder for years about the feeling of falling from something you thought was sturdy. When I asked Chris if he had ever had to replace an untrue memory with an accurate one, he wasn't sure.

I don't remember like you do, he had said, and you're just crazed by it because you usually remember *every little* thing you feel or anyone says or does.

Obviously not this one.

The news had rearranged my memory of what I thought to be true, of a story I had been telling myself, and others. Now the aspens were reminding me of that.

Because the aspens might have more messages, we returned to them each afternoon, after nights where snow blew in through the *tono* I had raised open for fresh air and sifted down over Bru sleeping by the stove. I'd wake up to stoke the fire and find him curled up under a significant dusting of snow—a strange sight, and even stranger to him. I moved his bed. Problem solved. Our routine established itself and my alone time flowed.

But after one puny week, the woodstove broke and interrupted my focus. I had told Chris not to call to check on me because I wanted the challenge of solving any technical yurt problems alone.

So I got one.

Standing up to my hips in snow, head level with the porch, I peered up into the long dark chamber of our metallic stovepipe and tapped on it. Then I banged on it. No bird trapped up there.

Great, I hissed, and then louder because no one could hear me, *just* great.

Unlike me, the yurt seemed relaxed. It had sloughed off

most of the snow. We had strapped it down by crisscrossing it with thick white ropes to combat the wind. They were encased and spun in ice. Icicles rimmed the roof. Every morning, I opened the door and broke through, splintering the daggers that had formed in the night. Now, above the shards of ice, the door was propped open to let the smoke out.

I just didn't get it. The stove clattered in the wind every night. Normal. I lit a fire and gray smoke puffed back out into the yurt. Not normal. Try again with *tono* open even more. Same response. Crawl out or be smoked out. Not normal. My investigation had come to an impasse. With numb hands, I decided to come back later that afternoon. With the cabin below, it was no real emergency; without other shelter, I would have had to problem solve like all those brave people who actually lived from the land. Mend it, freeze, or walk to a plume of smoke rising from a nearby house.

When we returned, I threw a wool blanket over Bru, wrapped a scarf around my face, and sat at the desk—zero degrees and debating. The white crust of earth was the same white crust of earth as before. It had nothing to say to me. I wanted to be cut from a capable cloth. I wanted to be good at this life while I was here. I made a mental list of why I should or shouldn't call Chris. Then I waited to know what to do. Meanwhile, Bru looked up at me with his black-rimmed eyes.

To call him or not?

I gave in.

Chris told me to try cleaning it.

I drove to town and bought a stovepipe cleaner. It was a long metal stick with a sea urchin metal top for scraping—who knew? As I pushed it up into the stovepipe, black soot floated down onto my face and made a black circle around me in the snow. That should do it. I should be back to the normalcy of starting a fire and depending on it for warmth.

This is the kind of shit I never figure out, I said aloud to Bru as he sat nearby, willing to partake in whatever was happening. I removed my dust mask and bent down next to him on the slope. I wanted to be the type of person who could say *I can hang with this*, that this three-day task brought me alive. But it didn't. I dragged my finger through the soot and found myself doing what would make me feel powerful again—making outlines of continents, of South America first.

When I am old enough to pull the heavy atlas from its navy blue box, I do. I don't know where I am when I do this: not Australia, maybe the Dominican Republic. My heart races with possibility. Gold letters spell A-T-L-A-S. I creak it open, run my finger across the clean crisp page of green land and blue ocean. It soothes me to do so, to stare at all the countries, inlets, and expanses, and to wonder what life might be like there, whether I'll find out one day, who I could be if I lived there. Even as an adult, when I spread a map over a counter, my breath will immediately slow, my fists will uncurl, recurl, uncurl, recurl.

Bru started to push at the soot with his snout. We dug and flipped and spread the soot and snow around together, madly. You cannot help but be pleased when a thing, even a stove, is unburdened of its muck, even if it doesn't know what its own muck is.

On a Thursday morning, I charged off to yoga for a break from The Land. There were other humans out there in the world.

Let me encounter them. Bru hung his head out the Jeep window, catching cold air into his mouth and then ducking back in to cough it out. The studio was tucked between a stand of firs on busy North 7th Street with Kmart across the way. I had gone to two classes here in January. Finding the right fit had been a priority of mine. I was cautious of rooms full of spandexed women sweating to lose weight, a bearded male guru spouting rhetoric to pious followers, or a heat intense enough to make your muscles do things unnatural to them. But this place was intergenerational, unfrightened of the word *fuck* or the word *compassion*, and part of what won me over was that a rancher in his sixties rode his motorcycle to class there. This style focused on heart opening.

My heart was open to everything—in theory.

You stay, I assured Bru. Always stunned to be in a world of cars and asphalt, I shut the car door and made a dash for the warm studio smelling of incense.

Anna, the teacher, was new to me.

I liked her immediately. She pronounced her name with a long *a*, making it sound foreign, which she was, Russian by descent. She corralled us into the small space. In her opening, she said that moving often as a child had asked her to meditate on place. She pointed out the window at the mountains.

We live in this amazing snowscape, she explained, and what got us here? I don't know. Does it even matter?

The class just stared at her.

I'm not even sure it does, she shrugged, beaming.

I sat cross-legged and felt exuberant about the words coming at me from a human being who shared my roaming experience. She made me want to be kind to myself. She moved us through postures to open our shoulders and then asked us to go into a backbend. I arranged my hands in the right place but did not push up. And then, she was standing over me.

She lifted a friendly eyebrow.

What? *You* can't do this? You can do this. I know you can do this.

Before I knew it, she had lifted me up into a U and the world was upside down and glorious. I hadn't been in a backbend since childhood and wasn't sure why. Blood rushed to my face, and my right wrist hurt, but what a perspective shift, a whole new proportion, a whole new landscape. After contorting my way down, I felt as if I'd been somewhere new.

As others rolled up their mats, I scooted over to Anna, noticing how quickly we inch toward what we know, our own version of belonging.

So, did you like moving a lot when you were little?

So-so, she said. My dad was a banker. It's kind of all that I knew.

We sort of have the same life.

We do? she smiled.

I moved too—a lot.

Tell me.

She was intrigued and I liked that.

Australia, Dominican Republic, Spain, Mexico.

A *Spaniiish* speaker . . . oooo. . . . Did you like it?

Yeah, I did. I like movement.

Me too. Sometimes I don't know what I'm doing here.

Me too.

Another student walked over.

Let's talk more later, she said, winking at me.

↓

When we got back to The Land, I sprang from the car and chased Bru to the mailbox. It was officially March, and the Canada geese had migrated back. They squawked over on the pond side, flapping their wings in celebration and leaving goose prints in the snow for us to find later. To avoid disturbing them, we would take our late afternoon adventures to the top now.

Some people called the West a horizontal place. Anyone with a decent eye could scan for miles and miles, past parched land, past migrating birds, over barns and horses and low-lying hills and eventually to the base of a mountain range. People like Anna and I were horizontal people—mile wide people. You can't grow up uprooting and not know that. Everyone around you is scared of change, but it is the only thing you know, so, as a default, you learn to be scared of its opposite. Slack water could drown a soul like me. Anytime I heard people say, for example, Oh, let's go to this restaurant, I always go there, I hid my cringe behind a blank smile. Did they only go to that place? Did they ever tire of it? Did they learn anything new, ever? I recognized my bona fide judgment and plain bad manners. Chris called me out on it all the time. But I rarely opined directly at the person —just snuck away quietly, fearful of being infected by the stasis.

Once, an American Airlines stewardess spied me lying at my mother's feet on the plane. I was barely old enough to write my own name. When she learned that moving to a new place was common for us, she gave me a set of wings and called me a "brave little mover." I loved that brave little mover more than I loved the woman struggling with the stovepipe. Whenever I moved, as rubber wheels turned, as jets left clouds behind, the simultaneous sensation of movement within me was undeniable, as if my internal landscape was shifting, growing in all the best ways, second by second, an accelerated stretching that someone standing still just could not get. It was easier to force growth by relocating.

Was I right back where I had started?

The vow to remain thirsty.

Later that evening, as the gloaming of blue sky, blue firs, blue snow, and blue yurt set upon us, we skied laps around the field and I cast around for a definition. Despite my distaste for stereotypes, I came up with one. Some people were vertical people; many of us were horizontal people. Some didn't ask whether life could be even better; many of us did. Some stayed; many of us threw a leg over the horse and went. Maybe it was that simple. And being continually restless, for me, or my friends, was part of our innate way, maybe part of a way necessary for this era. Being vertical would destroy me.

Done, I said to Bru as we clomped back onto the snow-crusted porch. I stood on the edge as sweat collected on my stomach. It was stark as stark can be out here. He walked back off the porch and dug furiously at a scent, unleashing sprays of brown soil across the snow. The sky darkened to indigo and my eyes squinted down to the valley below.

A lake appeared.

I squinted again.

It swelled up like a big blue eye. Somewhere, my canoe, lashed to a dock, awaited me. For a minute, the illusion took hold, held me at that threshold of what is and what could be. When I tilted my neck back to look at the sky, a cloud hung over us, shadow and reflection in a vat of falsehood.

Bru pawed at my legs. My cheeks had turned to porcelain plates.

Let's go in, I said. As I undid the lock and pulled the yurt door open, I knew that no living thing was solely horizontal or vertical. Our yurt lived above a slope that plunged 200 feet to where our well penetrated another 200 feet down into the earth, which meant that when I drank a sip of water, the water itself, down in that water table, could probably hear me gulp. All of which destroyed my theory that the West is horizontal. Because the mountains shot up and drew people who had not been born here. Nature was not exclusive in design and Anna had mentioned that we must root to rise. Phenomenal concept —root like a tree, grow up. Stop with the philosophy and get true with yourself, Molly.

And yet my root was my flight.

I knew what blood I came from.

Now inside, under the *tono*, I unwrapped a tampon. Bru scrambled up at the crinkle sound of the plastic. He sat down, saliva dripping from his jowls.

No, no, no, I laughed, *this* is not for you.

Had he never seen a tampon before? Or maybe I had avoided changing a tampon up here before. I took myself back outside. There was more to what that big blue eye had to say, but I wasn't able to see it right then. Under the now dark bowl of sky, I swept my eyes across the firs and opened a Ziploc bag to swap one cotton plug for another, feeling the heat of my insides meet the cold. Blood spilled on the snow. There—my red contribution to the white expanse. That is me. That is who I am; that is my ancestry. And I lingered with the copper smell of my own warm blood.

ꜗ

One of my goals had been to relocate as much of our firewood pile as possible while Chris was gone. He would be back soon— in only a few days. My solo weeks had flown by and the albino whale was still stranded by the cabin. I had hauled six loads up to the yurt each day, usually with snow pelting my face. But this day, I was careless. With only one empty three-gallon water jug strapped onto my pack board, I made my way down after a load. Bru idled in front of me, so I gave him a small shove down the hill. Let's go, big man. His movement always alerted me to where patches of ice hid under fresh snow. I knew most of them by now, so my legs splayed outward for balance.

But when one foot slipped, the slope snatched me with its gravity.

I fell and slid, bumping across rocks or sticks or whatever solid earth was in the way, until I slammed into the base of a tree. I'd done this before. I'd fallen with firewood or dishes or Tupperware on my back. I'd been clumsy; I'd bruised myself; I'd been Raggedy Ann.

I'm fine, I'm fine, I'm fine, I moaned aloud.

Bru leapt at me.

But that's it. I pointed at him. We're outta here today.

I had had it with attaching implements to my feet to be able to go anywhere. I could never get a grip. My sense of true traction had been defunct ever since the snow fell in October. Not far from here, the western side of the valley baked in sun. I wanted to walk on ground with no trace of snow.

Driving the back road was idyllic—flat, spare but serpentine in places, reminiscent of the lazy South, minus a canopy of live oak trees and moss. Bru panted out the cracked window and so did I. What seemed like eons ago, we had chugged along here during the blizzard that halted the yurt raising. Now, parked on the edge of a low ditch, we hopped out. Bru wore a leash and I wore sneakers. We walked down the dirt road like formal human and dog on an early spring stroll. He sniffed the yellow grass as if he'd never sniffed before. I could also smell the grass.

Gateway, this quiet ramshackle town of few, existed only a few miles away from us. It was the last stop before heading through the narrow canyon to Yellowstone. No hills protruded up to block the sun here, where the elevation was, I had recently learned, 4,975 feet, putting The Land at just above 5,000. I hadn't investigated this fact upon arrival in July, because elevation had never mattered to me. Some people built their whole lives around living at such-and-such elevation, as if it were a badge that proved an identity: tough, closer to the divine, and full of perspective.

Vertical.

A ways down the road, the coyote carcass surprised us both. Bru lurched back at the form and then forward at the smell. Its fur matched the grass. Maybe a farmer had shot it, and then had the dignity to toss it into the ditch, into a resting place. Birds had pecked at its hide. No other animal would use its flesh in the way it would have used another's flesh—disposing of it cleanly like a true scavenger. As we investigated, dust rose in the distance. The brown UPS truck was motoring toward us. I smiled. Of course we would collide into Brooks on a random day on a random road. The truck slowed. As Bru lifted up onto his hind legs to see in, I waved. Brooks smiled and pointed at his watch. Delivery rush beckoned, so he couldn't stop for a chat. We waved goodbye.

He and Marcie had hustled up to the yurt at the end of January. We asked them to bring headlamps and layers for their descent back down. Over dinner, they asked about the safety of city streets and Chris had pulled a typical line of his: Well, you wouldn't coat yourself in bacon grease and walk alone in the woods here; same sort of thing there. Marcie then told us that the rumor around here when my family's cabin started going up was that Johnny Depp was moving into the neighborhood. Which got us all laughing so hard at the stories people make up that at least two of us snorted up our wine.

But winter was almost gone. Layers were almost gone. I tipped my face up to the warmth, to the newness of a season change. This was like a normal outing, something normal people would do on a weekend. Spring was approaching.

On our way back, we stopped to drop off recycling near a trailer park in a gravel pit. I stepped out and met the sour stench of aluminum cans and plastic. Beneath my feet, the earth had dried to a shriveled crust. As the *clank, clank, clank* of my tossing rang out into the quiet, a warm breeze swayed over us. Where had it come from, what warm faraway place?

Hello, shouted a small girl on her bike, waving at me as she pedaled by.

Hi, I smiled back, shocked at her sudden appearance or that late winter could accommodate such an image at all.

You can't ride your bikes without supervision anymore, my mother tells me. This isn't good news. We have just moved from Spain to Mexico, where the road outside our home is concrete and perfect for bike riding. I love coasting down that hill and jumping my bike over the rusty grate, even though I fell once and my legs scissored the grate with one awful straddling whack. Pain pulsed in a place I didn't know had feeling yet. When I press her to explain why I have to be trapped inside now, she gives me a scary response. Bad people are kidnapping American children here and we have to be careful. I don't feel American and I don't understand how someone would know I'm American, unless I speak English to them, which I don't have to. You mean someone could steal me, or the boys? Yes, that's what I mean. Well, they can go steal a real American girl if they want to.

That had been so real to me then. It became dangerous to have a particular label, but also boring. Who wanted to be the American girl anyway? I was just the girl from many places. Driving back to The Land, snow patches amassed with each hundred feet until we bumped up our snow-mud driveway, lumbered into the cabin, and noticed a red blinking on the phone.

Brooks had left us a voicemail message:

> Heya, Molly, sorry couldn't stop today, had to make
> a few last deliveries. Wanted to tell you that a wolf
> pack has been around, come over from the west,
> from Turner's place. I hope you don't mind me
> being so honest about it. We seen 'em walking
> along your fence line and one or two of 'em took
> down an elk over at Yonder. Might not want to let
> Bru out on his own. Wolves like to get dogs. Okay.
> We'll see you around.

Some animal had been out there on that first night.
I squatted and grabbed Bru's square face.
You knew it; *you* knew it.

Whether wolves or lion or something else, an unknown thing had been lurking beyond the door.

Because Chris was almost back, I split a ton of wood. Now I could call myself a splitter of wood. It felt remarkable to swing that mallet and watch pieces fall to either side. Some people spent a whole lifetime with this chore. Did the muscle memory follow them into their dreams? Probably. I also broke my own rule of not calling anyone during my solo time. When I told Katinka about how stark this place had become for me, how unadulterated it was, especially in winter, she asked one question.

Do you feel pared down?

Sort of. I must sound pared down to you.

Just quiet, she said. It's good.

You know how I always tell people I'm from nowhere.

Yes, that's your line.

What if we all swapped our lines? Don't you think that would cause riots?

*May*be, she said.

Well, I've been thinking about it, with all this free time, how we're all trying to find our place in the world and no one is ever fully satisfied.

Oh, Molls, it doesn't have to be so intense, she laughed. You've found a place.

Not really, I corrected. Sometimes I feel like I can't remember anything I've done since I've been here, like it's this vague . . .

That's impossible, she interrupted. You remember moments in my life that *I* don't even remember. You are the memory-keeper for all of us.

Thanks, I said. That means a lot.

It's true, she emphasized.

Well, I said, I've been listening to The Land, just like you said, but I'm not necessarily more clear, and realizing that I probably shouldn't expect to be.

We never know what we might hear, she said.

Seriously, I laughed, I'm waiting for the big bang.

I wanted to know what was enough. I wanted it drawn onto a map for me. I hung up, turned the lanterns low to snuff the wick, and tucked myself into bed. It's hard to evaluate how you've changed without being able to survey yourself from afar. To see clearly from the center is impossible. My knowing was the outsider's perspective, which was why, at a distance, I called The Land *The Land* and terrain *terrain*, and belabored over whether I had become stark. People on the inside have no need for such mental footwork.

In the early night, the stovepipe rattled and woke me from half-sleep. I stepped out onto the porch and into a mist. Montana didn't do mist. It just was not done here, and yet here it was, blowing over me quickly and low in the dark. I turned to follow where it was going. But it wasn't a passerby. It kept coming from the west, like an endless gossamer veil being pulled across the surface of the earth. I opened my mouth to eat it. I wanted to sit down, but my legs stuck out bare beneath my down jacket. I squatted and let the mist pour over me, cool and moist—the strange sensation of being on a ship where you think you know where you are, who you are, but when the mist lifts, the landmarks appear and everything you assumed to be right is wrong.

You are asking the wrong question.

Excuse me?

It's hard not to be initially offended when a disembodied voice scolds you.

You are asking the wrong question.

The next morning, I woke with a clamp screwed onto my temples. My head. No wine. No whiskey. I folded my eyelids shut to initiate the pause necessary to cross the bridge back to remembering. My dreams had rarely taken a hiatus during my life. Without fail, they presented themselves each morning, so that I knew exactly what I had dreamt and maybe also what I should do about it.

My father and grandfather stood in a gray room.

I was facing them, standing also.

Molly, you cannot build an identity on having lived abroad for ten years.

How can you say that, Dad?

You were a little girl. You did not choose to move around.

He paused.

You just are not as global as you think you are.

He had never been so blunt.

My grandfather stepped forward.

It's true. I told your father the same thing when he was your age. We are not the wanderers you think we are. *You* are not what *you* think you are.

I was sure of internal bruising, a body part missing, a monster punching my face.

But what am I then? What the hell am I?

They never responded.

Out in the white expanse, I had sensed something coming,

yes. Someone had put me in a snow globe, flipped it upside down, shaken it hard and fast, so I was unsure of where I was.

The dream, was it true?

Pale yellow light filtered in. It moved across the floor and up the *khana*, signaling that I had slept well past my normal hour of winter's dark morning. The yurt seemed to circle and circle and circle with no end. Get up. I dangled my legs over the bed to shake the grogginess. Goose bumps traveled up my thighs to one small ugly spider vein.

I needed to get real with myself—to the facts, to pen on paper.

1. Four foreign countries do not constitute "all over the world."

2. Though I moved constantly in my twenties, I only lived abroad in New Zealand (barely counts).

3. My grandparents grew up in Chile until they went to college in America. Only as adults did they move.

4. My mother's family is sixth-generation Chicagoan. My blood is half them, so I am half rooted.

5. *Vagabond* connotes free spirited. My people just aren't that free spirited.

6. Elementary and middle school in Texas for five years. I forget to mention that. It seemed unimportant.

7. High school in Florida for four years. I forget to mention that. It seemed unimportant.

8. Everyone in America is a mutt. Being a place-mutt does not make me unique.

9. There *were* moments that I wanted nothing more than to live on a farm and never move again.

None of this information was new to me or to those who knew me well. I stared at the scribbled list. None of it was a secret. It was minutiae I had conveniently disremembered, wiped off the counter so that what remained could grow taller. My face flushed with shame. Why had I messed with the proportion?

C'mon, I mumbled to Bru and worked my way into the same jacket and pants and boots and out the door. We didn't go to the highway, though I considered it for a solid twenty minutes. The effort of doing so seemed futile now. Instead, we plodded through deep snow for hours. I veered away from our thin winding track so beaten down with use. It felt good to work my body. I didn't mind the ice crystals in my nostrils because cold leans on the edge of torpor. I wondered if the stars had ever surveyed me in a little white bed in a little white yurt in a vast white landscape and thought, *How quaint.* They must know better. The predators, cracked ice, aspens, blue eye, even the mist had all been pointing to this moment, or I had chosen to see in them what I needed to see. We are all our own meaning makers. I tried to straighten my shoulders, to invest in the eggplant shade of the mountains or traversing the backbone of The Land. My snowshoes snagged on snags. My paws pulled me through snowdrifts. My eyes skated over a valley swept clean by the wind every single day.

I now saw history here. I sat down in the snow. That's what I had wanted. History. A lineage. I had anointed myself with the only one I could: *I am from nowhere.* Because everyone has to be from somewhere; because no human thrives by being fragmented; because we all, out of necessity, construct a narrative about ourselves. My youngest brother liked to say that every person walks into a room with one card. You figure it out quickly because it is the one sure thing that will get you loved—by others and by yourself. Oh, I had used that horizontal placeless global woman card so often. Depended on it. Clasped myself to it. Now, wrenched back into a frozen world and a frozen butt, I understood it wasn't as real as I had made it out to be.

It was a myth.

More alarming were the questions that followed me around as I began to crawl through dimpled snow toward the band of green firs.

Now what?

Who was I without the myth?

At the medicine wheel, I stopped. Bru leapt toward me. With one gesture of my hand he knew to stay away and go leap elsewhere. Nothing had touched the snow here. No vole prints. No deer passing through in the three weeks since Chris and I had stood here. I held my ribcage and thought whether to undress myself, lift the white bed sheet, and crawl beneath the new terrain. Beneath all that heavy snow, I could soften, melt down deep into something soft and squishy, the most elemental part of me, the water, the blank slate, where four foreign countries could amicably quit their tenure of being my slipstream, where only this particular frozen ground and its frozen worms in this exact frozen moment could matter, where I could restore my sense of proportion, where I could no longer lean on something I held to be true, where I could no longer try to arrange myself into some pattern recognizable to others, or to myself.

But I didn't.

Not yet.

6

WHITE PICKET FENCE GIRL

April 2010

Then, what had been a flat white field for so many months began to undulate in waves of yellow and white, revealing the places quick to change, the places slow to change. Chris was pleased to be back and I was pleased to have him back. I stuck my hand in his coat pocket and we set out on a walk. We crunched on ice for a few steps and then padded on the soft yellow grass that gave way to mud.

The East Coast is so set in its ways, he said.

Not *everything* about the East Coast is, I said, leaning into him.

No, you're right, he said. But it seems harder to hold a dream there.

I knew he was talking about his own rooted childhood. Living in other places as an adult had freed him up to see beyond what he thought was possible—the experience, probably, of anyone who had spent eighteen years in one place with one set of people. But his tone was different, defiant almost, as if he had unhinged a gate and shut it behind him. I decided not to go into the details about my solo time with him right then. Wasn't sure it was necessary to explain that I suddenly felt remarkably undefined and wanted some of that definition he was running from now.

We're all just trying to define ourselves, I offered. You know, against or by our past.

Yeah.

The good old I am *this* and *this*, but not *that*.

I definitely do not want to be that, he said, I like this . . . with you.

Where the field dipped low, Bru ran along the fence behind us. A pewter sky hung above and, from here, we could see nothing but the rise of a slope. No sense of what lay beyond. I liked the unpredictability of this exact spot. As we stood quietly, I unzipped my jacket halfway to feel the warmer air and Chris bent down to pick at clods of mud that Bru then found interest in, pawing at them. But something was moving, a sudden movement up ahead, something large, brown.

Do you see that? I whispered.

Chris grabbed Bru's collar and stood up. Only a few hundred feet away, a herd of elk sat for an afternoon snooze—heads starting to sway back and forth to understand what we were. They turned in our direction and I stepped forward.

Easy, he said, let's leave them alone.

But my steps stretched longer, narrower, and then, without thinking, I started to run. One got up. Then another. The whole herd rose and, as if strung on a string, they followed each other away from me, trotted toward the faraway fence, and still, I accelerated. My legs strode out and the pounding of their hooves traveled back across the thawed earth to meet my approaching feet, and soon the thud of my heart sounded and something close to glee overtook me as I ran and ran— to do what? To be with them, to be a woman trying to get at something, to run with a herd, to know the genetic code of a creature that knew its place so well. The elk soared over the fence, one by one, until a few, startled, jolted back, desperate and stuck, spooked by barbed wire, by the chase.

I stopped.

Molly, stop! Chris's voice caught up with me, panting from behind.

Hey, he said, pulling at my arm now, what was that?

I know, I know. I'm sorry. I don't know what happened.

When you realize you don't know anything about anything, you start to want to know something about something. Though I wouldn't have confessed it to the world then, I was uncomfortable with my new lack of definition. My childhood story and the adult one spun from it had taken one last gasp and died on me. I couldn't hang out in the great empty space left behind. I needed to replace it immediately. Anyone who knows about elk knows that you don't run at them, or any animal, especially when they are gathered and resting. It's just rude. But I ran at them because I could smell them and see them and now wanted to belong to something, to whatever was in front of me.

The elk became specks in the distance as we left the field. I muttered *I'm so sorry* all the way to the yurt, all the way down the hill, all the way into a scalding bath. On the voicemail in February, my grandfather had wheezed, *I'm not sure what I am anymore*. I wasn't sure what I was anymore either.

I called a friend to share what I'd done to the elk.

Well, she said, sometimes you just have to love your own ugliness.

And I would continue to test that ugliness, as my relationship to The Land morphed and grew and became a desperate thing and then a quiet thing and all ugly and good things in between.

Part Two

↙

In April, small black bugs replaced the icicles on our yurt. They hatched and plastered themselves everywhere—on the pond's skim, on the canvas, even on leftover patches of snow. But winter lingered. From the cabin's northern roof, a sheet of snow slipped and froze into the shape of a surfer's wave curling in. I would towel myself off after a shower and watch it inch closer to the earth each day. We still stoked a fire in the yurt, and though the field on top might never see snow again, snowdrifts stayed paunchy and fat around us. Snow had cradled our shelter all winter. It was an obvious observation. But I wondered now what life in the yurt would be like without snow.

Chris continued to hurl himself off the yurt porch and belly flop into the powder. Bru loved this game. Leaning against the canvas, wrapped in my coat, I watched and smiled at this exuberant man, my soon-to-be husband. It didn't frighten me, the marriage piece. Maybe because a decade together had taught me that we all grow, that no one is static, that you didn't marry one person, but all the past and current and future people within that one person. Witnessing each other over a lifetime excited me. That same feeling had yet to translate to place —and if friends pointed that out, which they did, I just told them that it was different with a person. When Chris and I had reunited after long adventures, when I returned from four months in South Africa and he greeted me with an orange and a hug on the steps of a college dormitory, when the rash on my face from so much reunited kissing became painful, we couldn't have expected or even dreamed up in detail that we would one day move to Montana and build a yurt. Never. So, other things always lay ahead, another life.

Courtesy of my new computer battery, I started to write in the yurt for hours. Where snow had seeped in from the *tono* so many nights this winter, where a roaring woodstove had melted it into puddles on the floor, now wind and sun pushed at the canvas. The walls flapped like birds. The insulation crinkled and my desk rattled next to it. My fingers typed out sentences, and when I glanced behind me to read our small digital weather station, a gift from my middle brother, thirty-six or forty miles per hour wasn't an uncommon number. It was full living in the yurt for me now. Day and night.

It felt like learning how to breathe.

And there was much new learning. Such as how, but more importantly when, to plant a garden. Susan called to tell me she had planted her peas in town. I stared outside at our only viable garden plot. It was next to the shop and driveway and would be the sunniest spot down here near a hose, but it was still covered in snow. What if it didn't melt for weeks? Our planting would be behind. I marched outside to get a move on. Over a long morning, I dug it all out—three feet deep over a square big enough to park fifteen cars. Chris came home from buying wood and found me standing with a shovel in mud surrounded by a wall of snow.

Two days later, the snow melted from the garden spot anyway.

That was so *you*, Chris said, as we laughed about my rush to accomplish something that happened naturally in its own time. My *Almost there* still bumped up against his softer approach of *Getting there*. Now he was standing at the cabin's kitchen counter looking down at the list in my notebook.

What? I grinned.

It wasn't that epic: six raised beds made of creek stones, one garden shed crafted from aspen boughs, one herb spiral, two deer fences with a flower garden between them.

You might want to scale the plan down, he said, reaching for my palm.

But I want to do something useful here, to grow food and sit in a gorgeous garden.

But beb, we won't even be here the month of June. You don't have to define the whole garden right this moment.

But I want to.

But that's just another high expectation.

Let's just go and get started with the garden beds anyway, I said, twisting out of my seat and out the screen door.

Birds chattered as we dragged stones from the creek. We rolled them out of a watery home into place on dry land, much as I had with the medicine wheel. To plant a garden was a sure way of putting part of yourself into a place. It made a person feel that she belonged to something, an old ancient soil. I also wanted to meet my own insecurity face to face. Because *What is enough* was really *Am I enough*? For everyone. I understood that now, but still couldn't see how to solve the unworthiness without out a place or a new story.

Where I had clung to my youth abroad, and still did, I now clung to The Land.

Don't leave me.

As if it could.

The stones, some as large as our torsos, were free, free in their movement and free to us. No cost other than sweat. Diane would soon remind me that our season was at least two weeks behind town and that gardening here was gardening in the lumpy till left by retreating glaciers. When the rolling got hard, we lifted them into the Jeep and drove them to the garden, careful not to smash toes in the loud *tumble-tumble, thud* unloading.

Afterward, we drew our fingers through the cold creek and thanked it for letting us re-appropriate. The cottonwoods above us were still bare and brown. No green flush through their branches yet.

At the garden plot, a large pile of stones stared back at us.

Now what? they echoed.

All yours, Chris said to me.

Beyond the field, a truck rattled by on the dirt road, kicking up dust instead of snow. Chris needed to get back to his Chinese stool, a no-glue design. We had established that the garden was my project. No wood dust for me. No dirt under the fingernails for him. He squeezed my hand and walked away.

I bent over like a human wheelbarrow and pushed stones into place. They didn't run away from me. From this vantage point, it seemed unlikely that even a garden of raised stone beds would work in a land where our noses dried and cracked and bled upon arrival, where mountain lions stalked nearby, where wildness pushed at the edges of anything cultivated.

But I wanted to grow something here.

There, I had said it.

Like a plant or a life, or part of a life.

When I stood up to stretch, one white flat stone stuck out from the pile of streaked ones. So white it could have been whitewashed. A memory started to elbow its way forward, booted the others out of its way, determined to reach the surface where, finally, after all these years, it could take a long deep breath and declare itself.

The girl had wanted a white picket fence.

Do you think we can have a white picket fence? I ask my mother when we are living in Mexico, and maybe I've asked her before, when we were living in other places.

Where? she says.

The next place we move.

I don't know, Molly. That would nice, wouldn't it, but I don't know.

I leave her to her red beans and rice, and go outside and draw a white picket fence. Later, when I show it to my parents to convince them, though I'm not sure what I'm convincing them of yet, they will pat me on the head and we'll all go to bed. That night, I line my animals up around my twin bed. This is how I train myself to sleep on my back and wonder about other girls in other places and whether they wonder about me and whether we wonder about the same things. I fold my hands together and pray for a dream. Squeeze eyes shut. Pray for a white house with a red roof and a white picket fence around it. One tree rises up to the sky. I am a grown woman. I wear jeans and a white shirt, with my hair pulled up loose, my feet bare. My dog runs me. Somewhere there is a horse. Somewhere, though not nearby, there are other houses and other people. The dream will happen in my dreams. Then, a few months later, we will move to a white house in America. But it won't have a white picket fence. Instead, we will play on a wide strip of grass where electric high-tension lines buzz over us.

The girl *had* wanted a white picket fence. I emerged embarrassed, again. It shouldn't be such a shock when you admit something to yourself. But it always is. So I pushed another stone, the heaviest one, into place. I tucked my hair up under my hat, continued to move stones, and eyed the white rock in the corner. As much as she had dreamt of being a translator of languages, she had also wanted a home. Ugh. I moved further away, moved faster with the stones, but she followed me. Stay away, you white picket fence girl. If she was real, then she would squash global girl. Goodbye, distinction; hello, boring one. What was this, a battle complete with uniforms? These girls had no agenda. I did. Because ever since I had arrived here, I had liked The Land, liked it so much, more than any other place, that my liking terrified every cell within me. I had done what any neurotic woman does when goodness offers itself to her—pushed it away, which might explain all the neurotic meltdowns, all the huffing and puffing and trying to blow my own house down.

I stopped myself.

Me, a settler? Hmm.

Standing near the firs, surrounded by stones, cooled by wind, in the middle of an American state less populated than almost anywhere, I imagined what would happen if every single human, in one collective moment, revealed the impulses within that didn't match the image we each show to the world.

Texture. Complexity. Necessary collapse.

You, I said, pointing at the white rock before I turned to walk inside.

Spring plowed ahead. Farmers upturned fields. We could not escape the sweet smell of soil everywhere. We planted asparagus crowns. I planted cotoneaster shrubs as a windbreak. Brooks offered to lend me his beater of a blue truck to go buy two tons of compost from a goat farm. Then I borrowed his fence pounder for the deer fence. Then his knowledge on what kind of critters would try to get through. We would borrow a lot from Brooks in the next months, and his generosity would make me examine my own.

Toward others.

Toward myself.

Because, like spring, a child is generous in her clarity. She has not yet learned to shape herself to please others, or to please herself. The white picket fence girl started to talk to me when I wrote, when I sat under the aspens, when I clipped my fingernails. She got excited about her eleven best friends coming for a bachelorette party at the end of the month. She would get to show them this place. She let me know all about the importance of home, digging, knowing, letting go of letting go of letting go.

I wanted to integrate all these parts of me.

Do you remember me ever talking about wanting roots? I asked Chris.

He thought about it for a few minutes and then sat on the desk in the yurt.

Well, he said, you aren't as cut-and-dried as you think, Molly. No one is.

Then I called my mother and asked her. She explained that I had always loved new things, new schools, new friends, new binders and pens, that I hated, more than anything, to be stuck.

But did I ever talk about where I would live when I grew up? I asked.

Not really, she said, but you did seem to have a vision of home you wanted.

Where?

There was never a where, she said.

I thanked her and hung up.

There may never have been a where, but there *was* a growing up. I needed to grow up in a way I hadn't expected. Chris's brother Mike had gone back to Turkey for a final few months. He sent us an email from Syria, where he had traveled to a monastery in the remote hills. He wrote: *This trip will either get traveling out of my system or make me never able to settle down again.* It was an either/or way of defining himself. I related to that. But as I slept and woke in the yurt, strumming my fingers along the *uni*, watching snow fade away with each day of more sun, I could feel my own point of view struggling hard, like a burrowing vole, to expand its point of view. The real questions were, How do we choose to live, and was constant bettering a disease, and if so, why do we do it? And as I thought that thought, a rabbit darted across the field followed by a fox followed by a hawk followed by the wind.

Mud season was an in-between season. Snow had mostly departed, but nothing had greened. It was formless. It brought texture back to us. Our well-used path had no grip now, not even with my grippers. No deer tracks either. They knew to avoid it. But we didn't, at first. Our feet slid beneath us and soon we learned to skirt the margins and find grassy bits where we could hold on. Chris liked to pick his way up the ditch of hawthorns. I preferred to go up in a straight line through and over fallen branches. We never insisted on going up together. I liked that about us. The goal was simply to avoid a mud that had formed from thaw, not rain.

But one afternoon, after lunch, I climbed back up to the yurt along the path. It had done a lot for us. I had walked it at least four times every day for the past ten months. I didn't know what else I had done 960 times in that time frame. Not tea breaks. Not sex. Not showering. The slope had imprinted on me and I needed to walk it during mud season.

Even if things got messy.

The skin of snow had melted away.

So few people like mud. It is the ultimate inconvenience. No one chooses to schlog through unstable ground. I certainly hadn't. On the first steep stretch, the earth moved beneath me and it became clear that my only option was to get on all fours. I fell to my knees. I began to paw my way up, to push my hair back and smear my face with mud.

To connect with the connective tissue of The Land was to feel my own. It held everything together. Without soil, nothing could stand up straight because nothing could root, none of these firs, not me. And yet what was once solid was no longer, at least on the surface. My gloves clotted with mud. I began to claw like a maniac, using every finger to keep steady as my body weight pulled me down the hill. It felt good. I wanted a ritual. I wanted to own something for my own serious self. I wanted to hold it, to hold it tight in the way someone who has never held anything tight suddenly does. I grabbed a fistful of mud. The learning that this is mine and that is yours and mine is different from yours and I want mine and if you don't give it back to me I am going to scream and grab for it and make you sorry because you cannot take what is mine, mine, mine. It could be a toy truck or a way of being. None of us were that far removed from those early moments of identification and separation. Because without something to call *mine*, the abyss laps at your feet, pulls you closer, recognizes itself in you. Grasp, there was the word.

Loosen your hold, said The Land.

I listened and did and slid until arriving at a resting point not much farther above where I had started, and what ushered up was not a sigh or a moan, but a laugh so pure I didn't recognize it.

There were too many metaphors, too many opposing truths to sort out. Just hang out. I sat caked in mud and laughed until my shoulders hurt. I thought of my grandparents and how they must have slipped on mud too, in Chile or Belgium or Maryland. That right now, in the Northern Hemisphere of spring, right as I slid down the hill, my youngest brother lost balance on the Hudson's muddy bank, my middle brother dove through mud in a graduate school freeze-tag game, my mother almost bit the dust on her way through wet grass to the azalea bush, my father slid on a muddy sidewalk near his parents' home, and some woman I don't know trekked up a mountain alone, her hands mud-caked, losing footing, cursing herself for not yet being who she wanted to be, and in the one communal slip, we learned that we needed to do so before we could know anything at all.

With mud comes rain. I didn't expect Montana to be a place of much rain.

Hear that? I whispered, as Chris and I sat at my desk and shuffled paper around, finally making time to stuff our wedding invitations into envelopes. We had never heard rain in the yurt before—not even a suggestion of it—and it sounded, at first, like an old clock starting up again.

I raised my chin to the *tono*.

We live in a sound chamber, I said.

You know, Chris started, squinting at me, I'm beginning to love the place I live. That's dangerous.

Is it?

You of all people should think so.

Not fair, I said, and pinched his leg.

Really?

I'm just saying, I added, we all evolve.

Okay, he said, searching my eyes, something he only ever did when he knew I was upset, but this was different. This was more curiosity, a what-have-you-done-with-my-woman moment, and who, oh, who is in her place.

Later that evening, he reached around for my arm, pulled my back to his chest, and we stared out the yurt window. An owl stood on a fence post, silhouetted and hunting. We said nothing. No articulation necessary. No sound of my voice. No real idea of the change happening within me, or within us. The *pock-pock-pock* rain on the canvas continued and rose up to a full beat of 1,000 hands on a drum. We closed our eyes under the rush of a waterfall, nothing but that and our own hearts responding to it. We were being sung to. We were two humans under a massive weeping sky. I didn't know yet how to sing back.

I wanted to love myself. I wanted to integrate all the disparate parts of me into a whole self. But I didn't know how to do that. Snow insulated, but rain washed away old ways of being, if you let it. I wondered about the small black bugs. Had they lifted as one huge mass and flown away to another place, or did they hear the rain coming and crawl down between the porch planks to hang upside down like bats in a familiar cave?

Or did they do both?

↓

At the airport, one lone woman stood outside sucking on a cig-
arette. We raised eyebrows at each other in solidarity at the
late April snowstorm. It had come as a surprise to me, especially after the rain. On the way over, my two tires had carved
dark lines through a white land. I tucked my hands deeper in
my pockets and ran through the doors. The wall-to-wall carpet always made this airport feel snug to me. Inside now, my
breath no longer steamed. But where was everyone? No lines at
the ticket booth. No one was hanging out at the baggage claim
carousel. In fact, it wasn't even moving. I scanned and saw one
person. I waved him down.

Excuse me, excuse me, sir.

He limped over, no reason to rush, I guess. I realized that, like
so many of the employees here, he did it all. He checked tickets,
loaded bags onto planes, and greeted planes when they arrived.

I've got eleven friends flying to Bozeman today. What are
the chances?

Well, all I can tell you is that they're probably circling up
there somewhere. No one's landing today. Not today. Might get
rerouted to Billings. That's their best hope.

Really? No planes landing in Bozeman today?

Not likely. I just tell people, Welcome to Bozeman. We can't
fight the weather.

Okay, thanks, I said, and walked back out the door. When
the cold air blasted against my face, when I saw the empty, frozen parking lot, I understood that I was the only fool who had
come to pick up friends. Every other sane person had brewed
up some coffee, checked the Internet, and learned that planes
were not landing today. My enthusiasm had steered me here. I

was so eager to see and hug these women, to have them descend on this place where we could celebrate my upcoming marriage and I could share my life.

Back on the cabin's porch, I breathed in the stillness that comes from snow in every direction. The Land glittered. Chris and Bru had gone to stay at Susan's house for the weekend. It was quiet. It was solitary. It was good.

Three friends ended up in Billings. They rented a car and maneuvered their way through a highway snowstorm and slush and a speeding ticket. Everyone else zeroed in on Bozeman from the far reaches of the country after missing flights and finding new ones. One friend arrived on the late end of 2 AM. Another showed up in leggings and flip-flops.

We would have seventy-two hours together.

Hannah, Lauren, Jen M., Jen B., Kate, Laurie, Sam, Kimmi, Courtney, Katinka, and Piper jingled and jangled around the cabin like a traveling circus, squawking, cooing, shrieking, and laughing. I had set up beds: some borrowed futons, one inflatable pool lounger, a few bundles of cushions and blankets. As suitcases burst open with colors and scents, I stood apart with my butt to the warmth of a crackling fire and watched. My eyes found the exit, the window. Somehow, cottonwoods felt more familiar to me than the presence of my friends. It was as if I knew that soon we would pile into cars to see baby bison lean against their mamas at Spanish Creek and then go to our local hot springs. As steam rose around our red faces, as we soaked, they would ask me intimate questions, as friends do: how's your writing, what about your sex life, do you feel lonely, do you think you'll stay here much longer? Never one to shy away before, I was now unused to such expectant eyes. As hot water held me under the wide yawn of gray sky, I could see the creature that was now me, and she would float backward pretending not to hear because she wasn't as ready as she thought for those kinds of questions.

A day later, after wine and food and connection, we walked to the ponds. Green spears poked up from the matted-down sponge grass. Growth, finally.

It's so stark, someone said, but stark in a beautiful way.

I agreed that, yes, stark was the word—though this view of bare trees and blue mountains and white and brown earth had become so common to me my reference point for how it compared was lost. At the aspens, the clear, spring-fed stream wound at our feet like a river inhabited by small people. Here it was easier to understand the microscopic in a land that pulsed macro. I toed around for the soft edge and leapt across to the other bank. Others followed. But Courtney accidentally stepped right into the water. She laughed, pulling her dripping leg up and out. And that's when I saw it. A goose egg, white and large, nestled in the grass. I immediately reached for it and rubbed its sandpaper texture against my cheek.

Look, I said, lifting it to the sky.

Molly, no, scolded Katinka.

Oh shit, shit, shit, I muttered, and squatted to place it back.

Mollyyyyyy, said another friend.

I know, I know, I'm sorry, I'm sorry, I whispered at the egg, knowing that now it would never form into a chick because the mother would never come back to it because it smelled of the careless human who had, in her elation, touched it.

Run at elk. Pick up a goose egg. Nice.

That night, while others made enchiladas in the cabin and forgot about the egg, Katinka and I walked up to the yurt.

Can't believe I grabbed that egg, I said.

I was surprised too, she said.

It's like I want to ingest everything around me to know that it is real and that I'm a part of it, I explained. You know, I have *no* predominant sensory memory from my childhood because there were so many.

Maybe you just want to know this place finally, she said.

That's part of it, I agreed.

We lit a small fire in the woodstove. I took my clothes off and she looked at my posture, traced my shoulders while goose bumps ran up and down my legs. She wanted to give me a cranial sacral session as a gift, one of the many times she had worked on my body over eight years.

Your shoulders have gotten really strong, Molls.

Oh yeah?

All that yurt building, huh?

I stretched out on my bed. She stood on the end and put her hands on my head. As she worked, she told me about the wind inside me still, and the new grounding, and that my cranial pulse was "delicious." Somewhere nearby, the snow melted from fir boughs. I was relaxed, she repeated, in a way she'd never felt in me before. It took someone else telling me for me to know it.

But these feet, she added, you've got to spread 'em out, unbunch them. Spread out your toes. Let them really sink into the earth. Let them root.

↙

On our final evening, they all led me up to the yurt. I lit a fire. Someone lit our two lanterns. Everyone knelt back on heels or sat cross-legged on the wood floor. They had asked so many questions over the weekend. Where's all your stuff? We don't have that much. Isn't it romantic living here away from everything? Please, use a more nuanced word, you know it isn't all kittens and ribbons. Do you seriously walk up here every day? Yeah, but it's not any different from your walk-up apartment. This life seemed so foreign to them, which allowed me to again recognize some of the foreign in it. These were not soft women. Some had lived in the woods before. And yet their responses brought the radical of my own life into clear focus.

With so many women in the yurt, it felt as if the walls could explode outward and leave us with nothing but the stars pouring down. I could smell the attention turn to me.

Shadows flickered on smiling faces.

Someone handed me a red hand-sewn book.

It's all about geography, Moll, the geography each of us shares with you.

I sat up straighter and began to flip pages. The story of a cousin, a childhood best friend, college roommates who had watched me fall in love, writers had who encouraged me, friends I had been lost with over and over again.

They all knew about my tendency to bolt to a new place.

Thank you, I said.

It's a strange situation to confront an image of yourself given to you by others. Now that you are slightly more aware of your own proclivities, you wonder whether they are simply repeating a story you had told them or whether they actually see your essence. I smoothed back the pages of maps. Geography surfaced not as a myth created about myself, but as a real self. That *was* me. You can rearrange yourself in a thousand ways and never release the one image you hold to be true. Maybe because it is true. That me now needed some amending, but perhaps not in my usual way of reinvention by relocation.

I could have named how each of these women also grated against her own mild discontent. It was an existential question everyone faced: that we would be better off in a different situation. I would say, Lovely, you are enough as you are. But who accepts that? No one. Because the question propels us forward, when what we might all need instead is a kind of acceptance, one that pours through us like molasses to coat all our hard edges.

Silence sped into chatter. Everyone scooted over to look at the book. We huddled near the fire and The Land beyond the canvas walls hummed. Blades of grass stood still under a cold sky. And somewhere, off in the moon shadows, a small creature slunk along the fence, making its way, following a knowing it could not articulate, but also not worrying whether to do so was enough.

Kimmi tiptoed outside to pee and rushed back inside.

Oh god, she shrieked, it's so scary out there.

Soon, they went home, radiated back out to other geography. In their leaving, May brought constant rains. Water fell in rods from the sky, and from that soaked earth sprang small patches of green. The undergrowth spread daily and forecast an ease not found in winter. Bru rolled onto his back in the grass and then lounged outside all day. An eagle, heron, or crane would soar over the firs and into view and his eyes would trace it in circles as it flew west. He was the only dog I knew who watched birds fly. Maybe it was the only real movement to watch around here.

I called my parents to tell them of the change in seasons.

It's almost warm enough to hang laundry, I said, staring out the yurt window. My mother responded Yeah, but my father was silent. At the end of our conversation, he, a man who might never be land-based, made his opinion known.

One thing, he pleaded, his voice strained, please don't hang laundry. It's lowbrow.

Would I lie face down on the grass next year, and the year after? The ritual appealed to me now because, unlike my father, who didn't know how to make a home and probably never wanted a white picket fence in his life, I was thinking for the first time about what it meant to be land-based. The greening unfolded. Asparagus spears burst through the soil. We piled cross-country skis to put them away. Birds started to chirp well before dawn as if arriving at a gathering no one else knew about. Mist lay over the valley every morning. Tumbleweeds blew across the road, passing hundreds of robins that gravitated to the edges of the road, for bugs, for dryness, we didn't know what. Cottonwoods leafed out and exuded a perfume. Snow came and melted. The first yellow glacier lily bloomed. We cooked on our Coleman stove on the yurt porch and watched the season transition. We drifted to sleep under moons bright or filtered through clouds. I made plans to plant a cactus garden around the yurt. At night, we still lit a fire but no longer woke to stoke it. I dreamt of a Thai woman poking my nose with two magic wooden sticks, something I knew was good for me despite the pain. Gulping for air in the dream, I woke to my body gasping in response to smoke puffing from the stove. I hurled myself from bed and pushed the heavy door open. Cold air rushed in from the world and Chris, slower to wake, glanced up. How wise our subconscious is. We know what is happening to us before we experience it happening.

Integration was a word I understood only intellectually. When I wondered how to braid the two or five thousand impulses within me, my application looked like a houseful of mangy cats scratching and licking at each other all at the same time. A total mess of enthusiasm and denial and backtracking and leaping. Because change smelled of birth—wet, sloppy, metallic, unpredictable, and exactly as it needed to be.

Why do none of us feel adequate? I asked Katinka.

I don't know, she said, which I took as an acknowledgment that, indeed, none of us feel adequate.

Our journey to our wedding would be a reverse migration on I-90. Before leaving, we stared down our chute of preparation. There were bills. And they unnerved us. I tried not to think of that on the day I dug the trench.

I was burying chicken wire under our garden fence so that rabbits couldn't sneak in and eat our lettuce. My hands moved methodically, attached to a shovel that pierced the mud, loosened it, and pried it open. Geese honked and flew through light snow as it drifted in beneath white clouds. I unearthed a den of tiny gel eggs and apologized by putting the soil back. A crooked bend in the trench would have to do. Bru also participated in this strange act of removal. He dug and his claws got heavy with mud.

The worst part was chopping worms in half.

I couldn't help it.

They were everywhere. I hoped it was true that one worm could become two worms if split apart.

I yelped each time and Bru's eyes met mine to see what had gone wrong. He would come with us to the East. We would return married. But before any of that could happen, we had to deal with how the hell we planned to make money. We had given ourselves a prescribed time to make a go at being self-employed artists before having to find jobs that paid reliably. Chris had started to ramp up his furniture design-build business. Though I still had some savings, I was on the search for a part-time job because no one could depend on writing. And when we weren't counting up receipts, we were shoveling, designing a winch system for firewood, putting up a deer fence. We existed in mad dashes of doing. Tense might have described it best. Leaving our momentum for the four weeks of June made us both nervous.

When our health insurance bill arrived, Chris would bend over and rub his own head. Our intention for a peaceful candlelit night of writing wedding vows deteriorated, and fast. But in a tender moment, carrying groceries from car to cabin, we did speak about a pledge to help each other die one day. Would the push of living or how to live even matter then?

Breaking for lunch, I stabbed my shovel into the earth and left the worms behind. The creek roared with new rains, so much rain.

You're covered, Chris said, intercepting me in the yard with a hug.

I hadn't noticed the mud splattered all over my turquoise jacket.

We brewed up some heated discussions over the next few

days—about whether art was worth it, what exactly was worth it, how we foresaw the summer, whether we could slow down on the physical projects and engage each other and our individual visions of career and the raw experience of living on this land. I wasn't the type to let it go. It was a question of definition. I would grasp at our relationship as I had grasped at the elk and the goose egg.

We could build and build and never even notice each other or this place, I said.

You've been all excited about us and here, so what's this? he asked.

I'm allowed to have moods.

Well, the fence is almost done, he said. It isn't always going to be constant work.

I'm having a hard time trusting that.

Silence.

More silence.

More silence.

The eternal silence from him.

Okay, I continued, I just do not believe anymore in the idea that once X is completed, we can finally then enjoy Y. There is always going to be another X. So the cycle never stops. Honestly, it doesn't matter that we're living on the land; we're no different from Wall Street bankers.

So now we're bankers.

Noooo, god, I'm trying to make a point. I want more intention around daily life for us, how we used to be, to pay attention to us. I really want ritual right now.

Don't rely on me to give you ritual, he snapped back.

Well, that's supportive. Thank you. Do *you* think it's okay that we've fallen into a pattern of no weekends and all we do is work? Shoveling is still work.

So what do you want?

I don't know. I'm not blaming you or me. I'm just talking it out.

You aren't making sense right now, he said. None of your comments go together, so I'm going to take some space.

That was his way of ending the conversation. He cut his talk like a line of rope. But it didn't make it less distressing to me. In our most physically settled circumstance—our own home on land that could mean something to us—we were the least settled by the outlying circumstances. We had never not held proper jobs or not been in school. We had never not paid rent. We had never not made a distinction between work and weekend. And, illogically, that had all begun to make us unavailable to each other.

Wedding nerves, friends said.

Whatever, I said back, I don't buy that.

That afternoon, Bru paced the yurt porch, glancing from Chris slouched in the doorway to me lying down in sagebrush. He didn't know who to go to or whether to relax, which he would do later, by gulping down water once our exasperation wore off. My husband-to-be had backed into his own eddy again. His face had gone featureless. I got upset too. But, for once, I had nothing to say about it. Endurance had courted me with its hot steady breath. I asked the dark dank earth beneath me to swallow me whole. This was a time for the wild to inform the human on how best to live. This is what we do, isn't it, when we need connection?

Below us, the engorged creek, full of clouds and sky and

rain, rushed loud toward its river the Gallatin. I placed sage-brush sprigs over my eyes and thought of how murky the creek had become during spring. It was now a thick milky cord that ran down from the mountains, through the cottonwoods, through our lives. I wanted to reach across the abyss between who I was and who I wasn't yet. No, to grasp for something across the blank space of an abyss: for ritual, for a place, for what I never knew as a girl. Stones could aid the passage.

Newspaper bundles greeted me back in the garden. It was my last task before we headed out the next morning. Brooks had saved the black-and-white pages of the *Bozeman Chronicle* for us all winter, bound them in twine and brought them over. I supplemented by dumpster diving at Home Depot recycling. Now I could suppress future weeds.

Wind rustled evenly through the cottonwoods. I bent down, unfolded the newspaper, and began to spread it ten layers deep around the earth where the walkways of my future garden would be. The table saw whined inside the shop and its sound leaked out to me and the newborn grass. Chris was finishing another stool. We had recovered, as people do. You let go of one layer, another one surfaces; you let go again, you reach again; you let go again and you know it is the eternal process. He had pulled me into the kitchen and uncurled my fists one by one. We slow-danced to a Tom Waits song, something we never did. He was drunk on red wine and I liked it and said he should drink more often as he drew me closer and breathed, That's an awful idea.

I soaked the paper with a hose as I placed it. The smell

of damp paper on damp earth was rapture. Events, local and global, that happened during our first year here now floated up at me again: the Haiti earthquake, a school choir performance, something about Goldman Sachs. While the world had turned, we had moved here and built a yurt.

That had been our story, our small contribution, and we were still living it.

Lay down the past.

Let it compost.

To make space for the new, some parts of the old needed to die: maybe not the facts themselves but the stories woven around them. I had planted small seeds in dark garden beds. Now unseen, they would germinate while we were away—carrots, radishes, lettuce, beets, calendula, spinach, chives, arugula, kale, and any rogue transplants.

Grow, grow, I said, patting the moist soil with a bare hand, and the sight of my hand, now freckled and wrinkled and worn, reminded me of my young hand.

My mother calls them honeysuckles and they grow up the wall in our small backyard in the Dominican Republic. I pick them, pluck the yellow center out, and suck on it, like a honey straw. I tell my younger brother to do the same. He does, one hand pulling up his diaper rag. Then we gather the discarded red flowers and replant them in the cracks between concrete squares. Like this, I explain, showing him how to dig a little hole in the sand. We shove each flower into the ground and cover part of it over. I am convinced they will grow up tall and soon we'll have to weave our way through a forest of honeysuckles.

But surely those replanted honeysuckles withered in the heat.

I never noticed, though.

Had white picket fence girl and global girl coexisted then?

Our friend Piper had agreed to come water the garden and sleep in the yurt on her own retreat for a month. She wanted to be disconnected, she told me.

Hmm, I said, this place has actually moved me to feel more connected than ever.

We have to disconnect from one way of being to connect to another.

What of the verb *to belong*?

Not that I ever had. I had been conscious and unconscious of this as a child.

I knew I wanted *it*, but then decided that I was suited to being exotic and didn't really need *it*, well, partially because that made life easier, but I was still jealous of my friends who had *it*, and almost everyone did, so I grew into a woman who prided herself on not needing *it*, on being adamantly opposed to *it*, despite the friction of *it* within her. Yet here *it* was, some version of it, in the form of mud and paper and hawks, asking me to please continue to examine it.

There was never a where.

But now I had a where if I wanted one.

I had papered the whole place by dusk.

With inked hands, I touched my ribs and stared up the hill to acknowledge a garden created here, one that might last thousands of years or blow away in a few. A new awareness had grown within me. Part of integration involved failure. I didn't know yet, at least not in my bones, that you couldn't re-place the empty with another place. But I would try to. When people asked where I was from at an upcoming writer's workshop in Vermont before our wedding, I would not resort to my long list of nowheres. I would let my current life in Montana take up all the space of my story.

And I would not be apologetic about it.

Already, it felt dicey.

PART THREE

7

THIS IS THE PLACE

In a red Vermont barn, all the people we love sat around tables with plates full of brisket and salad. Chris and I had spent the week before zooming all over New England with Bru to see people—mostly, we marveled at the humidity and green and small scale. But now the wedding had arrived. My mother, host of the welcome dinner, stood up with a wine glass and began. She said a few words about the longevity of our relationship and even mentioned that if any two people could build a yurt together it was us. Already, a friend's mother had pulled me aside and whispered, Everyone needs a yurt. By yurt, she meant, a dream. And that's part of what my mother was getting at.

Then, lifting both arms, she explained that our family friends from many places had made an effort to come.

Look, she said, there's Cheryl from Australia.

Cheryl's eyes widened—*don't single me out, please.*

Too late.

Stand up, Cheryl, my mother asked, her voice rising with excitement, and Cheryl folded her napkin and stood up, unsure of what to do. Soon, she would not be alone. Momentum took over and my mother's speech snowballed into an epic toast of calling out almost everyone there.

And Barbara and Hugo from the Dominican Republic.

Stand up! And the Hopkins from Texas. Stand up! And the
Tangneys from Mexico. Stand up! And there's Susan Lilley,
Molly's high school English teacher. Stand up, Susan! And
there's Jackie and Cyril from Spain. Stand up!

Overcome with her own elation, she kept going and going
—naming what she saw as our support system, what I saw as our
transience. My closest friends shot smiling glances at me, knowing that I would be part humiliated, part proud of this moment.
I tried to avoid eye contact. Standing in the back of the room, I
wrapped my arms around Chris from behind and watched time
unroll for everyone to see. I was actually gratified as she called
out our past—because *What's next?* was still a true urge in me.
Everyone could see, in the flesh, this map of my youth abroad
and beyond.

She only stopped when she arrived at one table of Chris's
extended family.

And there's . . . she paused, I don't know who you are, but
stand up anyway!

Once the chatter and enthusiasm simmered down, once
people had gone back for seconds or out for a smoke break,
Chris's father got up. I didn't know what to expect from this
kind man of few words. He lit a candle and let us all gaze at the
flame that symbolizes love. Then, right when warm and glowy
feelings started to circulate, he blew it out. The room gasped.
He stood silently. What, oh what, did it mean? Slowly, as if it
wanted to provoke us more, the candle began to flicker—one
flicker, two—until it lit itself again.

Sometimes the flame goes out, he said. You have to reig-
nite love.

The collective breathed air back into that red barn. It was

a fine beginning—my mother naming the only thing my family knew, all our places, and his father, the representative of a family rooted in Maine, sharing the message that if you choose one person, as with choosing one place, you must continually stoke the fire.

As young kids, we had had no concept that there was a boy living a classic American childhood in the northern woods and that this boy would meet a girl who spoke Spanish and was as comfortable in airports as in any of the homes she'd inhabited around the world. Chris squeezed my hands and I felt a deep pinch of longing to be back in our yurt, just us, watching sandhill cranes.

On the day of our ceremony, gray clouds floated over green hills. Rain drizzled hard enough for guests to wonder whether we would still hold it outside. We did. Everyone stood under umbrellas as we walked toward each other through wet grass. I grinned at the perfect imperfection of it all, how appropriate the variable weather seemed for any relationship. It takes courage to love one person, one anything. This was the man I would walk through the mess of life with. It was a vertical choice made long ago by me, by us, one of the few choices that came for me with no doubt. It had been important to return to Vermont for our vows, the gentle landscape where we had found each other. Impatient as ever, I couldn't wait to get to him, and literally pulled my parents across the lawn with me. Under an arch made with two extra *khar mod* and a flap of yurt canvas, we held forearms and exchanged vows that acknowledged how we could love each other more completely—honest things like

Chris asking me more questions and me operating in softer tones. As it unfolded, as my brothers and close friends and Katinka and Mike stood nearby, a breeze, growing to a wind, yanked at the canvas, yanked at my dress, and threatened to blow all of us away.

A few hours later, while we all danced in celebration and a full moon rose above, something else entirely would happen on The Land. Our friend Piper would push open the cabin's screen door at dusk and find herself staring at a mountain lion. They would gaze at each other for milliseconds. Then the lion would bound over the irrigation ditch and up the path to the yurt and away. She was beautiful, Piper would tell us. Only a fleeting presence. Making almost no sound at all.

I would choose to take it as a good omen.

After the wedding, my brothers both asked, Are you really going back there?

I couldn't tell if they were jealous or incredulous.

Yes, I said.

What are you going to *do*?

What we have been *do*ing, hello.

Plus, now I had a new little seed of understanding tucked in my pocket—one I had yet to reveal to anyone but Chris. Two weeks earlier, at the writer's workshop, I had become, as planned, "Molly who lives in Montana." Though it felt painfully ordinary, I stuck with it and treated it as an experiment. One woman told me that I looked too sophisticated to live in a yurt. I challenged her back by saying, But no one is one thing. Later, at a picnic, one of the old guards of nature writing, a kind, compassionate man, listened to my questions as we both clutched paper plates. If everyone stayed put, wouldn't we abolish our capacity for learning? Wasn't it critical for my generation to heal intolerance by moving elsewhere, and maybe often? I really wanted to know.

Be a bard, he said.

What do you mean?

If the urge to travel and live elsewhere is in you, then do. But a person must also have a homeplace to speak *from*. A bard collects stories from other places. A bard also has her own stories from one place.

So you mean do both?

Yes, that sounds good to me if it sounds good to you.

I walked away thinking that, without knowing it, he may have just answered my life's question. Was it that simple? Anything familiar required reigniting, which could be defined as *leave, go away, and return to said thing to see it anew again*. A homeplace. I knew little about what a homeplace could be.

While away, I had missed The Land in spurts. Not at all. And then desperately, and I wasn't partial to the use of that adverb. In our absence, grass had grown and bugs skimmed on creek water and voles fled from raptors and deer bedded down under aspens and humans had taken off their coats. When we drove in on I-90, a repeat of our exact journey exactly one year ago, the entrance to the Gallatin Valley was no longer a stranger, with its mountains and wheat fields and homes. Neither was this short stretch of quiet highway. Hey highway, hey hey hey. We pulled off at our exit and shot south toward The Land with a heady anticipation.

Up the driveway, our faces out the windows, we both said,

Welcome back to the savannah. Grass creek mountains sweet smell—it was unmistakable. Grass up to our armpits. Bru pushed his black nose down on the ground and sniffed his way back into doing what he does. I looked for the familiar things: orange butterflies, cottonwood puffs, birdsong, lavender clouds rolling in from the mountains, wind sweeping through grass in roving bands of sun and shadow. Nettles and underbrush clogged the spaces where grass couldn't grow. Had I forgotten how to move in a landscape of predators? Nature had not asked us to be anything less than alert. I allowed myself to go there—a woman who went away from time to time like a bard, yes, but who came to know every bend of The Land, its moods and changes, and who wrote about it and who would die here, maybe against a tree, her shriveled skin and old bones sinking deeply into the earth.

My legs started right on up to the yurt.

Chris and Bru followed. We had never seen the yurt in summer. It looked like a giant mushroom growing in a green field.

We're back, I said.

We. Are. Back, Chris repeated.

Early July again and cottonwood puffs lined the roads like litter brushed to the gutters. It rained. Under a thunderstorm sky, thick with as much moisture as ever happened here, I wandered the garden, pulling at weeds already poking up through newspaper and wood chips. Lettuce and kale and arugula had grown into small sprouts. But a hailstorm in June had tattered them. Diane told us that she had come over to make sure the cabin hadn't been damaged. Golf-ball size, apparently. They would have bounced right off the yurt.

After we unpacked and stepped back into our life here, more

hail blew us across the valley. When it started to beat down on the metal roofs, I would peek out the cabin door to find Chris at the shop door smiling back at me through the sheet of chaos, small white pebbles scattering like mad across a green lawn. The green, it had been so easy to forget after months of winter's white wool carpet.

In the field on top, green alfalfa, tall and wavy, soaked my jeans when I walked in the mornings. But after a few days of sun, farmers everywhere in the valley cut their fields in diagonal stripes—the first of two or three cuttings. Now the air smelled of cow instead of horse, which made no sense to me, but there you go. Like actors in a play, square hay bales took up their positions in the field. Hello, hello, I mouthed, greeting each one as we crunched over sheared grass, a buzz cut, a bare earth, a bare soul. It wasn't tragic, but sharp and hot. Had the bales dropped down from the sky? I jumped on them and jumped off. They were made of stalks of grass, of air, of nothing, just like us.

It was here, transfixed by the long days of summer, that the white picket fence girl drew up her plans. Not for a white picket fence, but for something she could touch, something that would be hers, something that she could be *of.* She amazed me with her determination—as if to say that finally, geez, finally, she could go about her most important work now that I had removed her shackles and approved the concept of a bard. I stood on the sidelines and watched.

Questions hovered nearby: Is it that I'm in my thirties now? Could it have been any place? Am I just growing up?

I started to collect information.

Like this quote from Carson McCullers: "To know who you are, you have to have a place to come from."

I remembered a story told to me by someone somewhere. On his first voyage elsewhere, away from his home island where trees never lost leaves, a man entered college in the northern United States. When maple leaves turned orange and fell from the trees, he sat beneath them and cried. Now that man was *from* a place.

He wasn't geographically neutral, like me.

My homing instinct had always functioned like a river of dislocation, flowing in space, with no beginning or end, simply whatever was next. But I could choose to direct it now to a particular place, and naturally, with that intention, a hunger emerged. I wanted to know everything about this valley. How little I knew. I read a few books. People had come through here about 11,000 years ago. But no one had lived in the Gallatin Valley permanently before the white man. The Crow Indians summered here, along the creek, moving as nomads, which also means in relation to the land, in communion. When a whole community moves together, follows herds, to uproot is not to uproot, I think. They called it the Valley of the Flowers. That is, before fur trappers and the railroad and the otherworldly slaughter of almost all buffalo and subsequently the people who relied on them. Lewis's and Clark's journals say that Sacajawea knew of trails in the Gallatin even though she'd never been there.

Following deer paths along the creek, on the search for wild roses, around and over the old cattle fence, not much caring about the consequences of high grass, I let my face burn red in the heat and the thread of my thinking unwind. I didn't wonder about anyone else or envy their lives. I wondered about how wide a homeplace could be—a region, a state, even though land itself isn't aware of statehood—a country even, a continent. That it might change as a person grew up. Regardless, an innate call to definition existed in the world: I know this place, and this place knows me. Did all humans feel drawn to settle somehow? Even the sailor of high seas lives in a ship, otherwise known as a home moved along by waves.

You want, naturally, to care for that homeplace.

As evidenced by my incessant sweeping.

You are *really* into sweeping, said Chris, sitting on the yurt porch in his sarong and sandals. He had transitioned to summer. As had the yurt. No piles of blankets. No piles of coats. No snowy boots in the corner. No grippers. No mud tracked in. Door flung open to the warm air and birds. I loved sweeping the summer dust into a pile and then scooping it up with paper and launching it out into the grass. It all delighted me: the thick, loud, overgrown, abundant quality of late July.

I could be barefoot.

It was easy.

Chris had actually made mention of my newfound ease. Not that recent moments of frustration hadn't erupted, but something had shifted. I swayed like a dancer on the porch. I had also started teaching a creative writing class in town—a small financial addition, a larger sense of a world beyond building a yurt.

Full moon, I think, tonight, I said, propping the broom inside and joining him on the porch. In the grass, Bru rolled onto his back and stretched his legs out to keep him in balance, jowls long and loose. I yanked my shirt up for heat on my stomach. Was it Saturday, Sunday? Was this an actual weekend moment? We would spend the rest of the afternoon lying there, like sunbathers, watching larkspur and yarrow quiver as ground breezes rustled through the grass. And though neither one of us said it aloud, we both punched away thoughts that this time could be better *used*, that we were undeserving of such rest.

I would like to become a softer person, I said.

This place, he said . . . would be the place to do that.

Later that night, intoxicated by the smells of summer, we chased each other around the yurt, grabbing limbs, laughing, me shrieking, tumbling onto the bed and wrestling. I had learned to pull myself up on the *uni*, to rise above Chris and then down onto him, and again, my biceps taut in the moonlit dark. Because discretion about sex was sexy and that was my policy, I shared that image with no one, instead telling what it felt like to end a love-make heat by ducking under a small door, without bumping your head finally, into a sudden rainstorm that cooled our naked bums as we whapped and flipped our white ropes to slip a loose cover over the *tono*.

If you have lived so many somewheres that you have no somewhere to leave, then your journey might be finding a somewhere to simply be. That was it right now for me. Living without reflection was pure. I had never done so. I wanted to try it, though that effort would dwindle right away.

How about the ponds? Katinka asked.

We were mid-conversation, the standard back-and-forth of recounting our lives to one another. Phone pressed to ear, I paced the cabin's porch as far as the landline would let me go, barefoot and pleased by the brown tan lines from my sandals.

Oh man, frigid, I explained.

Chris and I had made a regular practice of shucking our clothes and diving in after a long hot day. What had been an ice rink now pulsed with heat, small bugs, tall swaying grasses, leftover goose poop, and pussy willows lining the edges. Body submerged, snout moving along the dark water, Bru swam like a sea monster. My pattern became a ritual. I dove from a rock, broke through water that caught my breath, and kicked up fast and away from the cold below to the warm surface. Did everyone have this holdover from childhood—a sure feeling that something would grab you down into the depths? Especially when you were naked and felt all slimy and one with the water. As Chris and Bru splashed in and out and in and out, I forced myself to float on my back and stare up at the blue sky. It's like true listening, I told Katinka, about my how my ears heard the low murky buzz of underwater while my face accepted the hot sun.

Like I'm in two places at once, I said.

She thought I sounded happy, and I suppose I was. It was our second summer—such a different kind of summer, one of being instead of building. My days were spent hauling goat manure around the garden, weeding thistles from between lettuce. Teaching and writing weren't a clear picture of reality yet; life required more work. But for now, I tried to channel all the people who would say, Chill and enjoy yourself.

Do you think contentedness and growth are the same? I asked her.

Molls, she laughed, just go play on that land.

I know, I know, I said, toeing the grass now, enough philosophizing.

But what really was the difference between contentedness and growth? I couldn't identify it. If someone asked me what delighted me, I would have said having to find my way around a foreign city or exerting my muscles and lungs to get up a mountain or studying a new concept. But maybe that was what advanced me, pushed me, or anyone, and my delight was not delight but learning. I didn't know anyone, not one person, who had been raised to seek basic contentedness. Perhaps contentedness seemed like not noble enough of a goal.

Katinka had to get cross-town for a gathering. I had to dunk my feet in the creek because tomorrow Chris and I were hosting our first get-together at the yurt. We actually knew enough people to have a real deal afternoon party.

Okay, I said, go catch your subway and then come visit me out here.

One day, she sighed, soon.

I tucked the phone into our hammock and stepped back off the porch and down to flowing water. The only crime of this place, or any place, was its familiarity over time—one day, a walk down to the creek might lose its novelty. For some people. As we pushed through grass and my bare feet avoided sharp rocks, one lone fly buzzed around my head, followed me right into the creek, where cold moved up my legs. No longer a thick milky cord running through the valley, the summer creek would have thrilled any fisherman, what they called gin-clear. They appeared sometimes, in waders, silent, casting back, trying to avoid the trees. Bru sloshed over to scattered rock islands. There low water butted up against a current that wrapped around tree roots and formed deeper pools for trout to hide among shadows.

It must be instinctual to bend at the waist and glance at the upside-down world between your legs. I'd done it five thousand times as a girl, together with my brothers, each one of us picking out the strange details of new vision, and where in that vision we would choose to live. The ceiling of silvery brown water coasted fast, moving between clouds of rock. Trees reached down to their feathered green ends, and even grass gave the earth a set of impressive bangs. I could live in a world where a person climbed out of a leaf house and up a trunk to get to the current.

Cars pulled up right after the afternoon lightning storm. It had crackled across the valley—sheets of rain descending, the sky a robin's egg blue—and now, in its wake, the electricity still clung to everything.

I directed people up the path to the yurt where Chris was waiting. We had perched in the yurt during the storm, watching it move, watching the grass stand even more green and tall to meet the energy of it. Now I would stay down by the steaming dirt driveway to make sure no one got lost. And there suddenly was Anna. The last to arrive. So enamored with the out-of-doors, I hadn't gone to yoga or seen her since our return. She jumped out of her car, eyes wide, and hugged me.

Hi.

Hey.

Whoa.

I know.

We had to seek shelter, she breathed as the story spilled from her, under these branches, ducked under our boards, on the edge of the lake. The sky turned dark dark purple, it came in so fast. Beautiful.

She and a friend had been paddleboarding up the canyon. While telling me more, more, more, she glanced around quickly to make sure no one else was around, yanked her bikini off, and slipped into shorts and a T-shirt. I watched us in this exchange. To live here was to be alive. You could not live here and not connect with your own animal self. No one could shush the elements and tell them to go backstage. I had come here for exactly that: to remind myself of the self who had run from lightning across a mesa in the desert, or had been serenaded by a bat colony while sleeping on a bridge over a river, or had spontaneously scaled a cliff above crashing ocean waves and barking seals and my own solitude. Part of it was just owning up to your own smallness. I wanted to live more of those moments because they were wild and they were teachers.

Anna rustled around in her car. When she was ready to go, she cocked her head and stared at me. I stared back from under my straw hat.

Yes? I laughed.

You look radiant, she said.

Thank you, I grinned. Everyone glows after a storm, right?

Sure, but, she said, pausing and waving her hand over my face, something is different.

We ran up the hill, panting as the ground breathed its sweet wet smell back at us. People had crammed into the yurt; most had spread out on the grass; dogs chased each other along the barbed-wire fence. Everyone was eating. The mixed ages pleased me: children, a few folks over seventy, and the whole range in between. We didn't know anyone well, but enough to gather a community. I had missed *that* element too, during the long, cold, yurt-building start to our life here.

Chris stood deep in conversation with two men. Anna ran into another friend from yoga. I walked right into the yurt to pour myself some lemonade over ice— ice melting in our cooler, but ice nonetheless. Inside, I found my new friend Darlene. She was a short spunky woman from Florida, double my age, dynamic and no-nonsense. We fell into a conversation about her unlikely landing in the mountains, especially these mountains, and then she asked me about where I grew up.

I told her.

I also told her that I liked it here.

You know, I explained, the whole settle versus wander thing we all have.

I don't think it's a bad thing not to be attached to place, she said.

Yeah, I heard myself say, but . . .

My mother visited a few days later. She had come to bask in nature, to see us and Susan, one of her closest friends, and to watch Bru while we took our canoe out on a river for a weekend. I didn't reveal much about my recent thoughts. I didn't mention the bard concept or that an urge for homeplace had risen like a steeple in me. *This* place appealed as my homeplace. But it wasn't my place and I did not know what my parents' recent intentions were for it—whether they would need to sell it one day, or whether they would move here and kick us out. I just hadn't allowed myself to sift through options or follow a thread further into the future than was comfortable. Despite my new rosy lens, The Land was still, as it had been in the beginning, an idea to me.

One evening, while we were gone, my mother and Susan slept in the yurt. For grins, they said. Because we had forgotten to carry our cups back up, they had had to sip water from shallow wooden bowls. I tried to imagine them cramped on our small futon, peeing outside in the morning, listening for sounds, and surely laughing, something they did well together.

We were tromping around the hillside beneath the firs, with gloves on, cutting stinging nettles to dry for tea. Almost August was the wrong time for harvesting this particular plant, but I wanted to anyway and my mother was humoring me by partaking. No longer the tender green leaves of spring, some had begun to flop over and wither.

So what did you think? I asked my mother.

The yurt is great, Moll, she said, but I think you have to be young to really truly appreciate it.

Fair enough, I said, nodding.

We strung a rope from one end of the cabin's porch to another and hung the limp nettle stems like wet laundry. They needed shade for drying. Especially surrounded by the mounting heat of summer, mounting not only around us, as heat waves returned and dry air dried even more and the eternal threat of forest fires presented itself. I could feel something old remounting slowly in me, even as it tried to rework itself. So when my mother stepped inside to cool off and shower, I kicked off my boots and fell back into the hammock to stretch out in my sweaty clothes. From here, this lower vantage point, as I drifted into relaxation, the nettles, now a sheet wall of green, could have been vines in the tropics reaching down to tempt me.

Come swing on me and see where you'll end up.

I am directing my brothers—again, in Spain. We have run down to the faraway willow trees, where we lean against the trunk of one and survey our plot. We are hidden inside by leaves that reach down to the ground like a green waterfall. Our plan is to make a home for sleeping. We'll be too scared to actually sleep here when the sun goes down and everything becomes dark. What if the porcupines crawl in or the crows attack the tree or the ghosts surround us? But those concerns don't stop us now.

Okay, I say, putting my hands on their shoulders, we have some chores to do.

What are they? asks my middle brother, wiping his nose.

Well, you can be the cook, because we need to have a dinner. You can make a soup, and then someone has to clean up and pick up all these extra sticks and pull back the leaves to make a front door.

Can I do that? asks my youngest brother, as if he is honored to take it on.

Yes, and someone has to go back out and collect all the treasures we need.

What kind of treasures? they both ask, eyes glued to mine.

I don't know yet, but I'll do that. You'll see when I get back.

As I push through the leaves and back out into the world, I don't even consider the fact that they follow my orders or that my rules are *the* rules in our trio. I start to skip along the parched low grass. Where to go? The campo rolls on forever past those hills and those houses, and I wonder how far to go and what to find and the freedom makes me bite my lip.

My daydream must have been long, because I only stirred

back to reality when the screen door creaked open. My mother stepped back onto the porch with a glass of white wine in hand. She looked glamorous—clean with hair blown dry and some mascara and lipstick, as if she were ready to go somewhere.

Did I tell you, she asked, that I'm going to Slovakia in a few weeks? I might not have even told you yet.

No, you didn't, I said.

Well, Mary and I are going together, because you know we both like the same kind of traveling. So we'll be walking across the countryside. We'll start in Budapest and then end the trip in Krakow. I've never been to that part of the world. I really can't wait.

That's great, Mom, I said, and rolled over to face the cottonwoods.

The Monday morning after she left, I dragged our heavy blue trashcan down the rutted driveway to the road for pickup. Cottonwoods fluttered on one side as I passed the garden, abundant now with herbs and lettuces and beets and small darting birds—and weeds. I always one-armed the trashcan and almost no longer heard the sound of it, like a train that jostled slowly over loose tracks getting looser. Under the sun, hawks coasted. Under them, I walked and thought about the word *mundane*.

Bru kept turning back to check in.

He knew that he needed to stay close down here, near the road, near the possibility of escape. Domestic tasks happened everywhere. I'd done them in every place I lived. The novelty of each new way always wore off. *Whoa, cool, I am sweeping dust from a yurt* soon became *God, there's so much goddam dust in the yurt.* We could only romanticize the life we saw from afar, or stepped into for a short while. I was sure most people, even the less flighty ones, recalled their lives in periods. We loved these periods because they were seasons and because we remembered them that way. But homeplace could lead to monotony—that was its appeal for so many people, wasn't it? Even with the bard model, this would be my life, dragging the same huge-ass trash-can over the same rutted road every single Monday morning. This sole domestic task suddenly felt like one of the many irritations preventing me from greatness.

The trashcan caught an edge and keened over to one side as I tried to yank it upright, but that turned its bulk around even more, so that soon I was wrestling the thing as it twisted my arm like a towel, and maybe I kicked it at the exact instant I let go so that its fall would be more brutal than necessary.

White trash bags.

Open and strewn everywhere.

Really, Molly?

Bru ran over to inspect the wounded victims. It didn't take me long, in my fury, to put the whole thing back together. With two arms, I wheeled it to the road.

I stormed into the shop so that Chris would ask me how I was.

He took one look at my face.

What's wrong? he asked.

I don't want to turn into a woman who spends her whole life baking pies and shit.

Oh-kay.

Well, I don't.

I don't think you're at risk for that, he laughed, and I don't think you've ever baked a pie anyway. How did we get from you taking the trash out to pie baking?

Same thing.

Is it a chore thing? Because we've both done chores our entire lives.

It's not about chores.

I didn't think so, he said.

It's about how to like myself, I said, and walked out to the trees.

With August now upon us, the landscape started to shift into full bleach-out. In the evenings, we lounged on the yurt porch and made dinner on our camp stove. Chris had not probed me further after the trashcan incident. It wasn't new to him. He knew to leave it to me. This was where I needed to make friends with the act of repetition, with the fact that I was still thrown off by hearing about foreign places, that I was still capable of envy, that the brick wall hadn't disintegrated yet, that learning didn't happen in a linear way, that it required going back over our same glitches, feeling our same feelings, until one day they simply weren't there anymore. We all regress in order to grow. And I was making an art of it.

I sat on a fold-up camp chair and wrote a few letters while he lit the stove. We both glanced up from time to time at the western horizon and a round orange sun setting over white grass. With the yurt door tied open, inside was outside and outside was inside. The breeze found its way inside, almost shy at first, but then coasted around the circle, puffing in between the *khar mod* and then slipping back out.

You know, I said, sometimes I think we were crazy to build this yurt.

Yeah, Chris said, retrospect is the human condition.

I mean, it's amazing that humans do what they do with the greatest hope and no guarantee of anything, I added, and we try to stack up all these things around us to make us *us*, but they aren't real.

What do you mean by things?

Places, people, jobs, hobbies, you know. You ski, but that doesn't mean that you *are* skiing. And with the Internet putting us in all these places at once, we could all be anything anywhere, or at least we think so. Where are we, then? How do we know ourselves, or even like ourselves?

By being wherever we are, he said, shrugging, less apt to pummel a thought to death.

I know, but that seems almost impossible.

As the words left my mouth, an owl, out of nowhere, whack-landed on the edge of our porch. Big yellow eyes. White fluffy body. It stared at me and wavered a bit, surprised by its own careless and sudden entrance. Then it gathered itself, turned a wing, and flew off.

Did you see that, oh my god, did you see it, beb? I said.

Yeah, he exhaled.

We both gaped at the now empty spot.

It's got to be the baby of the owl we saw last August, I said.

Maybe.

It was huge, but all fluffy, and isn't that nest down there?

I just can't believe it landed on the porch, Chris said, a plastic spatula dangling from his fingers.

Maybe it's learning how to fly, and then, oops, crash landing.

That's what it seemed like.

We crawled into bed that night bristling with the vitality of an eye-to-eye encounter with a wild animal. No different, perhaps, than a lightning storm that moves right down into your bones and jolts you. The big man Bru, snoozing in the yurt, had missed the whole thing.

After a few hours of deep slumber, a loud thunk on the roof woke me.

I nudged Chris.

Something's hopping around up there, I whispered. The owl?

We pulled the comforter away from our faces and peeked up through dark at the *tono* and an ever darker shadow perched above. It flapped its wings, then paused in an arc, like a swimmer displaying strong shoulders, balancing, cradling, blessing.

Unlike Chris, I didn't tuck back to sleep because the owl stayed for what seemed like hours—doing what, I don't know, swaying back and forth, catching itself. Was it watching us? Could it sense that we were in here? It must. Eventually, with one quiet whoosh, it made an almost silent departure.

But the mystical soon became, in Chris's words, annoying. Each night, the same owl would land on the *tono* and then skitter off, sliding claws down the canvas and then *tick-tick-ticking* back up to the top. It kept us awake with its antics on the roof and a mournful screech calling out into the ether.

Whoa, he or she is drunk, Chris complained.

Thank you for saying *she*, I said.

You're welcome.

We've both been drunk.

That we have.

So maybe this owl is just trying to figure out some basics, I offered as Chris folded a pillow over his face and ears. We had confirmed in our nature guide that it was indeed a juvenile great horned owl and that it probably didn't know how to feed or care for itself. Soon it would become what these birds were known for being: adaptable and nonmigratory. Not yet, though. It had not come to our yurt as a messenger from the great beyond. It just wanted food. I got it. I was sloppy in my search too. But it was much easier to have compassion for an owl.

We had been living on The Land for over a year now. If that was a marker of time, we needed a mark for it, especially since, in not so many words, we had decided that we would stay here for a bit longer. We wouldn't start the mad questioning of what was next. We would give it another six months. Long ago, somewhere on the northwestern coast of the United States, I had seen a compass carved onto someone's porch. It had moved me then as I wondered about the making of the compass—had it been an act of deliberate orientation? We are here. Our home is here. Most explorers, especially at sea, navigated through an endless blue span of water by the stars and also with a compass. They got lost. This was important. But they also found their way. Now every map had a compass rose printed in the corner. Whether anyone still used it was hard to know. Intuition had been co-opted by cardinal directions that had now been co-opted by a screen talking at you. Still, we are a species who likes to know where we are.

In all ways.

Map the body.

Map the mind.

Map emotions.

Map what you hold to be true.

Map what you hold not to be true.

Map your own worth.

So that each continent within moves in relation to the other continents within.

Standing on the porch, I surveyed Bru's claw marks, like sudden dashes, in our cedar planks. They scattered all over and then bunched up like a herd at the far edge. *They* were a map of what had happened here so far, of how many times he had run and skidded and leapt into snow, of how often his glee had made us laugh. One day, when he was dead, buried under a tree, a day that seemed so distant, we could come back here, run our fingers over the deep scratches, and remember him.

Chris fiddled with the plastic hand compass. Bru stood on the edge. I put one hand on his soft ear and then pointed generally north through the firs to Helena.

That way, I said.

Let's be a little more precise, he said.

True north versus magnetic north, I know, even though I've never really understood it.

Here, he said, showing me the little red numbers.

Let's make the compass as big as the moon, I said.

As Chris carved it into the porch with his crooked knife, I remembered my father's mother asking me, after our wedding, whether I was busier as a wife now. I had smiled to watch her reach into the deep recesses of her past for a phrase she may have asked her lady friends or been asked. The truth is that, as a young woman, she probably craved more of that busy—what

I, and most of my friends, considered classic mundane. She had loved Hawaii, where they first lived with their three little boys. It was a pleasant life, she told me once: walking down to the beach, maintaining her figure, living in a small bungalow. She would have stayed. Instead, they moved often, from Hawaii to post–World War II Japan to post–World War II Germany and beyond. Being "the other" became so familiar to her that, as a feeling, it became unrecognizable. Now I knew that she probably hadn't wanted that at all. She would have preferred to stare out the same window every morning, clean the same dishes in the same sink, tend the same pink flowering bush in the yard, and watch her family grow up, their height measured simply by the door they walked through each day. Maybe she would have pulled my grandfather aside on a weekend, smiled a sweet smile, and asked him to build a white picket fence for her.

Your turn, Chris said.

He had carved the compass.

It's gorgeous, beb, I said, and squatted down to do my part. As I filled in the groove with waterproof black Sharpie, again making a pale thing turn to a dark thing, a question pushed at my insides.

Okay, so what happens when people get attached to a place and then are forced to leave it, like real refugees or anyone moving for a job, or the place collapses in a hurricane, or the bond is severed somehow? I asked, knowing the answer, but wanting to voice it anyway.

Happens all the time, Chris said.

Exactly, I said, because don't you think everyone, *every* one, wants to settle into some place on some level?

I stood up and we stepped together into the compass.

Pressed into a hug, we could both fit inside it. Our arrow pointed north—whether it was true north or not depends on the onlooker.

But then, I added, how does anyone cope with that loss?

They just do, he breathed into my ear.

When Chris and Bru left for a hike, I knew there was only one thing I needed to accomplish that day. I needed to do it before they got home. I needed to do it at the latest point in the afternoon, when the sun cast a last warmth through the air and retreated behind trees, when clouds had settled over the meadow, when the pond had turned matte gray. Somehow, I had grown into a woman convinced that a pond monster was going to get me. It helped to have others around. If someone else was in the water with me, then I was safe, right? Or at least I wouldn't get sucked into oblivion without anyone knowing.

Now my urge to swim laps in the pond with my goggles presented itself.

I should be able to.

I would start with one lap and go from there.

I wore a swimsuit.

I stood on a rock and stared into the water, rubbing my thighs up and down, heart racing, mind starting and stopping with imagination. Remember the blue eye from winter, remember how it called to you, a canoe lashed to a dock. This could be that blue eye. Only it wasn't blue at this time of day. It was dark. Grass rustled on the edges. The muskrat was hiding somewhere. Fish swam too deep for me to see them. Of anything remotely scary I'd done in my life, this should not have registered on the list.

Clutching my goggles, I dove—and midair, for a brief moment, the feeling of everything being too late whooshed through me, that there was no turning around, that I had committed and now must see the thing through because you can't un-dive yourself. My splash was small. Cold water slid from my forehead to my toes. I told myself to relish it and that worked as I arced up to the still surface. It only took me a few seconds to blow on my goggles and arrange them over my head. Here we go.

But one freestyle stroke, one glance at the murky water beneath me, and I had had enough. It's one thing to assume that the murk exists. It's another to stare right at it. Breaststroke was it. Head up, I pulled myself through the leaden pond like a frog, as I'd done through the snow under the hawthorns. Just had to get to the end and then back. One full lap. Almost there. But why not just allow myself to get there eventually, wherever there was? I could do it and I was almost free of whatever weeds might curl around my legs, whatever fish planned to nibble on me, whatever toothed creature sat on the bottom and watched my frantic figure. When the end was near, though breathing like someone being chased, I forced myself to stop and tread water. I could fist-pump my success. I could soften into this pond. I could melt down into it and let the distinction between me and it fade. Wind skittered across the gray surface, sending ripples across to the pussy willows, and they absorbed the quiver and then sent it elsewhere. My wet head felt cold. I wanted to get out, but I didn't want to get out.

The thinking I had never understood until now flashed— that either/or could be replaced by both/and. Under the gray sky in the gray pond, my pink body made a note, not an articulation, but a gut observation.

The urge to go and the urge to stay could truly coexist.
Like a bard.

Because friends and family expected me to be wondering *What's next?* at this stage, they asked. I didn't know what to tell them. I was less enamored of the question than ever. I told one friend, Well, watching the moose that's been sitting on the hill for two days. One person's ordinary was another person's extraordinary. I was vague: We like it here. We like this valley. Maybe we'll stay a while and then leave and maybe we'll come back.

The mundane presented itself everywhere.

You think you are better than the mundane? The Land asked me.

Well, think again.

Sometimes whole days could be spent taking simple care. Harvest kale and find a dead gray bird wrapped in netting. Sorry, little bird: untangle its stiff body to rest it under a tree. Go to town to teach a writing class for girls. Leave Bru behind alone when I go because Chris has driven north to buy wood. Speed home to discover that our dog's separation anxiety is still an issue. Find him cowering in the corner of the cabin, floors splattered with diarrhea and vomit, expelled and then walked through and tromped around. Cradle his head to my chest and rub his snout and let him out. Watch him roll around in the grass. Wonder why he ripped wood from the front door. Realize he was desperate to get out. Realize I had left him too long. Pull rags from under the sink. Mop up putrid sludge and dig it out from between wood planks with a fork and then a paperclip. Disinfect every nook. Move like a person called to a vocation. Understand that something about this is holy, because what could possibly be more important than tending to the emotional lives of girls, the death of a small gray bird, and the well-being of the creature I love?

I wanted to believe that nothing was.

But if The Land and I were lovers, we might have tired of each other by now, given the popular modern narrative that exists about longevity of any kind. Oh, your wavy hair has gray flecks in it. Your giggle actually sounds devilish. The way you touch me, please do it differently. Can you get real, do you really love me, what does love even mean to you? The shiny gauze of new love always fell from your eyes when least expected. But after a decade with Chris, I knew some of the world beneath the gauze—one of sudden texture, narrowing and widening cobblestone streets, underwater dives to murky places that turned iridescent, and spins that left a person metamorphosed. The one faulty piece in the analogy is that land, unlike a human lover, exposes itself upon first glance. It has no secrets. It does not try to impress. It offers only balm and mirrors. Right away. My concern was not with the cottonwoods or our tidal wave hill. They would never disappoint me. What would was my own expectation of what life could look like here, even if I left from time to time. This landscape was one of absences. You wondered, Wait, is there more, is there more than carrying wood, carrying water, and watching trees shudder in the wind? Absence was palpable here. Maybe that was the point. Because, though I was not even remotely cut out to be a Buddhist, I had long ago memorized what Lao Tzu wrote, "When you realize nothing is lacking, the whole world belongs to you."

I knew The Land had more to tell me.

There were no simple answers.

Open your ears.

↓

On our way up to the yurt, as the mid-August sun softened to yellow for evening, we noticed a wide swatch of churned-up soil near the path.

The elk, I said.

Yep, agreed Chris.

I scuffed the ground with my sandal. Overcome with smells, Bru ran all over it like a possessed dog. Probably shelter from lightning storms. This would be a nice place to sleep at night, as a group, under the firs.

That's some serious erosion, I said because the hillside now looked like it could spill out from beneath us.

Elk don't care about erosion, Chris teased.

Of course they didn't. It was the same herd I had chased in April. They knew about the balance of run and ease. Where had they gone now? I hoped to see them up top in the field. But when we stood on tiptoes on the porch, even when Chris hopped onto a fence post to look, they were gone—somewhere else.

The next morning, Chris shook me awake.

What time is it? I grumbled at a man who rarely, if ever, was up before me.

It's 6.45. Come look out the window.

I sat up as he curled my hand around binoculars. Brown. Brown blobs. I stepped to the window with Chris, our heads pressed together. The whole elk herd was cresting the hill, munching on grass, mothers and tawny newborns, two bulls, one only a few feet away from us. Behind them, at this early hour, a stack of mountains cut open the sky. I didn't think to watch Bru's reaction, but surely his nose was glued to the canvas wall. Everything was a map to me now—even this, the voluntary arrival of the elk I had once run at in eager desperation. Could they see us? No. But I could see long lashes and bedroom eyes. I could see embodiment. The most mundane of the mundane of the divine. It looked so simple, so easy: eat this, live here, reproduce yourself, no other options.

8

A RUNNING CHAPTER

August 2010

As grains of darkness collected in the sky, as summer moved toward its strung-out end, as sagebrush twisted off into my hand, the juvenile owl grew up. In the sepia tone of early morning, she sat dignified on our woodpile. From the vinyl window, I pulled sheets around my neck and watched her silhouette watch the sunrise. Small birds circled around her, moved in and then away from her pointed ears, as if to make contact. But she remained unaffected. No longer screeching for food, at least from what we could hear, she focused on potential mice in the field. Her chest swelled forward, separate but in full relatedness to everything around.

She now inhabited her body.

It hadn't taken her long to know herself.

My parents had casually mentioned that times were tough, and knowing they could sell The Land if they had to, well, that helped. It wasn't definite and I wasn't surprised but it was a statement loud enough to prod at me, even on those silent mornings of watching the owl. What if they sold The Land? I had to dismantle the structure in order to see it anew. The parts, now isolated, would wait to be arranged in a new formation. Only then could I begin to categorize what I did know in order to know what I didn't know yet. The thing behind my ribcage had been quiet for a while—fewer shrieks, fewer but, but, but moments. But it was time to get real with myself. Again. Sure, I could be a bard. I could create a dynamic life of homeplace Montana and to-and-fro's elsewhere, often. But none of that was reliable. It was as unreliable as the wind. I wanted to feel connected to my own self, not to a new image I propped up of myself. To go from the placeless one to the bard wasn't that great a leap. We all had to live somewhere. I had to make a home. But I didn't want to keep running from that empty space within.

This place, it had become apparent, was a bird place—those that left for the winter and those that did not. Regardless, they all gathered this time of year, as grass crisped dry enough to snap with footfalls. They flocked to trees and chatted. Tiny birds. Magpies. Cranes. I liked the company. Birds knew to gorge on the ripening hawthorns, rose hips, and serviceberries now. Birds knew how to land. Birds also knew how to fly.

In the compressed heat of midday, I had tied the door open to a warm breeze. Whole flocks of sparrows had swooped in and out like unexpected gusts of wind, the whoosh of many small wings set at the same angle to make the sudden turn back out to the world of trees and sky. Writing at my desk, I usually heard them before seeing them. But one bird had just broken rank. Alone, it perched inside by the window and flicked its head back and forth.

Hey, I said.

That did not calm it down. The first small white shit landed on our cutting board. I sat still and debated trying to grab the

bird with a shirt or bag to then release it, techniques success-
fully employed in other places at other times. It would have to
fly past me to get out the door. There was no denying that I was
terrifying to it. I didn't want it to wedge itself accidentally in
the *khana* and make that awful, fluttering, I'm-trapped, straight-
jacket sound that birds stuck in a chimney make. Don't bang
yourself around trying to find the light. It would know what to
do; I just needed to guide it. I slunk to the floor, crawled over
to the other two windows, reached up to undo the Velcro on
the shades, and crept outside. My next move would have to be
less stealthy. I flipped the rope with a whack to pull the canvas
cover over our *tono*. Now, with the exception of the bird's current window and the open door, the yurt was a cave. Sometimes
you have to eliminate all possibilities so that only one brilliant
door is open.

I sat back against the yurt, let the sun warm my face, and
waited.

A few minutes later, the bird zoomed out like a torpedo.

It had found its way back into the familiar—trees, flock, air.
I got up and walked over to the medicine wheel with my cell
phone and a blanket. No Bru today. He and Chris had continued to make a point of man hikes. Strange to be utterly alone
and to feel blood shifting within me because nothing, hello,
was ever static.

Burrs and grass prickled the back of my legs. Blanket down.
From here, our new shiny solar panel looked like an extrater-
restrial object hiding out behind the yurt. My grandfather had
gifted it to us because the engineer in him wanted to start us out
on our married life with something practical. With sun gleaming down on it, the panel drew energy down into its cord and

under the yurt canvas into a battery that dispersed the sun for our use. What it brought to us was limitless charge on my computer, small light bulbs instead of kerosene lamps, music, and the subtle chuff sound of *power on*. Hearing the first mechanical noise in the yurt had taken adjustment on my end. I had to mourn the loss of utter silence. But soon, I was dancing on the porch, stomping my feet, and thrashing my head around. I practiced my handstand and fell over and then held it and felt like a girl all over again. No one could hear our music. By the time it reached the road below, it would be an echo mixed with wind and tree branches and clouds. Remoteness. Didn't everyone want remoteness and then sound to explode the remoteness into small shards and then quiet to glue the remoteness back together?

Some people escape sound for quiet; some people do the opposite.

I dialed Katinka's number. She had just bought an apartment in New York.

Molls? she answered.

It works, I said, I'm calling from the medicine wheel, didn't know whether I'd get reception. How are you? How's the new pad?

We're getting settled, she explained, and told me about buying furniture for all the nooks, about the shared rooftop patio and its view of the East River, about how good it felt to create a home that wouldn't have to be reconsidered every lease cycle. It, of course, came with some loss because to make any choice involves the loss of some other choice you could have made. She could have been here. I could have been there. She was sad not to live in the country or have her own herb garden, but that's why she could ask people like me to harvest some wild bee balm for her. Her life had knit itself around the city and, in that, she found comfort and community. We talked it out—laughing at how stubborn we, and most of our friends, had been about limiting our options. At. All.

So, how are *you* feeling about Montana? she asked.

I didn't answer right away. I picked at a stem of yarrow, rubbed its soft leaves, and brought the scent to my nose.

Well, I started, remember that time in Santa Fe when you took me to that run-down park to show me some meditation techniques, some breathing?

Yeah.

That was almost ten years ago, I said. Do you remember what happened? You asked me to close my eyes and take in a deep, long breath. It was probably the first time I had ever done that because gloppy tears started running down my cheeks. I couldn't stop crying. With that one breath.

I do remember.

That place, I explained, that place inside me, that's the place I want to know well, instead of deciding that this place or some other place or a set of places is going to soothe me.

But, she said, you're already good at being internal.

Um, not in a serene way, I laughed. I just see all of us—okay, not all, but most of us, and I'm the worst—grabbing for the perfect what, where, who, and elsewhere, away from ourselves. And then, once we have them, we crave a better version of them, like lunatics. Those are all external; those things don't last, you know?

I know.

I know I'm sounding all blah-blah.

Eating this raw cheese right now is enough, she mumbled with a full mouth.

Well, there you go, I laughed.

Don't you think that it's human nature to want something better? she asked.

Sure, I said, but it's exacerbated by modern life. For our grandparents, or even our parents, there wasn't this rampant Internet info out there about the 5,842 lives you can live and oh man, which one will you choose, and then what will that say about you.

True.

All I'm saying, I continued, staring into the dense firs ahead of me, is that the incessant search for those things hasn't produced a content person out of me, or other people I know. It's an epidemic and I'm not sure I want to be part of it anymore.

I can see that, she answered, but what's the real alternative?

I don't know, I said.

When the package arrived from Barcelona, I smelled it. Wrapped in twine and covered in blue and yellow stamps, its tattered overseas appearance made me giddy. It was our wedding gift from my mother's childhood friend Jo Ann. She had left Wisconsin as a young woman and made a life as an expat in Spain.

I waited to open it at lunchtime, when Chris would step out from the cool shade of the shop into the hot blinking day.

Guess what came today?

More pans for the kitchen we don't have, he said, smiling.

No, I sighed, punching his arm, a package. From Spain.

He took one look, touched it, and then made a suggestion.

Let's open it at the yurt, later, after the work day.

You. Are. Killing me, I said, because I had no willpower to wait.

But in the slow buttery light of evening, sitting on our bed in the yurt, we finally pulled two frames from the crinkled paper. He unwrapped one. I, the other.

Lithographs.

I ran my fingers over them, looking from one watercolor to the next—one gray, the other salmon pink. They were the same print of a human torso, from chest to butt, bent in a sensual posture of movement. Like trees.

It's your favorite gift, isn't it? Chris asked.

Mm hm.

We hung them from the *khana* with fishing line and debated on which one each of us preferred. His hand on my knee; my hand on his knee. It occurred to me that I had not torn open this package from a foreign place and immediately wanted to get on a plane and go there, or elsewhere. I had not worried about where I wasn't, or what I wasn't. Instead, on the wall of our yurt, two images of a body reminded me of my own body.

It was the start of another map.

If you want to belong, abandon the ideas. Do as the animals do. Go to the body.

One thing I knew how to do as a girl was run. Usually the fastest in my class, I leapt over concrete walls and down boulevards and across soccer fields with surety in my limbs. But after our move to America, as my double digits increased, the acute awareness of my particular body hit me: brown hair, blue eyes, pale skin, and freckles. I started to wonder whether I liked those attributes. Then puberty hit and breasts grew and self-consciousness changed the way I moved, the way I ran. Like everyone, I was herded into the sea of comparison, where we washed out and in with the tide, unsure of our placement, rubbed so raw by saltwater we fell away from our true selves. We all have a shell. Most of us find problems with it.

I had lost my run.

Now I wanted it back.

Any of my friends would have told me that I still had it with the bike races and triathlons and hiking, and hell, you chased those elk, but they didn't know. My frame wasn't slender. Over a distance, I jogged with heavy flat feet, not flying over ground through the woods like a nymph.

I laced up my sneakers on the cabin's porch. Bru circled me and nudged his wet nose repeatedly against my arm.

Where you two going? Chris asked, opening the screen door.

On a run.

Nice.

Yeah, screw the flat-footed theory, I said. That just can't be true. You know, there are places on the hill I haven't even been.

He sat down next to me and wrapped an arm around my shoulder.

No bear spray? he asked.

Nope.

Hey, he said, leaning into me with a look I'd seen before, that's a new Molly.

Well, get used to her, I said, and stood up to go.

Bru and I bounced away toward the hill. Here, 8,000 miles

away from where I was born and three decades closer to the setting sun, I would run again. The early steep climb never got easier, and it never would, not for me, not for Chris, not for anyone—it was something about the angle. Stamping my way up, I wanted to make ritual surrounded by the smell of green. This path had been, and was, the constant real up-and-down of life. Just pay attention. Halfway up, panting and red-faced and admittedly less glory bound than I had hoped to feel, I branched east off our packed-down trail, across the hill, on a more flat path through the animal corridor of thick firs. Bru had followed habit and dashed right up our worn path. He turned to check in.

This way! I hollered.

He leapt back down to me, surging through the air like a squirrel, and we continued, kicking up sticks and soil and fir needles. It was good to move only with the purpose of moving. Sun filtered through trees and dappled the ground. Nettles drooped green leaves, resigned to the end of a season. Dust collected in my socks. In places, the soil had morphed into a dark brown frothy mess because the elk had hoofed around back here too. They had traveled far to get here and traveled far again to get back high into the mountains.

I found my footing. I wanted my feet to touch every inch of The Land, not to claim it, but to make contact with this particular earth. We could map the world in footfalls.

At a wall of hawthorns, I ducked and crawled up to another animal trail. Thistles scratched at me. Thin lines of blood on my thighs. Battle wounds. My flushed face pleased me, as did repetition paired with movement. It was movement and movement meant possibility and possibility, turns out, meant relief. For our final ascent, at a vertical bank, Bru tumbled backward once and dashed away to find a better approach. But I made a choice. Grabbing handfuls of grass, I leaned in and yanked myself up. Crested hill. Because my legs weren't slogging uphill, I was finally flying. The flat grassland felt like a downhill. Bru emerged near the yurt and I sprinted at him, careful not to twist an ankle on the sponge grass. I clomped onto the porch and bent over. Blood rushed. Lungs pounded. Legs itched. Fresh air burned the edges of my throat in a way that made me think *Yes yes yes*, this is life, this is exchange.

My sweat dried quickly.

I pulled my shirt over my head and collapsed on the cedar planks. Nothing like a straw hat over my face and the sun warming it and me. My mind fell into dreams of southern India, a place I had never been, and tree fronds and fuchsia flowers and tea fields and people and the complex history of nationhood. Cedar smells roused me, a cheek now compressed, and there, underneath my hat, Bru had become my tiger. Paws hung over the porch's edge, he sat erect with a long strong tail that swooped up.

You, I said.

He glanced at me.

He was fully contained, like the owl. Not at all concerned with bettering himself. I pushed up to sit and scoot back to the warm canvas walls. I started to pluck at the taught ropes strapped across our yurt. They made such great sounds. They would be encased in ice again, for months, though it was impossible to believe so on a summer day like today.

This yurt was also contained. I reached for my innards, for the space between my front and my back. In high school, a Muslim friend had told me that she felt embraced, literally held, by her culture and religion. An Episcopalian friend had said the same thing. A Jewish friend had said the same thing. I could go on and on. I'd heard others say so about hometowns or even partners. It made sense. But that whole prospect continued to make me nervous. It could all *poof* disappear one day, and then what? What were you left with but an empty framework of yourself? Chris always insisted that we had to blow our own minds, couldn't rely on anyone else to do it for us, not even each other. And he was right.

The woman who ran didn't know how to contain herself yet. I got up and started back downstairs, but stopped off the porch with the sun behind me to make shadow shapes on the white canvas: warrior, antelope, crocodile, V-shape, hands on hips. Bru meandered down our narrow path through the electric white grass. I followed and, on my way down, touched everything, spoke to it, asked about its ability to contain itself. Only humans lose our essence and then spend a lifetime trying to find it again.

It was in me somewhere, somewhere, some where.

I ran into September, into coldness. I needed to run out the questions, and if that meant circling back on myself a thousand times, then that's what it meant. Snow dusted the mountains blue. We stoked fires in our woodstove again. Some mornings, I ran through the wet slap of alfalfa, grown back up for second cutting, and waterlogged my sneakers. The wild grass wasn't much easier. It grabbed at me so that I lifted my feet high high high like a dressage horse until I got to the rocky area of the juniper tree and then back up, calling Bru back from chasing mice, unzipping my vest and realizing that, suddenly, I was hot. I needed to get up earlier. I needed to move this way everyday.

My feet didn't have any answers for me. They knew how to get me from point A to point B, and that had been valuable and would continue to be. But they were also the farthest body part from my center—grounding, for sure, but not the *it* of the it.

Running took me under fir trees, where we had weeded the hill so long ago, where I now stared up into the splay of evergreen branches and palmed the bark. An old friend once said to me, When you stand under a tree, you know who you are. I wanted to believe it was so easy. *How* do you know yourself? I actually needed some concrete understanding of that. The willow in Spain had been my first exposure to a tree in my backyard. Like the willow, the yurt sheltered me. Both were covered dens with an opening to the sky. The same shape.

I had no name for the shape until someone gave it to me.

In yoga, late afternoon light faded away from the windows. My practice had actually become a practice. I attended four times a week and lifted my toes like a serious devotee in order to strengthen or, let's face it, create my nonexistent arch. Other than to teach an occasional writing class, it was my only venture into town twenty minutes away, so grocery and library runs bookended my trips.

Anna asked us to close our eyes.

I want you to each imagine a dome, she said.

A what? someone asked.

A dome, she repeated.

Let it fill the space of your torso; build it within your ribcage, she said. Use it as a space to greet yourself.

It's good that our eyes were closed. I wanted to burst out with, Stop it, just stop it right now. It was my go-to line, often laughed, anytime something resonated and hit me so hard with its truth I could do nothing but wave these words at it to ward it off. Because, when you've spent your whole life trying to figure out what you belong to and someone tells you to go ahead and make a dome inside yourself, you either run for the door or clasp your hands together. There's no in-between reaction.

I stayed.

But after class, I drove straight to the highway. The ramp greeted me: *Hey, stranger, where you off to, stranger?* Nothing felt urgent as my wheels eased between a faraway truck and a faraway sedan. I wasn't leaning forward on my seatbelt. I wasn't trying to conjure up a feeling. I simply needed to make an introduction.

Highway, meet Dome, I said, first pointing across the valley to the yurt no one could see from here. It had taken me until now to recognize that we had built a dome and slumbered in a dome and watched the stars light up from our dome. So many domes. The trees—willow from Spain, firs, cottonwoods. But those weren't *the* dome. Abstract as it was to me then, I really wanted the highway to know that there was a dome within me, within every person. See, it's there. It's here. I wanted to know it. None of my hammer skills were going to help me create that dome. It would take longer than three months. It might never be finished. But, shit, it needed to start now.

Leaves began to turn yellow. It was a true autumn—no early freeze like last year—and the valley would soon light up with golden paths marked by aspens and cottonwoods grown along rivers and creeks. Diane called to tell us that this, yes, this, was a more common seasonal pattern. As the world around me turned to letting go, I secretly read about domes. Meanwhile, Chris was formulating other plans.

When he snuck up on me with a grin before dinner, I said, Okay, okay, with a fist full of silverware. The thought of building an external structure made his usual slow sentences almost tumble over each other. But I wanted to be assured that our lives wouldn't be overtaken by another project. In fairness, we had talked together about adding a timber frame shed next to the yurt—woodshed in winter and shade area in summer. I had suggested that we could plant a xeriscape garden to connect them: my way of unspooling the thing in our minds that allows us to believe something is possible, even when the likelihood is small. So don't let the claws come out, Molly.

He was ready to get going.

What about the wood? Won't that be expensive? I asked.

Yeah, but we can get it from the hill.

You mean chop trees down.

Yeah.

He must have noticed a look in my eyes.

We'll only take standing dead trees, he said, and it won't be hard and it won't take me away from building my business and yes, it will take a little longer than if we bought wood but, it'll be free and no, I won't kill myself.

It was hard to resist his enthusiasm, the way his body bounced a little in the telling, and so I stuck to facts.

Do you *know* how to cut down trees? I asked.

Yeah, mostly, and Mike can show me the rest.

His brother Mike had returned from Turkey and was on his way to Montana, a place he thought might offer him some stability. After so much relocation and dislocation, he was eager to settle in and build something physical with his hands in one place with one purpose. He wanted to help us. Have at it, I would tell him when he arrived. We actually, by some ridiculous stroke of thinking, had the tool for the job. For some reason, I had agreed that we should spend almost all of our wedding money on a large chainsaw that, to me, was loud and dangerous. It also had a mill on it, and this, I was told, made four-sided beams from trees. We had debated between that or a medicine cabinet of essential oils that would last ten years. The tool won out.

So once you fell the trees, how do you get them up the hill?

We'll use the winch, he said, shrugging the shrug that usually meant he wasn't completely confident about what he was saying.

Are you serious?

Trust me, he said, we'll cut the logs and notch them below. They won't be as heavy as you think.

The winch was our latest addition to yurt life. Chris had put it together. Somehow, with 400 feet of reeled steel cable lodged in the ground up top and connected to a wooden cart on wheels below, we could now winch up our firewood. Even that had been precarious. If the winch snapped, the person cranking it risked a death slap from the wire. Already the winch had given once, suddenly, and sent the cart crashing all the way through the firs down to the bottom, releasing the smell of mint and holy shit from the understory. When it worked, we could relocate almost one hundred logs in one go, what would have taken me over ten trips with the pack board. If Chris thought we could haul big timbers on it, I needed to trust him.

Okay, I'm in, I said, but let me lie down and think for a second.

Face down, I inhaled the smell of grass and wind. My pep for building physical structures had waned after the yurt. I didn't want to waste my life away sawing into wood; *waste* was my perspective, because the process didn't invigorate me as it did Chris. I wanted to build internal structures now. But life involved more than internal structures. We needed a shed and someone had to build it.

Back in the yurt, Chris had stacked dishes and swept.

Okay, I said, grabbing his hand, I really am in, but I don't want to be responsible for it.

As if I had ever been responsible for any of these projects.

No problem, he said, squeezing my hand back.

I'll help put the frame together, I added.

Great.

And winch it up.

Got it.

Just no felling trees for me.

No problem. Mike and I can do that. We probably won't start until October.

When we made agreements that felt good to both of us, I snuggled closer to Chris, and he to me. As he twitched to sleep, my eyes followed the edge of our *tono*. When we name a thing, it becomes alive. The word *dome* had come into my consciousness and stuck there. Now the history kept me awake. Many thought the Persians were the first to abandon square corners to build domes, though it seems that every early culture incorporated the structure into their lives. The dome was made of the strongest architectural feature—an arch. It would hold up anything. Bricks. Mortar. Dreams. Visions. Grief. Early people must have known this, for whether in Rome, the Ottoman Empire, South Asia, China, Russia, the Americas, or all over the Middle East, the dome held space, often for transition rituals. Some were ancestral homes for the dead. But as early as the late

Stone Age, the dome also had celestial significance. You could see it. Everywhere. Not only in a modern observatory. People climbed each other's backs to paint stars on the walls. People prayed there. Some domes were opulent. Others were made of sticks or ice blocks. Domes were places of prayer, places of royalty, and also places of everyday humble living. They still were.

A dome didn't have an attitude. It could exist anywhere. And maybe early peoples gravitated to the dome shape because it already existed within them.

While Chris planned his cutting down of trees, I peeked under almost every tree for ideas. My dome would be made of pale orange stucco flecked with mica. Past the open-air windows, desert plants grew, and past them, ether and white pulsing light available for everyone, all of us. There was no white picket fence here. This was a matured version of home. I could draw this light down from the top of my dome and into the minute crevices of my spine. No one could destroy my dome. No one could set fire to it or smash it or change it. It was the only for-sure thing.

As fall unwound and I wrote and taught adult writing classes and worked my lungs, my runs became easier. I didn't fly across the landscape, per se, but some kink had undone itself and there were actual moments of feeling graceful. Bru would bound ahead as we lapped the field. Afterward, when we paused in the grass on the hill's edge to sit and catch our breath, when dead vegetation poked through my stretch pants, I would take in the valley—ground bushes turned reddish orange, the yellowing of trees, the brown descent into a new season.

One day, though, my eyes stuck with the dark firs stretched along the hillside, offering cover for wildlife traveling from the mountains, for me. No one could see me up here. No one but the tall fir just there.

Come climb me.

What?

Come climb me.

What if I fall?

You might.

I can't believe you are talking to me.

Believe it.

Fine.

I slid down brambles to reach the tree's base. Sorry, Bru, you can't follow me up here. He leapt up, paws on the trunk, to watch me ascend. Branches fanned out evenly all the way up. I hadn't climbed a tree since when, when, when. My hands gripped rough bark and sap, sticky sap, the smell of pitch and a break through small branches with my head. Sticks fell into my eyes. Was that the sound of my breath or my lack of breath? Trees of my youth spoke to me—the willow, great protector, the gnarled *barranca* trees, the waxy magnolia leaves, the oaks dripping with moss. I hadn't ever felt the blood in my body match the sap flowing up and down the tree, rooting it down and rising it up. Roots held the tree up, yes, but the inside, cells drawn from other trees, from faraway trees, from forests combed by humans and from forests no one would ever see—that made it grow into its destined shape and then fortune allowed it to tweak that shape. The tweak was necessary. Bloodlines teach us how to stand. Later, we have to teach ourselves how to keep standing.

So often that involves amending the *how*.

Scamper up, up, up, the only direction anyone wants to go. Until I glanced down to Bru's small head.

The branch beneath my foot snapped. I pressed myself against the trunk, hands clutching branches as my leg dangled. But when another branch took the burden of my weight, the view opened before me. Crows flew by. The tree was the tallest point for miles, for the whole valley swept across and up to the Bridger Mountains. I breathed as the tree breathed. John Muir once wrote about being in a tree during a storm. If you stuck with the movement, you were fine and not flung. When we slept in the yurt, when wind ripped through the firs, when their boughs slapped the wind back, was this its utterance of selfhood?

No one ever wants to climb down.

It shouldn't even be called climbing down. Dropping down is more accurate. The surge of upward peters out to a calculated downward. You let gravity pull at you and hope for the best. I moved like an insect, carefully and at all right angles.

At the bottom, Bru sniffed me with urgency as if to ask where I had gone and what I had brought back. We crawled back up to our sitting spot. In the sagebrush, I picked bits of sap from my hands and turned back to greet the great fir from the ground now. It knew how to hold itself.

You are the climbing tree, I said.

And you are the climbing woman.

What's next was accentuated for me by autumn—always. I had an affection for the end of September in any place because it brought those first few glorious weeks of new places, new schools, new jobs, new starts. Even though nature moved toward hibernation. Black bears had begun to topple trashcans in our neighborhood. Diane called with updates: Saw a bear this afternoon; might be headed to your place. We winched more firewood up the hill. I weeded large thistles from the garden. And I still didn't care about what's next. Not really. Not in a palpable way.

As cold settled over the valley, my running turned to walking. I just couldn't muster the same get-up-and-run in the cold. If we had let the fire go out at night, the chilled air seeped into every pore of the yurt. Bru would shake his collar to wake up.

On my first dawn walk, the pink glow spread up and over the backsides of mountains. Birds chattered outside. Crows sat on fence posts in the soft light. Magpies flicked their black and white feathers. There could be new here. New need not mean *I am relocating to* x *place tomorrow*. My impulse took me to the climbing tree, where I did not climb but instead curled up like a deer on sponge grass to feel a living floor beneath me.

It was here that I closed my eyes and entered the dome.

When I felt like saying, Get over yourself, the dome encouraged compassion.

You can feel like the only person on earth at dawn: arise, begin, start over, wake up again, know possibility. I had never been one for sunsets. They could weigh on me like a wet wool blanket. The end. But dawn was something I could catch in my hands. On my way back, I usually wondered if Marcie and Brooks were awake across the fields in the green house. She rose early to tend her last flowers for the farmer's market. Earlier that spring, she had invited me to come over "between sets of hail" for a tour. As we padded through rows, as she named varieties, she announced, I don't do wimps.

Wimps did not survive here, apparently.

I thought about what that meant.

I was both a wimp and a non-wimp.

To learn kindness toward myself was new—so new to me, and most of us, it could be called brand-new territory.

We ended up at a party up the canyon. I moved away from the shiny pig roasting in a pit and ate crackers and strawberries from who knows where. Though most people in Montana prided themselves on meat, even brought their own game to cookouts, the vegetarian in me was still wary of animal flesh. I had tried Brooks's elk jerky. But soft flesh was a whole other prospect. Chris locked into conversation with another man. I mingled around the yard and introduced myself to new faces. Dogs ran amuck. Horses in corrals nearby stood quietly. I swapped story, as you do, with each person. How had people gotten here, why had they gotten here, and what did they think? Most were about our age, late twenties to mid-thirties. I heard myself explain the yurt, laugh about the process, talk about New York, and then say, Oh, all over, when people asked about the where of my childhood.

One younger woman and I stood together by the drinks for a while. I could tell by the tightness of her face that she tended toward privacy. But her dam had started to crumble. She oozed sadness. She had moved here from her small hometown in the Southeast a few years ago. Had odd jobs. Now she felt neither here nor there.

What's your gut? I asked.

I don't know who I am here, she said, but if I go back, then I'm a failure.

She sipped on her beer and I toed the ground, trying to come up with something helpful to say or ask.

So, where do you feel most alive? I asked.

I don't know, she answered, blinking back at me.

Her boyfriend walked over and the conversation veered in another direction. I made my way over to the fence with her words. They were strong, familiar words. Failure. Had she been a close friend, I might have tapped her chest and asked about *that* place, told her how knowing that that place existed, even if I didn't know it well, brought me relief. But she was all sagging shoulders. All forlorn. All in the middle of it.

I followed the fence back to our Jeep, leaned against metal doors warmed by sun, and watched. What I saw was a group of walking narratives—all of us, mostly strangers to one another, weaving in and out, crunching on chips and salsa, nodding, expressing, and assuming postures that supported our narratives. It helped us categorize each other. It helped us categorize ourselves. I am an ocean person. You are a desert rat. She is a city dweller. And who could blame me, or any of us humans?

We were bred to be storytellers.

But maybe all we really wanted, every last one of us, was to be loved.

Eventually, the crowd slipped down across the dirt road to another house and we followed. The owner of the house approached me as I looked out a window at the same coppery creek that ran by our place. She had a twinkle in her eyes, this older woman. She seemed to have harnessed some calm I never saw in myself or my peers. Her parents had once been newcomers, she told me, one of the first to settle permanently in the canyon.

Whoa, I said.

Everyone has to be a newcomer sometime, she said.

How 'bout you, she asked. Where do you live?

Oh, in a yurt down the road.

Oh, yeah, she said, where?

I told her.

Ooooo, she said, so *you* are the ones who bought that beautiful piece of land.

No, no, I corrected, not us. My parents bought it.

We're squatting, Chris added from behind me.

Nothing wrong with squatting, she laughed.

But I don't see a yurt there, her husband jumped in.

Oh, it's up on the hill, I explained. You can't see it from the road, but it's right behind the firs, about a five-minute walk up.

So, he said, shaking his head, you mean I would have to walk up that hill to see your yurt?

Yep, I laughed.

Well, I'll bring my horse then.

He wasn't kidding either. When he left the room, she reached for my forearm and stared into my eyes.

We, all of us around here, were wondering who was gonna buy that place. It's the prettiest piece around here. Your parents aren't going to develop it, are they?

Not that I know of, I assured her.

Ah, she sighed, thank you, thank you.

I didn't know when I would see her again, or if. The crowd picked us up and swept us out the door, and when I turned to wave goodbye, she cupped both her hands and blew me a kiss.

↓

Anticipating the long rest of winter forces us to say goodbye to so much. I plucked dead stalks of chard from the garden. I picked dark purple berry after berry from the hawthorn bushes near the yurt. Birds dove down to do the same. Heyoooooo, I called out with each turn. Rose hips tasted of apple, fleshy and fresh. I liked that I could know about them. One weekend, sitting on the yurt floor, organizing my books and papers, I told Chris about the young woman at the party.

Well, strangers always tell you their life story, he said.

Not really, beb.

Yeah, really.

But she was paralyzed by the decision to go or stay, could barely hold herself up, it seemed, and that is just so common these days, you know?

I know, he said.

But you don't struggle with that.

No, I struggle with other things.

True, I said, kicking at his legs.

It's the price of options, Chris suggested. Because if staying in a nine-to-five geology job at a computer had been my only option, I would have found a way to make it work, in some random state like Pennsylvania, and might have even been happier because of that simplicity.

Do you really think that could have happened?

It could have, he insisted.

I. Don't. Know.

It could have.

Okay, here's a more concrete list, I said, and handed it to him.

1. Goat manure to supplement garden beds.

2. Plant bulbs.

3. Don't let Bru out at night: wolves.

4. Someone nearby to plow us out in winter for a rate that won't break us.

Good list, he said, matter-of-factly.

We fell into silence for a while, as he sat at my desk, sketched furniture designs, and punched numbers into his calculator. I had spread all my papers out across our dark wood floor, now waxed because the bare feet of summer did not enjoy splinters. When organization mode hit me, when deep clean happened, it all came out: essay drafts, bills, lists, receipts, old notes that didn't need to be kept.

Chris snapped his notebook shut and stood up.

Gotta go down to the shop to test an idea, he said, stepping into his boots, but I'll be back up in a few hours. You can keep Bru.

No, you take him, I said, but come here first.

I pulled his head down and brought his forehead to mine.

When he left, I stoked the fire and settled back down to my cross-legged position on the floor. I made piles. I shuffled papers. I wrote new lists. I unfolded a receipt for my wedding dress. Oh, how resistant I had been to the whole concept to begin with, what a trial it could have been, given my history with dress-up and dresses.

On one of our visits to America, I must be nine and we are at a party with my mom's Chicago family. My dress has a bow that ties in the back and big puffy sleeves. But my cousin Lauren, who is younger than me, prances around in a strapless purple dress. I retreat through the crowd of tall adults to find my dad. On a couch in the corner, I sit on his knee and tell him that I don't feel pretty enough or good enough. He whispers in my ear and assures me that I am. It feels like we are conspirators because somehow I sense that he always feels inadequate when we are here too. Or maybe it's how anyone feels everywhere. Lauren is dancing and flashing a movie star smile for a pod of clapping adults. Later, she'll tell me that that was her way of making herself feel good enough. My dad is into trying new activities every time we move, and it will continue until I am an adult: the wetsuit hung over our rattan chair in Australia, the running sneakers in the Dominican Republic, the full horseback-riding outfit plus leather crop in Mexico, the lease of a 300zx sports car in Texas. And did he even try to take up golf in Florida? Did he actually depart from blazers and buy a corduroy jacket when his new job involved land conservation?

I will grow up watching him try to remake himself into a shape that pleases him with each new place. His excitement is infectious—it bubbles over, and my brothers and I like to splash around in it. But it never really works. He always ends up disappointed with himself. When you move all the time, you never have to face yourself. He can rarely sit with one place, or one situation, because he is incapable of sitting with himself. It isn't the same with my Mom. She wavers, sure, but maybe she has a core that my dad, the global traveler, doesn't.

He is convinced that, in each new place, he can finally be the man he wants to be.

I will grow into a woman convinced of the same thing.

If you are convinced of that, you depend on the act of going.

Or you choose not to.

I shook myself from the daydream and stared up at our *tono*. Thank you, yurt; thank you, trees; thank you, owl.

↓

Winter was on its way. In mid-October, the grass outside our yurt sparkled blue with frost, but there was no snow like the first snow last year that slowed our yurt process. I grabbed Chris's hand and we stepped further into a blue-gray world.

Lie down with me, I said when we reached the sponge grass.

I did not want to charge the moment by turning to love on him, or have him love on me, no. He hadn't rested here for longer than a minute and I thought he should know about it.

This is more comfortable than our futon, he said, arms flung out wide.

We are growing up, I said.

Mmmm.

Below, somewhere, Diane had found a ten-thousand-year-old flesher on the creek bank. Above, here, a few generations back, a woman descended from one of the early families of this area, and this land, had asked for her ashes to be spread here and they had been. Maybe homeplace is wherever you end up when you are adult enough not to overcontemplate, when you've been there long enough that memory embeds and you let go of the other lives you had once imagined.

When do you think we'll ask ourselves what's next? I asked.

You never stopped asking yourself, Molly, he laughed, propping himself up on an elbow. That question will always be part of you. It's not a bad thing. It's constitutional for you.

I didn't sit up.

For once, I was the quiet one.

Body deep in grass, I could not see mountains or roads when my head turned. Chris squeezed my leg and wandered off to share twilight with the four mules at the fence. I could hear him mumbling to them far away. He had told me that part of the phrase *Getting there* was that you never actually got to the *there*. There was no rush. You ambled and watched the scenery move past you.

And this, on a cold night, is where a person slips, slips in the horizontal sense, so that all the beings within her, within every-one, make themselves known. I became a deer bedded down, a canoe floating down a calm river. I am my great-grandfather pushing his spectacles back. I am a daughter living in a dusty mining camp. I am a man who kisses a woman. I am a woman who kisses a woman. I am a woman who falls off a ship and becomes a castaway on an island. I am a boy full of sorrow in a ditch full of trash. I am the dead owl Chris will find on a dirt road and move under a tree in ceremony. I am the canoe again, moving fast, but the river never changes, and maybe neither do I. I am all these things and they are me, and we, well, we are here. I know this only because for one second, I am also con-tained, because for one second, I am me.

The fast thuds of a run, ground vibrations, and then hot breath over my face. Bru was strafing me. He jumped from side to side, leaned over, and let his black jowls hang low and close. Get up. Come with us. South of us, the headlights of two cars snaked down a mountain and we wondered why, where, who. Our yurt breathed like a living thing in the distance. We walked back to the orange glint.

These had become normal days.

But we can't be a canoe floating down a calm river all the time. On a few nights, while Chris slept unknowing, I stood naked and cold on the porch like a gorilla woman and wept into the low clouds. It was a combination of relief that never feeling like enough was the central issue, and sorrow that never feeling like enough was the central issue. When you realize you've never loved yourself properly, you have to howl about it. But not only for myself—for the young woman at the party, for my father, for my cousin, for everyone who felt less than, for my whole generation trying to hedge against emptiness, trying to fill it fast with whatever they could find.

Gorilla woman was ugly.

She clawed at her sagging breasts.

But you must adore her and her messy process. I had to love that she was trying to translate an idea into a feeling. I had to love that she couldn't find her way out. Soon, she would learn to find her way in—beyond the concept of the dome and into the dome, where she could contain her own everything and wake up one day to say and mean, I like myself just as I am, and that the "am" could still be fluid.

There is good weeping. There is always backtracking. I didn't want to rely on any external situation. I didn't want it to define whether I was worthy or not. But it seemed impossible not to, because some innate part of me still believed that it was easier to find yourself by going elsewhere—to anything better than the current this. You don't just sit in a rocking chair. No, you go, go, go. The going forces the growth.

If you run far enough, you end up back at the spot you started.

Gorilla woman made a few appearances—and I knew she would continue to throughout my life. It wasn't a bad thing. It was exactly what needed to happen. My dawn walks disintegrated into the stuff of the past. The crisp early mornings couldn't lure me out of a warm bed anymore. Instead, I twisted into the covers like a glowworm, bound up and protected. Not unexcited about the season ahead, I welcomed the natural act of turning in, along with the white white white blank space. But a body has to gear itself up for perpetual goosebumps. It's just part of the drill.

A second winter, Katinka said to me.

Bring it on, I said.

And one afternoon, overcome with a silliness, I leapt off the porch in my sneakers and went on a last run. Bru catapulted right into a somersault and kept going, running back to circle me and then sprint ahead. Cold nipped at my ankles. Every time he hurled himself at me, I bent down and paddle-played him, from one of his sides to the other, jumping from right to left, crouching so that he would crouch, and then bolting so that he would bolt. He always made serious eye contact during that game.

At the climbing tree, the running stopped.

I fell back into my ritual of lying down here.

The sponge grass held me, thin clouds passed over, and the bounce of a basketball somewhere below echoed out across fields and fields and fields. Then, as if he had planned it all along, Bru stood above me and set one paw on my chest, then another, and the bulk of him pushed me down into the earth.

What are you doing, big man? I laughed.

It wasn't that complicated.

It was a preparatory move.

Animals know where they belong. They don't belabor. But he wasn't pushing me into this place, he was pushing me, again, into my body, myself.

9

THE DEER SPEAKS

October 2010

Grasshoppers had come and gone over the summer without me noticing. On our first day here that July, they had
sprung about sure of their own lives. Standing in the sun
and wind, I had been aware of them the way a child is aware of
a new sensation. But now, on the edge of our brown field, cap-
tured in the desolate air by the fence, hundreds of grasshoppers were dead—their papery husks still clinging to grass blades.

Hey, look, I said to Chris and Mike, who were walking
with me.

They squatted down. The dead only returned our study of
them with vacant eyes, filament legs, and plated shells. If a breeze
had blown, each one might have been holding on to the mast of
a ship as it creaked under weather. Maybe they had died mid-
meal. They would be back next year. Mike stood up, and then
Chris did, brushed off his pants and continued on with Bru, all
of them less impressed than I was by the corporeal part of death.
You couldn't be on this land and not recognize it—a bleached
bone, a shredded carcass, or the ashen residue of a snowstorm.
I stayed and removed one of my gloves to touch a few of these
insects. I rubbed my face in the warmth of my sweater and wondered whether their brittle limbs would let go when snow fell.
There would be many deaths to witness in the coming months.

Chris and I had talked about hunting. Though he owned a rifle, he had never killed an animal, let alone a mammal. And now he was mentally bracing himself for that possibility. It was only about food for him, not sport. To stock a freezer full of wild game would be the best way to include meat in our diet. Game was a remarkable resource of this place and it seemed unfortunate not to tap into that. I had wanted to start eating meat, but still felt squeamish about the whole thing. It wasn't something he took lightly—the shot. When he spoke about it with me, his words came out extra slow and he touched the corners of his eyes.

It gives me tears, he would say.

My only experience with dead hunted mammals involved our yearly visits to America. My uncle, the same one who taught me how to shoot a gun, would lead us kids onto his screened porch and lift us up one by one to greet Sunshine, the hairy black boar head mounted on the wall. It always scared me. As I squirmed, he would demand in a low growly voice, Touch the tongue. That was the ritual. Before he let any of us down, we had to do it. It was part of his banter with us. So I would squeeze my eyes shut, suck in a deep breath, and reach out quickly to touch the tongue.

But that was taxidermy.

Not blood and guts and last gasps.

Even a bird wasn't the same as a mammal, from what I had seen so far.

When Mike came over, we often stalked grouse through the hawthorns, pushing back thorny branches and ducking under thick mats of brush—all four of us, two brothers, me, and Bru. The whole landscape had not turned brown. Hidden under here, the ground was covered in small bushes of red, orange, and some rogue green leaves. It had been a snow world when I had last slithered through here on my belly, so sure that a mountain lion would stalk me and eat me.

The afternoon that Chris spotted a grouse on the ground, Mike handed him the gun. Chris aimed and pulled the trigger. The sound startled Bru and he ran off into the woods for hours. I stood there, trying not to cringe, as Mike opened the gullet to show us chokecherries spilling out.

Wow, I said, wow.

Back at the cabin, Mike fried up the tiny breast meat and I forced myself to eat it. It tasted, to me, like sponge grass.

As autumn quickened, so did all our preparation: for hunting, for winter, for our shed, for whatever else would come. Chris and I continued discussions of how to make life work financially in this place, how self-imposed sabbaticals to foreign lands might take shape, how to create a both/and bard situation, and how to have a backup plan for when and if the current plan suddenly evaporated. Had we considered that living in a yurt full time for much longer was not a sustainable scenario? Not really. One step at a time. But without a joint project anchoring us to a schedule, we settled back into our normal selves, distinct from one another, drawn to different tasks. In the early mornings, while Chris slept with a pillow over his head and Bru chased chipmunks in his dreams, I wrapped myself in a wool blanket and sat in front of a dying fire. My dome had become a real place when I closed my eyes. I blew small prayers into the stucco walls. I drew elaborate maps, erased them, drew them again. Sometimes, my younger selves showed up—the white picket fence girl, the one who hated America, the traveling translator of languages, even the unaffected teenager, all of them—and together we circled the would-be map like a pack of dogs, sniffing, retreating, and moving in again to understand the object before us.

Meanwhile, Chris and his brother took on the shed. I loved having Mike around as he transitioned from Turkey to Montana. Somehow he was able to blend his angst about life with humor. He insisted that, once he turned thirty-five, it was over. What's over? I asked. *It*. It just is. Come on, I had teased him. No, it's over, that's all there is to say. I appreciated that someone else nearby seemed as raw and freshly hatched as I was.

He had recently offered a reflection.

See, Mike explained, Chris says *Go travel*, and you say to him, *Fine, buy a chainsaw*, and that's why you two work.

It was a simplified sentence about our relationship, but true. If ever there was a man who had no hold on me, it was the man I had chosen. His tether was long, sometimes too long, but he was the only consistent thing I'd done in my life.

In orange construction hats, they shuffled around the base of a standing fir tree like little boys eager to perform. Out of the trunk, they would be able to create the pieces for our timber frame. In an attempt to avoid getting too serious, we had given the shed a playful name, the Copacabana. I didn't know anything about trees falling. I didn't like the idea of a tree falling by human hands. And I really didn't like the idea of Chris being nearby when it did. I actually wasn't against cutting down trees out of necessity; though later, when I first heard the moans from a newly felled live tree as water sizzled up through its exposed flesh, I would feel awful about it.

Bru and I watched from the cabin's window.

Be careful, Chris, I said aloud to myself, like a woman convinced that everything good is going to be taken from her.

They ran around the tree, chain-sawing a notch on one side, checking the other side. Not long afterward, Mike shouted a warning and Chris stepped aside. The tree leaned slowly, then let itself fall in a way that signaled it knew to be dignified at this moment.

There are moments to be dignified. I was generally good at those, but not always.

A week later, we were ready to raise the frame of our shed. The challenge would not even edge close to that of erecting our yurt. When we thought back to it now, we laughed—a negative temperature blizzard, carrying everything up a hill, how eager we had been. We picked a Wednesday afternoon. We zipped our coats up. We were more tidy and organized than ever before. Though weather forecasters had predicted heavy snow within forty-eight hours, Chris said, We're pros at the last-minute situation. The predictions would be incorrect anyway. Under the warm bright sun, anything seemed possible.

If anyone had seen us from a distance, they would have assumed we were on a covert mission. On the ground by the yurt, one of two twenty-foot-long beams lay prone but pegged to its legs. And here is where I had not understood how this would work until I actually saw it. In the yonder days, though people only used other people, not horses, I imagined that they might have tied many long leather ropes from a wooden beam to a team of horses. As the horses walked forward, their strength would raise the beam on its legs, an almost assembled structure, as a group of people, usually a whole neighborhood, guided the structure up, steadied it, filled in the foundation with rocks.

Instead, we had two of us, a metal cable, and a winch. Mike would have helped, but he was out of town and we couldn't wait. Chris had hitched a metal cable to the beam. This long cable fed up and over a strengthened fence post, now tall as a telephone pole, and out for what seemed like a quarter-mile to the winch, now relocated to the middle of the field.

I would be the team of horses, via the mechanized winch.

He would be the neighborhood.

I'm nervous, I groaned. Where are you going to stand? What if the cable breaks?

I'll be fine, he said, putting a hand on my shoulder. Just ratchet it in nice and slow. We had already tested our walkie-talkies. Not able to see one another, we at least needed to hear one another. These beams were no joke. If one fell on him, he would be stuck, squashed, dead maybe. It would be impossible for me to lift it off.

I ruffled his dark head.

Okay, let's do this, he said, smiling.

I watched him skip back through the field, the sight of him smaller and smaller until he slipped through the fence and was gone. My walkie-talkie eventually beeped and he told me we were good to go. One hand on Bru's collar, the other on the winch, I began to ratchet, cranking the cable back onto its spool. The clicking sound reassured me. Please, let this be easy.

The beam began to move. It rose higher with each click. It rose slowly like a pharaoh sitting up from a long deep rest. This was actually working. I just needed to keep steady. I kept steady for a good long long long while.

Then something gave.

The winch released.

The cable flew out.

I started running before the beam had fully fallen. I ran screaming, because I couldn't see him, screaming, oh god, oh god, oh god, screaming his name. My feet beat into the earth like the feet of those before me who had tried to chase death away. The fence was far. I wouldn't be able to see him until I got there. Get to the fucking fence.

He was on the ground—moving, sort of, patting his sides, checking himself the way he had checked me after a bad slip on ice once. I rushed to him. His eyes flicked up at me when I scooped my arms under his to pull him up. He let me lift his shirt. My hand ran over a red triangular bruise from shoulder to shoulder. I wiped away speckles of blood. He shook like a man who rarely got the shakes.

You okay? I asked, smoothing his shoulders.

I dove, he said, but it still hit me.

Later, he would tell me that he barely made it. Someone less nimble wouldn't have fared well. Bru sniffed him all over. When I knew he was okay, when I knew he hadn't smashed any bones, when I knew he could breathe, we sat in the grass away from the beam.

He sipped some water.

Watching that one simple life-giving act of replenishment, I noticed my concern percolate. What had happened finally registered and my monologue shot off like a flare out of nowhere, as if that's what he needed then. It escalated in intensity with each word, even as he hung his head and picked his shoelace.

Beb, I don't care about this shed. I don't care about any of this at all. I only care about you. It isn't worth it. You could have had your head pulverized, or gone paralyzed, your legs shattered, your back broken. You could have died, over a shed. Who cares about a stupid shed? You haven't been taken out by a lion or bear or avalanche here, and now a shed, god. This should be nothing on our list of priorities. We need to scale back and not do things alone like this; it's just asking for it, and I can't handle that; I can't handle a risk that isn't worthy of being a risk.

I know, he sighed.

But he had already recovered. He kept looking back at the fallen beam and wanting to inch over there. I could just tell. We had regrouped together many other times: canoes flipped in white water, car accidents, and falls down mountains. Despite all my fear of predators, nothing bad had actually happened to us here. Certainly not by the hand of nature. Just the man-made beam. Man-made felt preventable somehow.

That afternoon, we disregarded good sense and finished the shed anyway.

We did it.

We did do it.

The timbers smelled fresh. Because we had run out of money for a corrugated steel roof, the frame would stay a frame for a while. Dusk had pulled a blue sheath over The Land. Chris scrambled up to straddle the beam eleven feet from the ground. I sawed a branch from a fir for our blessing and held my thumb over its wound. Blessings had become common for us now —burning sage or juniper or arranging rock statues. I didn't need to tell anyone about them. But they were important to us because we now had a place to offer them.

I climbed up, using the pegs as footholds, and remembered shimmying up soccer goals and jungle gyms and anything at school that allowed me to flip upside-down and see a new world.

Chris used his drill to secure the branch to the beam. I stared at him, in his olive green army jacket now, hair sheared and a twinkle in his eyes.

Well, maybe you'll write about this one day, he said.

Maybe.

We gazed across the field and in the other direction, through a V in the firs out to the valley. Like kids, we swung our legs madly and smiled across the beam at each other.

Could it be that we were prepared for winter already? We stacked wood in our new shed and covered it with a tarp. I planted poppies, *Echinacea*, and mountain bee balm on the edges of our garden, though none of them would surface in the spring. Mountain lion tracks appeared in the freshly fallen snow. Hello, lion. We poured brandy over snowballs and ate them. A friend emailed me to say, *Don't ever write about the pristine silent winter, make it hot, messy, external, I don't want to read about dormancy and holing up*. But winter was pristine and silent and dormant. When the key to our yurt froze in the lock, we loosened it by taking turns to suck on it with a warm mouth. Once, we sucked on it together. Had that happened last year? I could not remember because memories started to overlap as they do when you live another same season in the same place.

Nature *is* movement. Even the empty space inside us moves. Leonardo da Vinci, man of the body, man of art, was obsessed with motion or movement because "where there is life, there is heat." Everything must move. The water in the creek was like the blood in my body. Even death wasn't a settled state.

Because the start of this winter smelled different than the start of last winter. No push on our end to close in a shelter.

Crows gathered. Voles burrowed deeper. Every living thing desired more life. It was the hardwire of being a creature. Even those creatures who didn't live with the constant human fate of questioning. I was sick of trying to come to terms with how a person could both seek *and* also feel that she was enough as she was. The two forces struck me as critical for living. They also struck me as mutually exclusive. Live with the paradox, Molly, I told myself when brushing my hair, dragging the trashcan out to the road, drinking ginger tea. There are no true answers anyway. Make it real, put it in my hands, to touch and feel and taste and know.

Chris and Mike hiked into the Madison Range to hunt elk for a weekend with Gregg, the guy who had led the team of seven as we hauled the yurt stove uphill. I stayed home picking tiny hairs and seeds from rose hips before drying them. The man was hunting and the woman was preparing herbs. Sometimes, you just can't fight what you prefer. I forced myself to leave the warm yurt for Anna's Halloween party. Susan had offered to keep Bru for the night, saying, If you want to party late, know that you can sleep over in town. No need to drive home that late. When I let myself in to her home to drop him off, smells of cloves and a simmering soup floated from the kitchen to the entrance right as she did.

Oh, darling Molly, you're a bird!

I *am* a bird, I said, smiling. Over the years, I had been a license plate, a pair of scissors, an octopus, French fries, and even, in New York, the Depo-Provera birth control injection just to make a political statement about what male doctors do with women's medicine. But now I had gone primal, wrapped myself in scarves of red and teal and gray, folded a beak out of a few coffee filters and attached it with an elastic strap.

We must paint your face, she said, pulling me upstairs to her bathroom.

I had never been good at being "made up" by someone, or even myself, and made an art of avoiding it altogether. The idea that something about me would be prettier if we did this and that had never sat well. But Susan had known me since that first year we moved to America, and being here, in her home, surrounded by her zebra skin and paintings of Italy and pear brandy, was comfortable.

She sat me down and slid open a drawer of makeup. Bru curled into a ball by the bathtub. As she sorted through eye pencils—an artist looking at my face and then back down at colors —we started talking.

How, oh how, is that yurt life of yours?

She spoke with an emphasis I didn't even have about my own life.

Oh, it's good, I said, living here, well, especially on The Land, is actually making me examine where I came from, why it matters, and the many things I need to let go of.

Wow, she responded and drew a blue line down my nose.

But, I laughed, I've never been a shining example of grace as I go about things.

No, no, no, she said, drawing across my cheeks now, you've always been intuitive, Molly, ever since you were a little girl, you always had this inner knowing and you've always pushed yourself to grow. More than most.

Yeah, I guess.

Oh, but I've seen a change in you, she insisted, glancing all over my face in a way that made me feel seen and also embarrassed. You have really come into yourself here. You've become who you are, Molly May.

Look at you, she squealed, turning me to face the mirror.

There I was.

A blue and red bird with my own blue eyes staring back at me. I didn't know whether it was another mask or my real self, or at what point a person knows this about herself. But my eyes did look serene.

Thanks, Susan.

All I had to do was bring out what was already there, she said, as I stepped into my boots to scoot out the door.

When I walked into Anna's party, she moved toward me.

What kind of bird is this? she asked, fluffing my scarves. I didn't have an answer. The thought *desert bird* emerged as the night progressed, though I may also have been an owl. Birds had never caught my attention as a girl. I had been a soft animal person: horses, dogs, and hamsters. But birds could migrate and see below and play in the wind. They had beat wings over our yurt, flown into our yurt, stood on fence posts just outside our yurt. They knew a dome. A few years later, Anna would tell me that, in Russian, *doma* means home.

The party was small. People sat cross-legged on the floor. I poured another cup of wine and Anna leaned toward me.

So, she asked, does this bird fly away or stay?

While I flew around like a bird that night, Chris, Mike, and Gregg carried a cow elk out six miles in grizzly country. Most people take a horse to carry out the meat. But they butchered it in the field and left the head, skin, and guts under trees. One leg in one backpack, another leg in another, elk arms strapped to human arms. Chris hadn't shot it, but he had at least brought straps for the potential of a carryout. The bloody trail through snow wasn't ideal, but it was necessary. That felt real to me. It terrified the part of me that couldn't deal with moths dying in the shower. But it also seemed like something everyone should experience.

What did it feel like, I hammered at Chris the next morning, to carry a dead creature down a mountain?

He was brewing up some coffee and, as usual, slow to answer at any length before he had eaten a decent breakfast.

It was what we had to do, he said.

I know, but was it strange?

Not as strange as you would expect, actually.

Hmm.

Being the one who shoots the animal is probably the hardest part, he explained. Everything else is sort of mechanical.

With that comment, I snuck over to peck his neck in small abundant pecks until he said, Stop, stop, stop, and pecked me back. Here was my earth element husband, feet and mind planted firmly on the ground.

Let's go fly our kite, yes? I said, holding him from behind with a hug.

What, right now? he mumbled, halfway through a serious stack of pancakes.

No, finish eating, but then let's go, we *have* to before it snows again, or I'll just go.

No, I'll come, just give me a sec.

The top was the perfect place for kite flying. For our wedding, an old friend had gifted us the exact green kite we asked for—one that could swoop and do a few tricks but ultimately just soared. Years ago, in New Zealand, I had concocted elaborate plans and ordered special carbon fiber rods and nylon to handcraft a kite for Chris's birthday. It never got made. We moved and the dream of it got left in the drawer of our drafty harbor-side rental. But we each had a thing for kites, especially me. Up here, Bru transformed into the lean tiger he was. He would go insane at the piercing sound and chase the dragon in the sky, back and forth, back and forth, back and forth across the field, until the dragon came to its senses and landed limp on the ground where a dog could take stock of it with his frothing mouth. After less than ten minutes of Chris maneuvering some dives and spins, the froth was noticeable.

Here, all yours, Chris said, handing me the base.

As Bru sprawled his whole body out, panting, I waited a few minutes to give him a break. Spots of snow dotted the field, but most of it had melted. Under the expansive gray cloud sky, I pulled the white line in a bit, wrapping it carefully around the base with my gloves, not unlike the winch actually, a spool.

Okay, big man, I warned Bru.

I started to walk and then run, glancing behind me as the line pulled taut and the kite rose, caught by a breeze, an updraft, higher and higher until it was high enough for me to stop and work the line. The wind wasn't strong, but it was enough. As dense clouds parted momentarily, light beamed down and the kite flickered and my eyes saw spots—an exquisite disorientation that spun and spun and spun me around with no sense of gravity.

This was my first memory ever, this staring up at a kite in the sky. I am young, the youngest I will ever remember. The sand is warm and my blue bikini bottoms make me proud as I toddle next to my handsome dad. This is the beginning of my life. This is Australia. Everything about this place is soft. I can fall and it is so soft. It is soft anywhere I go. I can go in any direction. There are no straight lines here. I follow his legs, but when I look up to see him, blurs and white dots hurt my eyes because the sun is bright. Ah, there is his face, smiling, and he is holding something in his hands and he says, Watch, though I can barely hear him over the roar of ocean waves. The blue thing in his hands is flapping. He uncurls it and keeps uncurling and suddenly, with a loud pop, it turns into a floating shape and moves away from us, and he tells me, Look, look, it is attached to a string. I gasp and it is the first time I hear my own excited voice. His hands move fast. As they spin backward, the floating shape goes higher, higher, and I squint to see it, and now it starts to dive and dance and play and my dad is laughing and so I laugh too, and we are laughing together.

When the boys and I are old enough, he'll let us hold the base and we'll lose control of it and the kite will deflate and fizzle down or crash-land violently into the ground. It's okay, he'll say, you'll get the hang of it. The kite cannot exist or fly without its base. Right around this time, I start to pay attention to the thing behind my ribcage. It lets me know what I feel when I feel something. With one hand over mine, he will teach me how to let the string out carefully and then roll it back in at the right time. Because when the kite is about to lose its lift, it needs to touch back in with home. Once it does, I can roll it back out again to catch the wind, but it's got to come back home, back home, back home in order to go higher, to go higher, to go higher. That's the rule.

We all have a learning moment as children that only focuses into meaning once we are older. I stood in that field, with my man and my dog, and watched the kite soar and dart. You must go away to learn but you must always return.

The kite swerved, and though I tried to reel it in fast, it crashed hard.

Oy, I wheezed.

We walked out across the brown field and squatted down by the lifeless being.

Broken, Chris said, with a shrug.

Well, shit, I said.

That's the end of this kite, he laughed.

Can we fix it? I asked, as he pulled nylon apart to inspect the kite.

Uhhh, no, it's shattered. We'll have to get a new one.

Okay, then.

The first week of November tugged us into that sudden darkness before clocks fall back. Our sun rose well after eight in the morning, or at least I thought so. The sky stayed monochrome, not bothering to include a cloud here and there. Last year at this time, my boots would have sunk into muddy snow on the dirt road by Willem's and Diane's place. Chalk dry now, the road led around a corner to the sunset behind our hill. Out that way, three wolves had taken down an elk, and many years ago a mountain lion had backed a woman and her dog out to her car. Plumes of smoke rose from everyone's chimney. I wondered if people could see our yurt smoke on the hill.

After such a mild season, the first real snow hit hard.

I was cutting kindling, still working my spastic moves to avoid finger dislocation, when wet snow began to fall. It fell like rain does, with no space between the empty sky and the snow. I blinked up to white dots dusting, no, burying, what had been brown field for so long. Take note, take note. This was it —the great descent into the great white months in our great white tent.

Snow coated my eyelashes before I thought to tuck the ax into our woodpile. There is a certain champagne energy with the first sticking snow. I had only experienced it during college because our very first sticking snow in Montana, sparkly as it was, had severed our yurt building process. It came down harder.

When I pivoted to rush inside, Chris and Bru burst through the yurt door toward me. We charged, all three of us, into the white field. Bru took the lead and flung himself, flipped on his back and up again to continue the arc of his run. Bulked up like a snowman by his down jacket, Chris ran in front of me with his hands in the air. His silly made me smile. Without a yurt or shed project, we hadn't spent consistent time together recently, which was actually a good thing. You can't truly see a thing if you are pressed up against it all the time. The space had given us perspective on each other. One evening, he had gone out of his way to tell me that I had mellowed. For a man who said little without being asked, it had been a waterfall. Now he tumbled forward into a roll and Bru sped back to leap over him as they pawed at each other and wrestled. I watched and ran at them, leaned forward into my own cartwheel, clumsy in snow, and landed only to fall down again and make angels. We had entered the white place: a landscape both serene and severe.

That night, we danced like ghosts for hours. We made new tracks. We crossed our tracks. Soon no one knew whose tracks were whose, only that we had made them together, and that they would be gone by morning and that somewhere, buried in deep snow, some trace of them would be left.

When our tracks were, as suspected, covered by morning, I stood by the yurt and understood that there was no great map that would steer me to what place or self might be enough. If we put something on the map, it gains importance. If we cut something out of a map, it loses importance. If something is off the map to begin with, it doesn't exist. We map out our plans. We are creating new maps all the time. Once, in a bookstore, I came across an old map of the Soviet Union before its fall in 1991. I remembered the event well because it had almost coincided with our arrival in America. The historical map was useless now in terms of accuracy. It was misinformed for the present moment. But all maps are misinformed. The moment they get made, something has already changed. We evolve.

Enter the temple where the maps were made.

Inside, all the myths, all the attempts and failures and stepping-stones were tucked into the walls, some rolled up, others tacked up, some recent ones open on the floor. So many dead. So many yet to be born. Each map deserved as much reverence as the next. Each map was a narrative. And there were thousands, layers of them, because yearning was a human condition. Yearning propelled every move I had ever made: for an apple when hungry, for touch when untouched, for an adventure when routine-bound, for an adventure when eager, for an adventure when insecure, for a yurt in Montana when in need of self-acceptance. Without yearning, I would have never engaged the question of why yearn for more.

The yearning of today was the steady of tomorrow.

No one was *one* thing.

That's right, no one was one thing.

I had never been placeless. Someone is only placeless when place has been taken from her. Instead, I had been simply without a place. I needed to remind myself of celebrating and then letting go. It felt good, initially, to hold on, but then it just hurt. What would the narrative of not holding on look like?

On the day Chris shot a deer, I answered my phone in the Jeep. I was careening home from teaching and watching the mountains reach up everywhere.

Hey.

Hey, he breathed into the phone.

I could tell he was outside and that something had happened.

What's up?

I shot a deer, he stammered.

Where?

Here.

I'm coming.

He had gutted it and dragged it down the hill already. It lay in a pale brown heap just off the irrigation ditch. Chris stood over it. I approached him, touched his shoulder, looked into his eyes, and saw a blend of competing emotions. Squatting down, I touched a still warm body with fur thicker than expected. I had never seen a newly dead large animal this close before. The life had vanished without question: eyes blank, velvet nose cold against my fingers, nothing but a sheath for what had spurred the soul to eat, mate, play. What did I say to this creature? Was there anything to say? Chris had hidden behind his shop to watch as the buck moved west under the firs. He watched it for a good long while and contemplated. This is what Chris would do. Do I do this now; is it the perfect shot; am I ready to kill this animal? When the buck raised his head, Chris exhaled and sent a bullet speeding to drop the animal right between two small trees.

I was lucky, he said. He just went down, only flinched, didn't run.

The slight shake in his voice always alerted me to the stirring of something strong within him—especially after moments when he had done something hard he had wanted to do but had never done before. I would likely never hunt myself, but he would again. This was his first and, just like any first, the overwhelming excitement and sorrow and pride of having crossed a threshold you can never turn back from must have been immense. He had worn gloves to gut the deer. But a wipe to the brow had left a streak of blood across his forehead. I stood up, grabbed his hand, and squeezed it.

We would butcher and eat this meat, a concept still so brand-new to me I could have been watching a film about someone else's life. But first, we had to hang it from a tree for a few days to let it cool off. Because white-tailed deer grow up within a five-mile radius of where they are born, we knew that we had probably met this exact deer before, as a speckled babe bolting and collapsing as they do when learning to walk.

By eating the deer, we would be eating The Land.

This was the real I had been waiting for.

We leaned on each other.

It gives me tears, Chris said.

Me too.

The Deer Speaks

↓

I went to the highway to ground myself in the near and far of geography. The same three exits. The same gray strip of road. On my way back, I pulled over on a dirt road near us. It rose high and low and generated deep snowdrifts that always deserved respect and distance. None so far this winter. Near the ditch, under a white sky, I sat in my car and stared at the tidal wave of The Land.

Hidden by a bank of dark firs, our yurt seemed a dream of the mind, not alive to anyone who would pass by. But I knew exactly where it was, between which trees, to the right of which drainage. What would I tell people when I was an old woman? That it had felt like living on the top of the world, that I woke up to the whole valley beneath me, and when hawks coasted by they were at eye-level some of the time. And that, in the wind, because the winds were untamable, the climbing tree swayed violently on the edge, and from there, if I wasn't careful, I could tumble off the plateau, though I now knew that people out here call it a bench. I would somersault all the way down that vertical, gathering nettles and fir needles and stones and snow until I became one magnificent whirl, and I would go past the place where, at night, a mountain lion shared the path, past the place where I fell and slid with pots and pans, past the place where Bru fled into the moonless eve, past the place where we panted holding our heavy yurt door, past the place where the owl stood before us, past the place where the deer dropped dead when Chris shot it; yes, I would tumble past all these places, so that when I landed they would be rubbed into me.

But I got to decide. Did I want them rubbed into me? I had

not been so sure, then so sure, then unsure, and now I just was. Because when you stare back up all of that uphill, you get to say one thing: I did that. You get to write a letter.

> Dear The Land,
>
> I'm probably not going to stare at you for the rest of my life. I know this. It would not honor all of who I am. But you continue to show me myself. Thank you for tolerating me and for making me now want to remove the word tolerate because I am not to be tolerated I am to be loved and you have taught me so.

Three magpies balanced on a fence nearby. Their movement caught my eye.

It wouldn't matter what I was doing or where I was. One day I would die and now I was alive. America, the word that horrified the almost ten-year-old girl releasing crabs on the dock, was made up of people who had left somewhere else. Americans were a migrant people. Turns out, I was one of them.

At the cold end of November, I was now going home to prepare myself for butchering a deer. The Land had been an idea to me when we first arrived. Places had been ideas to me my whole life. But not anymore. Our dead deer was not a new job or a strategic plan or a Facebook update or a new identity or an advancement of self or a fragment of a fragment. The deer was not an idea. It was a life.

No one tells you that a trachea looks like a pearly white vacuum hose. I don't know what I expected, but not that. I held it in my glove and stared. It could get tacked up in a museum. It was the passage place for voice. The buck had made buck noises with this trachea. The buck had asserted itself with this trachea. The buck had uttered his last sound with this trachea.

But the holy is also mundane.

A few minutes after wanting to fall on my knees for the trachea, I dropped it into a plastic grocery bag, along with the penis, the balls, the strings of fat. Later, we would dump it out under a tree somewhere. For now, it all needed to be out of the way. The day had begun when Brooks and Mike came over to help. We strung the deer over a rafter on the porch to hang. As they pulled the hide off, it made a sort of clean ripping sound when it separated from the muscle. The meat was purple. I had not expected that either. Because it was now exposed, we had to work fast. When it was my turn to duck into the cabin away from the cold, I watched the three men circle around the animal, slicing muscles from bones, their breath in clouds. It amazed me how the muscles came away as whole pieces, intact, the mark of a design. No hacking to be done. We could almost have put it all together again and snapped the deer to life.

Instead, we dismantled the deer.

At one point, Chris spread apart the breastbone and said, Look, Molly.

I leaned into the cavity, an empty space once full of organs, once halved by a diaphragm. It was a whale. It was a leaf. It was an instrument. My fingers ran across the white ribs and the purple spaces between, white and purple stripes. So these were real ribs. I needed to revisit this place. Mike smiled at my awe and showed me the bullet hole—a small splinter of bone and coagulated blood. Bru lingered on the edges, nosing at the hooves, licking at the wooden porch, hoping to find a taste of blood. We were careful to make sure he didn't, not wanting him to associate the meat with the deer. Everyone but me set to work on removing the limbs. I wanted to watch, so I held the grocery bag for pink and red and white bits. The deer banged around as they yanked at it. But its center, held open now by a stick, stared right back at us: a dome. The internal was on display and I had never seen it before.

I wanted to crawl inside.

It would be a liberating theology to fully believe, in your bones, not your head, that you belong to yourself. Not to a place or a way or a tribe. If you did, then no external could affect you either way. The owl had shown me her interiority. The trees had shown me my shape. Now the deer made it real. My dome was my here *and* my elsewhere. I could physically touch it.

If butchering was considered a gruesome act, then few had taken stock of how we filet ourselves every day. As the heavy limbs came off, each man handed them to me. I barreled through the cabin door and placed them on the counter: shoulder, haunch, another shoulder, another haunch. I thought back to the woman standing in the tall grass a year and a half ago, hankering for an experience, and wished we could share this moment. This was new. We would pull on latex gloves soon and start cutting the meat, or processing, a verb so sterile I didn't want to use it. What would start as a gentle and slow removal of connective tissue would turn into a late-night fatigue where small details matter less. When Chris and I fell away from the counter and into a shower, I would scrub the smell of blood from his winter beard as water ran down our backs. It wasn't a bad smell, but being separated from its origin sharpened it. My dreams would be the underwater kind, dense from blood and the pleasure of neatly organized white packages of meat now lined up in the freezer. When my forearm met his forearm as I turned in sleep, or my foot rubbed up his leg, or we embraced back to belly, I would know muscle and that we are all animals made of purple meat and open spaces.

But we weren't there yet.

We're going to flesh the hide, explained Chris as he and Brooks walked to the shop.

I've got to head back to town, said Mike.

I'll deal with the carcass, I said, because I no longer wanted to be a woman who could not tolerate the debris and mess of a life that is lived.

Then suddenly, I was standing on the porch alone—alone with the body, a grocery bag of bits and a bucket of legs and fat. Where to take it? I needed to drag it far away from the cabin so that coyotes and lions and birds could find it undisturbed by us and us undisturbed by them. Only the antlers would stay here.

Strapped into my snowshoes, I began to move east past the hawthorns, the place of alligator eyes in wood and crawling and fear and relief. Deep snow pulled me down. As I labored under the first load, cold air stung my already raw winter throat. Bru heeled at least five feet behind, aware that he shouldn't even be following so he had better stay discreet.

The day was bright and white, a land covered in crystalline snow.

At the farthest spot, bordered by creek, ditch, and forest of hawthorns beyond, I dumped the bucket and then the grocery bag. Red on white and a blood smell that signaled *come here, come here, come here.*

Go on, I growled at Bru, and he scattered.

The creek burbled along, not yet covered by blue ice.

It was good to be alone.

On my last walk out, I held the ribcage in one hand and the furry head in the other. It wasn't easy. Both threatened to slip, even under equal weight. I stopped every few steps to rest. The trail of blood was faint, just drops in some places. And as I continued, voices began to gather around me: the voice of the deer, the voice of wind, the voice of me, and the voices of my ancestors, and not because this was some big drama moment, not because hunters don't do this every day all over the world, but because the voices wanted me to listen.

They got loud.

Inhabit yourself, they said, and though I had learned the concept already, it felt like a great pulse being offered to me, a reminder, a tempo with which to reset my life. I smiled as we do when we know something has changed and it won't ever change back.

Okay, deer, here you go, I said.

I placed the head down first and ran my hand along its soft ear to thank it. Why had I been so scared of being sentimental when we first arrived here? With my boot, I scuffed the snow to make a flat area for the ribcage. Then the head tucked into the ribcage and the circle was complete. Everything was turned inward so that, once the foragers got word, it could freely go outward.

CODA

What I didn't know then, surrounded by snow, what none of us know about our own future lives, was that, in a few years, we would still be living here. And, in an attempt to accommodate our increasingly busy lives, we would move our yurt, that nomadic structure, down to this very spot along the creek, near the deer's resting place. The medicine wheel would stay. When money dried up further, we would take on part-time jobs and then leave them when we could, and then my parents would announce that they probably needed to sell The Land to support themselves, but then they would pack up boxes and move into the cabin instead. And Chris and I, well, we would stay. The mention of foreign places would continue to unseat me, but I would laugh at myself and then listen. I would ski by our old yurt site with Bru and happen upon a set of huge elk antlers sticking up from the snow. I would write these exact words and then sell them on the same summer day that I stood near the climbing tree in the sagebrush and peed on a pregnancy stick. And just as another winter ended, just as the green wild grass started to poke up again, just as it pokes up almost everywhere on the planet, on a day of strong winds, my daughter would spill out of me and meet The Land that taught me about myself, and all of this, every last moment of it, would be as permanent and impermanent as tracks in snow, because I would also let go of what I thought I knew about the woman who is me, and let go of each story I told myself, and let go of going, and then let go of not going, and continue to let go as new translations formed: let it all go down the creek and we, together, would go again, we would move away, and maybe come back, go elsewhere, somewhere, with enough, or just enough, already within.

Acknowledgments

A book is not born solely of an author, but of the many people who support her. Thank you to Starling Lawrence for his generosity and for normalizing the publishing world. Gail Hochman took a chance on me and continues to grace me with her coaching and straight talk. Dan Smetanka swept into this project with humor, breathed life into it and insisted on the right cuts, the right additions. I could not have asked for a more collaborative editor. My writer's group in New York read many versions of proposals. I thank them—Ethan Todras-Whitehill, Felice Bell, Kate Torgovnick, Scott Lamb, Jennifer Gandin Le, Alex Morris, Joie Jager-Hyman and Theo Gangi —for appreciating the nature girl in me and making the writer's life feel real and possible. It's no small task to read a manuscript. Thank you to those who did so. Hank Lentfer reminded me of reverence and irreverence. Bill Morris caught some glaring mistakes and pushed me to clarify. My cousin Lauren Besser vetted my character and encouraged my madness. Courtney Martin has, through her kindness and willingness to invite people into her fold, been instrumental to my life as a writer, and more importantly, as a human. Kimberlee Auerbach Berlin's honesty, laugh, friendship and knack for story have saved me over and over again.

I can think of no one wiser, no one so attuned to transformation as Janice Conti. My gratitude for her guidance is beyond these words. Susan Lilley's example and mentorship allowed me to choose poetry. Katy Smith Abbott said the right thing at the right time. Samantha Dabney has brought delight into my creative practice and life. Hannah Miller has listened to and held my urgency many a time. I thank Jen Marlow for sharing so many of my visions. Katinka Locascio still teaches me how to breathe. Thank you to those who kept me energized and understood: Jen Bloomer, Laurie Richmond, Kate Seely, Brendan Curry, Paul Whitlatch, Anna Ourusoff, Dr. Holcomb Johnston. I am also indebted to all of my writing students, who become part of my fabric and teach me in turn. Susan Dabney brought us to The Land. Her exuberance for life and art is intoxicating and my deep thanks go to her. Brooks and Marcie Gehring and Diane and Willem Volkersz welcomed us with open arms—a person could not ask for better neighbors.

My family has been an amphitheater of support. Linda and Moe Kautz have not batted an eye when our whims took us across an ocean, or across the country, or beyond the land of reasonable employment. Mike Kautz, a man of words himself, keeps the questions alive. My brothers are my limbs; thank you to Alex for melting candles and leading the way into art, thank you to Peter for his matter-of-factness and for asking, always, about when I was going to get down to writing a book. My parents, Mary and Ken, are impossible to thank adequately. They introduced me to an expansive world, fostered my love for the globe and have encouraged my instinct. That we live on The Land at all is a testament to their constant big-heartedness.

Living with a creature makes me a better creature. I thank Bru for asking me to step away from writing on the computer and come play outside. Chris has been my grounding and inspiration ever since he offered me an orange on a snowy day. Without him, so little of anything is possible. And Eula, fresh to this world, has only just begun, I know, to teach me about surrender.